CIMA

NEW SYLLABUS
PRACTICE & REVISION KIT

Intermediate Paper 4

Finance

BPP Publishing
January 2001

First edition January 2001

ISBN 0 7517 3830 1

British Library Cataloguing-in-Publication Data
*A catalogue record for this book
is available from the British Library*

Published by

*BPP Publishing Limited
Aldine House, Aldine Place
London W12 8AW*

www.bpp.com

*Printed in Great Britain by W M Print
45 – 47 Frederick Street
Walsall
West Midlands WS2 9NE*

We are grateful to the Chartered Institute of Management Accountants and the Association of Chartered Certified Accountants for permission to reproduce past examination questions. The answers to past examination questions have been prepared by BPP Publishing Limited.

CONTENTS

	Page number
Question search tools	
Question and answer checklist/index	(iv)
Topic index	(vi)
The exam	
The exam paper	(viii)
What the examiner means	(ix)
How to pass Paper 4	(x)
Background	
Useful websites	(xii)
Syllabus mindmap	(xiii)
Question practice	
Questions	**3**
Answers	**63**
Exam practice	
Mock exam 1	**157**
• Questions	
• Plan of attack	
• Answers	
Mock exam 2 (Pilot paper)	**183**
• Questions	
• Plan of attack	
• Answers	
Mathematical tables and exam formulae	**212**
Order form	
Review form & free prize draw	

BPP PUBLISHING

Question and answer checklist/index

The headings in this checklist/index indicate the main topics of questions, but questions often cover several different topics.

Questions preceded by * are **key questions** which we think you must attempt in order to pass the exam. Tick them off on this list as you complete them.

			Marks	Time allocation Mins	Page number Questions	Answers
PART A: THE FINANCE FUNCTION						
*	1	Objective test questions: The Finance Function I	20	36	3	63
*	2	Objective test questions: The Finance Function II	20	36	4	63
	3	Objective test questions: The Finance Function III	20	36	6	65
	4	Financial management	20	36	8	66
	5	Stakeholders	20	36	8	68
*	6	Policy decisions	20	36	8	70
*	7	Merchant bank	20	36	8	72
*	8	Market efficiency	20	36	9	73
	9	Treasury department	20	36	9	76
PART B: SOURCES OF LONG-TERM FINANCE						
*	10	Objective test questions: Long-term Finance I	20	36	10	78
*	11	Objective test questions: Long-term Finance II	20	36	12	79
*	12	Objective test questions: Long-term Finance III	20	36	14	80
*	13	Objective test questions: Long-term Finance IV	20	36	16	82
	14	Objective test questions: Long-term Finance V	20	36	17	83
	15	Objective test questions: Long-term Finance VI	20	36	19	85
	16	Objective test questions: Long-term Finance VII	20	36	21	86
	17	Bardsey plc	20	36	23	87
*	18	S plc	20	36	25	90
	19	Z plc	20	36	25	91
*	20	Newsam plc	20	36	26	93
	21	MRF	20	36	28	96
	22	ABC plc	20	36	29	98
*	23	Armada	20	36	29	100
*	24	Risk and market efficiency	20	36	30	102
	25	Cost of capital	20	36	30	104
*	26	Leisure International plc	20	36	31	105
	27	Crazy Games plc	20	36	31	107
	28	Jeronimo plc	20	36	32	110
PART C: SOURCES OF SHORT-TERM FINANCE						
*	29	Objective test questions: Short-term Finance I	20	36	34	112
*	30	Objective test questions: Short-term Finance II	20	36	35	113
	31	Interest rates	20	36	37	115
	32	Yield curve	20	36	37	116

			Marks	Time allocation Mins	Page number Questions	Answers
*	33	Excess cash and money market instruments	20	36	37	117
*	34	4D plc	20	36	38	119
*	35	RT plc	20	36	39	121
	36	Expandalot Ltd	20	36	39	123
*	37	Overdraft usage	20	36	40	124

PART D: WORKING CAPITAL MANAGEMENT

			Marks	Time allocation Mins	Page number Questions	Answers
*	38	*Objective test questions: Working Capital Management I*	20	36	41	125
*	39	*Objective test questions: Working Capital Management II*	20	36	43	125
*	40	*Objective test questions: Working Capital Management III*	20	36	45	126
*	41	*Objective test questions: Working Capital Management IV*	20	36	46	128
	42	*Objective test questions: Working Capital Management V*	20	36	48	129
*	43	Moribund plc	20	36	50	131
	44	Ratios	20	36	51	133
*	45	YZPK Packing Co Ltd	20	36	52	134
*	46	Improving cash flow	20	36	52	136
	47	Phoenix plc	20	36	53	138
*	48	Ripley plc	20	36	54	140
	49	Recent research	20	36	55	143
	50	Whichford plc	20	36	55	145
*	51	Discount	20	36	56	146
	52	MP Ltd	20	36	57	148
*	53	Overdraft	20	36	57	150
	54	Keswick plc	20	36	58	152
	55	Fenton Security plc	20	36	59	154

MOCK EXAM 1

	Questions	Answers
	157	169

* Questions 56 – 61

MOCK EXAM 2

	Questions	Answers
	183	195

* Questions 62 – 67

BPP PUBLISHING

TOPIC INDEX

Listed below are the key Paper 4 syllabus topics and the numbers of the longer (Section B) questions in this Kit covering those topics.

If you need to concentrate your practice and revision on certain topics or if you want to attempt questions that refer to a particular subject, you will find this index useful.

Syllabus topic	Question numbers
Beta factors	34
Capital asset pricing model	26
Cash flow forecasting	17, 46
Cash management	48
Cash management models	35, 48
Cash surplus	33, 47
Convertibles	19
Cost of capital	25
Credit control	45, 49, 50
Creditworthiness	55
Debt factoring	53
Debtor management	48, 55
Dividend growth model	18, 27, 28
Efficient market hypothesis	8
Equity finance	18
Financial management	4
Financial management decisions	6
Financial objectives	4
Financial services	7
Gearing	20, 54
Interest rates	31, 33, 35
Investor ratios	17, 20, 27, 44, 54
Leases	21, 22, 23
Long-term debt finance	18, 26
Market efficiency	8, 24, 28
Merchant banks	7
Operating cycle	43
Overdrafts	36, 37, 53
Overtrading	36
Payment terms	52
Portfolio of investments	19
Rights issues	23, 28

Syllabus topic	Question numbers
Risk	24, 34
Settlement discounts	51, 53, 55
Share prices	25
Shareholders	5
Shareholder wealth	4
Short-term investments	33, 34
Stock exchange	7
Stockholding	45
Trade creditors	45, 54
Treasury function	6, 9
Weighted average cost of capital	22, 26
Working capital cycle	54
Working capital management	49, 50, 51
Working capital ratios	17, 44, 45, 47, 53
Yield curve	32

BPP
PUBLISHING

THE EXAM PAPER

Format of the paper

		Number of marks
Section A	Objective test questions	40
Section B	Three questions from five	60
		100

Time allowed: 3 hours

Analysis of pilot paper

Section A

1   20 objective test questions

Section B

2   Treasury departments

3   Measures to improve cash flows; investing cash surpluses

4   Gearing ratios; WACC; debentures *versus* preference shares; merchant banks

5   Factoring services; cash discounts

6   Rights issue; issue of convertible loan stock

WHAT THE EXAMINER MEANS

The table below has been prepared by CIMA to help you interpret exam questions.

Learning objective	Verbs used	Definition
1 Knowledge What you are expected to know	• List • State • Define	• Make a list of • Express, fully or clearly, the details of/facts of • Give the exact meaning of
2 Comprehension What you are expected to understand	• Describe • Distinguish • Explain • Identify • Illustrate	• Communicate the key features of • Highlight the differences between • Make clear or intelligible/state the meaning of • Recognise, establish or select after consideration • Use an example to describe or explain something
3 Application Can you apply your knowledge?	• Apply • Calculate/compute • Demonstrate • Prepare • Reconcile • Solve • Tabulate	• To put to practical use • To ascertain or reckon mathematically • To prove the certainty or to exhibit by practical means • To make or get ready for use • To make or prove consistent/compatible • Find an answer to • Arrange in a table
4 Analysis Can you analyse the detail of what you have learned?	• Analyse • Categorise • Compare and contrast • Construct • Discuss • Interpret • Produce	• Examine in detail the structure of • Place into a defined class or division • Show the similarities and/or differences between • To build up or complete • To examine in detail by argument • To translate into intelligible or familiar terms • To create or bring into existence
5 Evaluation Can you use your learning to evaluate, make decisions or recommendations?	• Advise • Evaluate • Recommend	• To counsel, inform or notify • To appraise or assess the value of • To advise on a course of action

BPP PUBLISHING

HOW TO PASS PAPER 4

Revising with this Kit

A confidence boost

To boost your morale and to give yourself a bit of confidence, **start** your practice and revision with a topic that you find **straightforward**.

Diagnosis

Sets of **objective test questions** are included for each syllabus area. Use some of these questions as a **diagnostic tool**: if you get many of them wrong go back to your BPP Study Text and do some revision; if you get the majority of them right, move on.

Key questions

Then try as many as possible of the **longer (Section B) questions**. Obviously the more questions you do, the more likely you are to pass the exam. But at the very least you should attempt the **key questions** that are highlighted in the **question and answer checklist/index** at the front of the Kit. Even if you are short of time, you must prepare answers to these questions if you want to pass the exam. They incorporate the key techniques and concepts underpinning *Finance* and they cover the principal areas of the syllabus.

No cheating

Produce **full answers** under **timed conditions**; practising exam technique is just as important as recalling knowledge. Don't cheat by looking at the answer. Look back at your notes or at your BPP Study Text instead. Produce answer plans if you are running short of time.

Imagine you're the marker

It's a good idea to actually **mark your answers**. Don't be tempted to give yourself marks for what you meant to put down, or what you would have put down if you had time. And don't get despondent if you didn't do very well. Refer to the **topic index** and try another question that covers the same subject area.

Ignore them at your peril

Always read the **Pass marks** in the answers. They are there to help you.

Trial run for the big day

Then, when you think you can successfully answer questions on the whole syllabus, attempt the **two mock exams** at the end of the Kit. You will get the most benefit by sitting them under strict exam conditions, so that you gain experience of the four vital exam processes.

- Selecting questions
- Deciding on the order in which to attempt them
- Managing your time
- Producing answers

Tackling objective test questions

Of the total marks available for this paper, objective test questions comprise 40 per cent.

The objective test questions (OTs) in your exam contain four possible answers. You have to **choose the option that best answers the question**. The three incorrect options are called distracters. There is a skill in answering OTs quickly and correctly. By practising OTs you can develop this skill, giving you a better chance of passing the exam.

You may wish to follow the approach outlined below, or you may prefer to adapt it.

Step 1. Skim read all the OTs and identify what appear to be the easier questions.

Step 2. Attempt each question, **starting with the easier questions** identified in Step 1. Read the question thoroughly. You may prefer to work out the answer before looking at the options, or you may prefer to look at the options at the beginning. Adopt the method that works best for you.

Step 3. Read the four options and see if one matches your own answer. Be careful with numerical questions, as the distracters are usually designed to match answers that incorporate common errors. Check that your calculation is correct. Have you followed the requirement exactly? Have you included every stage of the calculation?

Step 4. You may find that none of the options matches your answer.

- Re-read the question to ensure that you understand it and are answering the requirement

- Eliminate any obviously wrong answers

- Consider which of the remaining answers is the most likely to be correct and select the option

Step 5. If you are still unsure, make a note and continue to the next question. You have an average of 3.6 minutes per 2-mark OT question. Some questions will take you longer to answer than others. Try to reduce the average time per question, to allow yourself to revisit problem questions at the end of the exam.

Step 6. Revisit unanswered questions. When you come back to a question after a break you often find you are able to answer it correctly straight away. If you are still unsure have a guess. You are not penalised for incorrect answers, so **never leave a question unanswered!**

After extensive practice and revision of OT, you may find that you recognise wording in a question when you sit the exam. Be aware that the detail and/or requirement may be different. If the question seems familiar read the requirement and options carefully - do not assume that it is identical.

USEFUL WEBSITES

The websites below provide additional sources of information of relevance to your studies.

- **www.ft.com**

  This website provides information about current international business. You can search for information and articles on specific industry groups as well as individual companies.

- **www.economist.com**

  Here you can search for business information on a week-by-week basis, search articles by business subject and use the resources of the Economist Intelligence Unit to research sectors, companies or countries.

- **www.bpp.com**

  Our website provides information about BPP products and services, with a link to the CIMA website.

- **www.strategy-business.com**

  This website includes articles from *Strategy & Business*.

- **www.invweek.co.uk**

  This site carries business news and articles on markets from *Investment Week* and *International Investment*.

- **www.pwcglobal.com/uk**

  The PricewaterhouseCoopers website includes UK Economic Outlook.

- **www.bbc.co.uk**

  The website of the BBC carries general business information as well as programme-related content.

- **www.cimaglobal.com**

  CIMA's website. Includes student section.

SYLLABUS MINDMAP

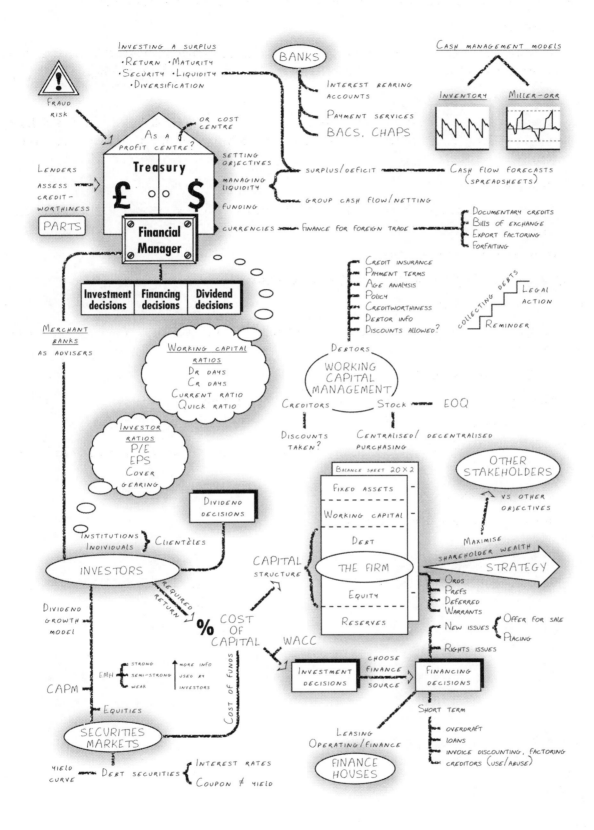

BPP PUBLISHING

Questions

THE FINANCE FUNCTION

Questions 1 to 9 cover the finance function, the subject of Part A of the BPP Study Text for Paper 4.

1   **OBJECTIVE TEST QUESTIONS: THE FINANCE FUNCTION I**   *36 mins*

1   Which of the following functions is not normally included in the role of a company treasurer?

   A   Budgeting
   B   Banking
   C   Currency management
   D   Funding management

2   Which of the following is generally assumed to be the principal financial objective of a company?

   A   Maximising profit retentions
   B   Maximising operating profitability
   C   Maximising the wealth of the ordinary shareholders
   D   Maximising dividends

3   Which of the following is concerned with how well an activity is achieving its intended effects?

   A   Earnings
   B   Economy
   C   Efficiency
   D   Effectiveness

4   Which of the following is not one of the '3E's' of 'value for money'?

   A   Earnings
   B   Economy
   C   Efficiency
   D   Effectiveness

5   What is any group or individual whose interests are directly affected by the activities of a firm called?

   A   Agent
   B   Investor
   C   Shareholder
   D   Stakeholder

6   Which of the following is a disadvantage of having a wide range of shareholders in a business?

   A   Shareholders will have a wider range of objectives.
   B   There is likely to be greater activity in the market in the firm's shares.
   C   There is less likelihood of one shareholder having a controlling interest.
   D   There is a greater likelihood of a takeover bid being frustrated.

7   What is any person or organisation who brings together providers and users of finance, whether as broker or principal, known as?

   A   Business angel
   B   Venture capitalist

C   Merchant banker

D   Financial intermediary

8   Of what type of market is the following statement a definition?

'A short-term wholesale market for securities maturing in one year, such as certificates of deposit, treasury bills and commercial paper.'

A   Capital market

B   Stock Exchange

C   Alternative Investment Market

D   Money market

9   Which of the following is not an example of an institutional investor?

A   Bank of England

B   Pension funds

C   Insurance companies

D   Unit trusts

10   In which of the following projects would a venture capital organisation be the least likely to invest?

A   A business start-up

B   A management buyout

C   Renovation of a production facility

D   Replacement of an existing production line with a process using a new technology

Total Marks = 20

2   **OBJECTIVE TEST QUESTIONS: THE FINANCE FUNCTION II**   *36 mins*

1   Which of the following forms of new share issues would normally be underwritten?

A   Introduction

B   Offer for sale by tender

C   Placing

D   Rights issue

2   Which of the following organisations may not act as financial intermediaries in the UK?

A   Department of Trade and Industry

B   National Savings

C   Pension funds

D   Clearing banks

3   Which of the following is *not* a method by which a company can obtain a Stock Exchange quotation for its shares?

A   Offer for sale

B   Placing

C   Rights issue

D   Introduction

4   Which of the following is not a feature of a capital market with 'strong form' efficiency?

A   Share prices change quickly to reflect all new information about future prospects.

B   Transaction costs are not significant.

C   No individual dominates the market.

D   Individual share price movements behave in a random way.

5   Identify which of the following is not an advantage of a well established stock market.

A   Capital is allocated productively, benefiting society as a whole
B   Shareholders can sell shares easily
C   Firms can readily obtain long-term funds
D   Current market prices fully reflect available information

6   The efficient market hypothesis exists in a number of forms that relate to different levels of information processing efficiency. In the semi-strong form of the hypothesis, which of the following types of information will not influence the share price?

A   Past movements in share prices
B   Publicly available factual information
C   Announcements of mergers or takeovers
D   Specialist information

7   Which of the following UK capital markets is *not* operated and supervised by The London Stock Exchange?

A   Primary market
B   Alternative Investment Market
C   Gilts market
D   Over the counter markets

8   Which of the following is not a reason why a company might seek a stock market listing?

A   Access to a wider pool of finance
B   Improved marketability of shares
C   Enhancement of company image
D   Protection from being taken over

9   A company is making an offer for sale by tender. It wishes to raise £2m from the issue, and has received the following bids. How many shares should be issued and at what price? Issue costs may be ignored.

Price tendered per share	Number of shares applied for at this price
£	
1.50	200,000
2.00	500,000
2.50	600,000
3.00	200,000

A   200,000 shares at £1.50, 500,000 shares at £2.00 and 280,000 shares at £2.50
B   200,000 shares at £3.00 and 560,000 shares at £2.50
C   666,667 shares at £3.00
D   800,000 shares at £2.50

10   With which of the following is the efficient market hypothesis primarily concerned?

    A   Information-processing efficiency
    B   Operational efficiency
    C   Allocative efficiency
    D   X-efficiency

Total Marks = 20

3   OBJECTIVE TEST QUESTIONS: THE FINANCE FUNCTION III   *36 mins*

1   Somer Halliday plc, an unquoted company, has obtained a Stock Exchange listing, with its shares offered to the general public by means of an offer for sale. Not all of the shares put on offer were bought by the public, and these unsold share were bought instead under a previous agreement by a number of financial institutions. This agreement by the institutions to purchase Somer Halliday plc's unsold shares is known as:

    A   A placing
    B   Sponsorship
    C   Underwriting
    D   An introduction

2   When a company decides to make a rights issue of shares, the main advantage of issuing the new shares at a deep discount is:

    A   To improve the prospects for a successful issue
    B   To avoid concerns about a fall in the cum rights share price
    C   To avoid a large increase in the share premium account
    D   To avoid having to pay underwriting costs

3   Deferred equity can be described as

    A   Shares that are entitled to dividend only after the main class of ordinary shares has been paid a dividend

    B   Securities that are not yet ordinary shares, but could be converted into ordinary shares at a future date

    C   A class of ordinary share that has less voting rights than another class of ordinary shares in the same company

    D   A golden share

4   Which of the following statements is true?

    A   Since 1960, the proportion of shares in the hands of individuals has fallen by approximately half

    B   New issues of share are a more important source of funds for firms in the UK than cash retained from profits

    C   An investment trust is prohibited from borrowing

    D   A company that has moved into profit has the advantage of increased levels of cash

5   Which of the following factors is not a possible disadvantage of flotation on the Stock Exchange?

   A   Having to write off the costs of flotation against the company's profit for the year

   B   The pressures of being expected by investors to achieve continual growth in profits, earnings and dividends

   C   Dilution of control and ownership

   D   The need to comply with stringent Stock Exchange regulations

6   Which of the following is not a reason why a public company might revert to private company status?

   A   To avoid shareholder expectations of annual growth in earnings per share and dividends

   B   To avoid the danger of a takeover

   C   Because the plc's share price was overvalued

   D   Because the plc's share price was undervalued

7   Which of the following is not generally a function of financial intermediaries?

   A   The provision of investment advice and information
   B   Reduction of risk via aggregation of funds
   C   Maturity transformation
   D   Prudential control

8   Which of the following is not normally a function of the treasury department of a large firm?

   A   Currency management
   B   Funding management
   C   Credit control
   D   Short-term investment

9   Equity funds in their company can be increased in a variety of ways. Which of the following are examples of this?

   A   Ordinary shareholders taking a dividend payment
   B   Ordinary shareholders taking up a rights issue
   C   A company buying back its own shares
   D   Ordinary shareholders taking up a debenture issue

10 An investor who makes all his investment decisions just by analysing historical share price movements as a basis for predicting future price changes is acting as if he believed that the stock market has

   A   Weak form efficiency
   B   Semi-strong form efficiency
   C   Strong form efficiency
   D   No efficiency at all

Total Marks = 20

If you struggled with these objective test questions, go back to your BPP Study Text for Paper 4 and revise Chapters 1-4 before you tackle the longer questions on the finance function.

If you would like a bank of objective test questions which covers a range of syllabus topics, order our MCQ cards using the order form at the back of this Kit.

4   **FINANCIAL MANAGEMENT**   *36 mins*

'The objective of financial management is to maximise the value of the firm.'

Required

Discuss how the achievement of this objective might be compromised by the conflicts which may arise between the various stakeholders in an organisation.

Total Marks = 20

5   **STAKEHOLDERS**   *36 mins*

(a)   'Financial managers need only concentrate on meeting the needs of shareholders - no other group matters.'

Discuss.   **12 Marks**

(b)   Many decisions in financial management are taken in a framework of conflicting stakeholder viewpoints. Identify the stakeholders and some of the financial management issues involved in any two of the following situations.

(i)   A private company converting into a public company.

(ii)   A highly geared company, such as Eurotunnel, attempting to restructure its capital finance.

(iii)   A public company offering to run the UK National Lottery on a not-for-profit basis.   **8 Marks**

Total Marks = 20

6   **POLICY DECISIONS**   *36 mins*

When determining the financial objectives of a company, it is necessary to take three types of policy decision into account - investment policy, financing policy and dividend policy.

Required

(a)   Discuss the nature of these three types of policy decision, commenting on how they are inter-related and how they might affect the value of the firm (ie the present value of projected cash flows).   **10 Marks**

(b)   Describe the different functions of the treasury and financial control departments of an organisation and comment on the relative contributions of these two departments to policy determination and the achievement of financial objectives.

10 Marks

Total Marks = 20

7   **MERCHANT BANK**   *36 mins*

When a company seeks a listing for its shares on a stock exchange, it usually recruits the assistance of a merchant bank.

Required

(a)   Explain the role of a merchant bank in a listing operation with respect to the various matters on which its advice will be sought by a company.   **10 Marks**

(b)   Identify the conflicts of interest which might arise if the merchant bank were part of a group providing a wide range of financial services.   **10 Marks**

Total Marks = 20

8   **MARKET EFFICIENCY**   *36 mins*

(a)   Describe the main forms of market efficiency.   **12 Marks**

(b)   Discuss *two* of the following in the context of the efficient markets hypothesis.

   (i)   The role of technical analysis (Chartism) and fundamental analysis

   (ii)   The purchase and sale of shares using 'insider information'

   (iii)   The increasing popularity of index-tracking funds which track stock market indices

   (iv)   Companies using creative accounting techniques in their accounts   **8 Marks**

                                                              Total Marks = 20

9   **TREASURY DEPARTMENT**   *36 mins*

ABC plc is a UK-based service company with a number of wholly-owned subsidiaries and interests in associated companies throughout the world. In response to the rapid growth of the company, the Managing Director has ordered a review of the company's organisation structure, particularly the finance function. The Managing Director holds the opinion that a separate treasury department should be established. At present, treasury functions are the responsibility of the Chief Accountant.

Required

(a)   Describe the main responsibilities of a treasury department in a company such as ABC plc and explain the benefits which might accrue from the establishment of a separate treasury function.   **12 Marks**

(b)   Describe the advantages and disadvantages which might arise if the company established a separate treasury department as a profit rather than a cost centre.

                                                              8 Marks
                                                              Total Marks = 20

SOURCES OF LONG-TERM FINANCE

Questions 10 to 28 cover sources of long-term finance, the subject of Part B of the BPP Study Text for Paper 4.

---

10   OBJECTIVE TEST QUESTIONS: LONG-TERM FINANCE I   *36 mins*

1   Which of the following methods of issuing shares could be used by a company that is being floated on the stock market for the first time?

    A   Offer for sale by tender
    B   Prospectus issue
    C   Rights issue
    D   Placing

2   Where shares in a large company are already widely held, so that a market can be seen to exist, the Stock Exchange may grant a quotation. No shares are made available to the market, neither existing nor newly created shares. What is this process called?

    A   Placing
    B   Introduction
    C   Share split
    D   Scrip issue

3   The following information has been extracted from the accounts of Whitewater plc:

	£m
Earnings before interest and tax	800
Debt interest	100
Earnings after debt interest	700
Tax payable	200
Earnings after interest and tax	500
Number of shares in issue	250m
Market price per share	£20

What is the EPS (earnings per share)?

    A   £2.00
    B   £2.80
    C   £3.20
    D   £0.20

4   The following information has been extracted from the accounts of Whitewater plc:

	£m
Earnings before interest and tax	800
Debt interest	100
Earnings after debt interest	700
Tax payable	200
Earnings after interest and tax	500
Number of shares in issue	250m
Market price per share	£20

What is the price/earnings ratio?

    A   6.25
    B   8.0
    C   10.0
    D   40.0

5   The following information has been extracted from the accounts of Whitewater plc:

	£m
Earnings before interest and tax	800
Debt interest	100
Earnings after debt interest	700
Tax payable	200
Earnings after interest and tax	500
Number of shares in issue	250m
Nominal value	£1
Market price per share	£20
Payout rate	60%

What is the dividend yield?

A   4%
B   80%
C   120%
D   6%

6   The following information has been extracted from the accounts of Whitewater plc:

	£m
Earnings before interest and tax	800
Debt interest	100
Earnings after debt interest	700
Tax payable	200
Earnings after interest and tax	500
Number of shares in issue	250m
Market price per share	£20

What is the dividend cover?

A   0.6 times
B   1.67 times
C   2.33 times
D   2.67 times

7   Dukes plc has 4 million £1 ordinary shares in issue with a current market price of £5 per share. It decides to make a 1 for 4 rights issue at £4. What is the theoretical ex-rights price of the shares following the issue?

A   £4.00
B   £4.50
C   £4.80
D   £5.00

8   Dukes plc has 4 million £1 ordinary shares in issue with a current market price of £5 per share. It decides to make a 1 for 4 rights issue at £4. What is the value of a right per new share?

A   £1.00
B   £0.80
C   £0.20
D   nil

9   Dukes plc has 4 million £1 ordinary shares in issue with a current market price of £5 per share. It decides to make a 1 for 4 rights issue at £4. The rate of return on the existing funds is 10%, and it is widely expected that the rate of return on the new funds will be 12.5%. What is the yield adjusted theoretical ex-rights price?

BPP PUBLISHING

A   £4.00
B   £4.80
C   £5.00
D   £5.80

10   Which of the following forms of annual payment to investors made by a company is not tax deductible?

A   10% debentures
B   8% loan stock
C   8% bond
D   6% preference shares

Total Marks = 20

11   **OBJECTIVE TEST QUESTIONS: LONG-TERM FINANCE II**   *36 mins*

1   Which of the following factors is the least likely to affect the actual market price of convertible stock?

A   The price of straight debentures with the same coupon rate of interest
B   Market expectations of future equity returns
C   The market price of redeemable preference shares
D   The length of time before conversion takes place

2   Which of the following are not features of a finance lease?

A   The lessor is responsible for the maintenance of the asset.

B   The agreement may split the lease term in to a primary period and a secondary period.

C   The capital value of the asset must be shown on the lessee's balance sheet.

D   The leasing company is normally a bank or finance house.

3   The dividing line between finance and operating leases is determined by the proportion of the value of the asset which is in the contract. An asset value above which of the following percentages would cause the lease to be classed as a finance lease?

A   95%
B   90%
C   85%
D   80%

4   Which of the following would not be appropriate to a small company seeking government finance?

A   Regional Enterprise Grant
B   SMART Award
C   Teaching Company Scheme
D   PONZI Scheme

5   The following figures have been extracted from the accounts of Cockcroft plc:

	£
Ordinary shares of 50p each	750,000
Reserves	750,000
8% preference shares of £1 each	250,000
10% debentures	250,000
	2,000,000

The ordinary shares are trading at £2.50 each, the preference shares are trading at £0.80 each and the debentures are trading at £120 per £100.

What is the gearing ratio for Cockcroft plc based on book values?

A   40%
B   30%
C   25%
D   20%

6   The following figures have been extracted from the accounts of Cockcroft plc:

	£
Ordinary shares of 50p each	750,000
Reserves	750,000
8% preference shares of £1 each	250,000
10% debentures	250,000
	2,000,000

The ordinary shares are trading at £2.50 each, the preference shares are trading at £0.80 each and the debentures are trading at £120 per £100.

What is the gearing ratio for Cockcroft plc based on market values?

A   13%
B   16%
C   18%
D   21%

7   The dividend growth model can be stated as:

$$k_e = \frac{d_0(1+g)}{P_0} + g$$

Which of the following definitions of terms within the formula is incorrect?

A k_e = cost of equity
B d_0 = current dividend
C P_0 = market value of equity (cum div)
D g = expected constant annual growth rate in dividends

8   What is the cost of capital for Mitchell plc, assuming an equity beta of 1.2, an expected market return of 15% and a risk free rate of 10%?

A   18%
B   16%
C   15%
D   12%

9   Ravenscroft plc has 10% debentures that are currently quoted at a cum interest market price of £90. Corporation tax is 30%. What is the cost of the debt?

A   7.8%
B   8.8%
C   11.1%
D   12.5%

10 Which of the following assumptions underlying the use of the WACC in investment appraisal is incorrect?

    A   The new investment does not carry a significantly different risk profile from that of the existing entity.

    B   The new investment is marginal to the entity.

    C   The capital structure is reasonable constant.

    D   The new investment is in the same business area as the existing operations.

Total Marks = 20

12   OBJECTIVE TEST QUESTIONS: LONG-TERM FINANCE III   *36 mins*

1 Which of the following is the source of finance which a company can draw upon most easily in practice?

    A   Cash generated from retained earnings
    B   New share issues
    C   Rights issues
    D   Bank borrowings

2 The following information relates to CDE plc.

Earnings per share   42p
Dividend cover   2.1
Dividend yield   1.6%

What share price is implied by this data, to the nearest 1p?

    A   20p
    B   55p
    C   88p
    D   1,250p

3 What does the 'relationship of the fixed cost to the total cost of an operating unit' refer to ? (CIMA *Official Terminology*)

    A   Operational gearing
    B   Leverage
    C   Financial gearing
    D   Capital gearing

4 Which of the following is not a valid reason why the directors of a company might decide to retain earnings rather than pay them out as dividends?

    A   Finance from retained earnings have no cost as a source of finance.

    B   The shareholders generally wish to make a capital profit.

    C   Retention of earnings avoids the possibility of a change in control resulting from an issue of new shares.

    D   Retention of earnings allows the directors to undertake investment projects without involving the shareholders.

5 A company's balance sheet shows the following long-term funds.

	£
Ordinary share of 10p each	100,000
Reserves	650,000
6% preference shares of £1 each	400,000
12% unsecured loan stock	250,000
Total long-term funds	1,400,000

The mid-market price of the ordinary shares is currently 240 pence on the stock exchange. The unsecured loan stock trades at £80 per £100 nominal. The preference shares trade at 75 pence each.

Calculate a figure for the market value of the company's securities (equity *plus* preference shares *plus* loan stock) that you would use to calculate the weighted average cost of capital.

A   £850,000
B   £1,740,000
C   £2,850,000
D   £2,900,000

6   Which of the following factors is not likely to affect the actual market price of convertible stock?

A   The price of straight debentures with the same coupon rate of interest
B   Market expectations of future equity returns in the company
C   The market price of redeemable preference shares
D   The length of time before conversion takes place

7   Which of the following statements relating to the warrants issued with loan stock is not true?

A   If growth prospects are good, the warrant will usually be quoted at a premium above the minimum price prior to the exercise period.

B   A warrant is a right given by a company to an investor to subscribe for new shares at a future date at a price to be decided by the market.

C   The purpose of warrants is to make the loan stock more attractive.

D   Warrants are normally issued as part of a package with unsecured loan stock.

8   Which of the following statements is true of an operating lease?

A   It is only possible to cancel the agreement during the term at significant cost.

B   With this type of agreement a company sells assets to a finance house and the finance house receives regular payments while the firm uses the asset.

C   It is a short-term lease that can easily be cancelled.

D   It is a contract for a specified term, normally equal to the expected asset life.

9   Which of the following ratios cannot be used to measure the financial risk of a company's capital structure?

A   Price/earnings ratio
B   Gearing ratio
C   Debt ratio
D   Interest cover

10   A quoted share has a beta factor of 1.25. The market risk premium is 9%. The risk-free rate of return is 7%. Using CAPM, the required rate of return is:

A   9.5
B   11.25
C   15.75
D   18.25

Total Marks = 20

13   OBJECTIVE TEST QUESTIONS: LONG-TERM FINANCE IV   *36 mins*

1   Fulmer plc has decided to calculate its gearing ratio according to the formula: prior charge capital/total capital employed. At which of the following levels of gearing would it be low geared?

A   25%
B   50%
C   75%
D   100%

2   A company has decided to calculate its gearing ratio according to the formula: prior charge capital ÷ equity capital (including reserves). At which of the following levels would it be highly geared?

A   50%
B   75%
C   100%
D   150%

3   What is meant by systematic risk?

A   Risk arising from the inclusion of debt in the capital structure of a firm

B   Variability of returns caused by factors affecting the whole market which cannot be eliminated by diversification

C   Diversifiable risk that is specific to sectors, companies or projects

D   The risk of failure of the financial system

4   Which of the following statements is not characteristic of a company with a rising level of financial gearing?

A   There is increased variability in the level of shareholders' earnings.
B   There is increased risk of financial failure.
C   There is a rise in the level of interest cover.
D   There is a fall in the level of variable costs.

5   Eltron plc, a consultancy company, has a number of different types of creditor in its balance sheet. Which of these carries the greatest default risk from the point of view of the 'lenders'?

A   £100,000 bank overdraft
B   Ten year £250,000 bank mortgage on the company office building
C   500,000 10% preference shares, nominal value £1
D   2m ordinary shares, nominal value £1

6   What is meant by the term 'tax shield'?

A   A scheme to make use of tax havens to reduce tax liabilities of a firm

B   The treatment of interest as a business expense, making borrowing cheaper than equity when calculating the firm's cost of capital

C   The use of tax rules for the carry forward of losses in trading companies

D   A scheme to avoid double taxation of profits earned in one country and remitted to another

7   Which of the following is not a feature of the cost of capital to a company?

   A   It is the return that investors expect to be paid for putting funds into the company.

   B   It is the minimum return that a company should make on its own investments.

   C   It can be estimated from the average market returns.

   D   It can be used in investment appraisal.

8   Which of the following is a feature of a finance lease for capital equipment?

   A   The agreement may split the lease term into a primary period and a secondary period.

   B   The capital value of the asset will not be shown on the lessee's balance sheet.

   C   The lessor is responsible for maintenance of the asset.

   D   The lessor is normally the manufacturer of the equipment.

9   Ordinary shares in Multizip plc are quoted at a mid-market price of £3.60, with a par value of 50p each. The market value of its long-term debt is equal to its book value. Corporate tax is at a rate of 30%. The company has the following market structure.

	£m	Cost of finance %
Ordinary shares	5	15
Reserves	10	15
Long-term debt	8	10

   What is the weighted average cost of capital of Multizip plc?

   A   12.2%
   B   13.3%
   C   13.5%
   D   14.1%

10   Which of the following factors make leasing attractive to the lessee?

   A   Operating leases can provide a form of off balance sheet finance.

   B   Leasing restricts flexibility in a period of rapidly changing technology.

   C   The implicit interest rate on a lease may be higher than that on other loan finance.

   D   The supplier of the equipment is paid in full at the start of the lease.

Total Marks = 20

14   OBJECTIVE TEST QUESTIONS: LONG-TERM FINANCE V   *36 mins*

1   Which of the following is hire purchase (HP) a form of?

   A   Vendor credit
   B   Lender credit
   C   Acceptance credit
   D   Finance lease

2   A 20-year bond with a nominal value of £100 and a coupon of 6% (annual) is due for redemption in six years time. The next interest payment is due in one year from now. The market rate of interest is now 12%. What is the approximate market value of the bond?

A   £24.67

B   £36.55

C   £50.70

D   £75.37

3   PRT plc has one million shares in issue and is preparing to make a one-for-four rights issue. The current market price of the shares is £2.00. At what price should the new shares be offered so as to avoid a drop in the share price following the issue? You can assume that the earnings performance of the new funds will be the same as on the existing funds.

A   50p

B   £2.00

C   £4.00

D   £8.00

4   Saffron Ltd has 100,000 ordinary shares in issue with a nominal value of £1 and a market value of £2.50. It is proposing to make a one-for-four scrip issue. Mr Normal holds 200 shares in the company. How much would he have to pay Saffron Ltd for his new shares?

A   £200.00

B   £125.00

C   £50.00

D   Nil

5   A company has 1m shares in issue, which have a nominal value of £2 and a market price of £8. The company is proposing to double the number of shares in issue by means of a stock split. What will be the effect on reserves of this action?

A   Reserves will increase by £1m

B   Reserves will decrease by £1m

C   Reserves will decrease by £4m

D   Reserves will be unchanged

6   The figures in the table below are an extract from the profit and loss account of MKE plc. Reserves are £4.5m. There are 3.5m ordinary shares in issue (nominal value 50 pence each) with a market price of £2.

	£
Profit before tax	2,500,000
Less tax	750,000
Profit after tax	1,750,000
Dividend	500,000
Retained profits	1,250,000

What is the dividend cover?

A   5 times

B   3.5 times

C   2.5 times

D   9 times

7   The figures in the table below are an extract from the profit and loss account of MKE plc. Reserves are £4.5m. There are 3.5m ordinary shares in issue (nominal value 50 pence each) with a market price of £2.

	£
Profit before tax	2,500,000
Less tax	750,000
Profit after tax	1,750,000
Dividend	500,000
Retained profits	1,250,000

What is the earnings per share, to the nearest 1p?

A   100 pence
B   36 pence
C   50 pence
D   71 pence

8   Which of the following factors are company directors likely not to take into account when setting the level of dividends for the year?

A   The law on distributable profits
B   The previous level of dividends
C   The liquidity position
D   The level of other creditors

9   A company has made an issue of 10% debenture stock 2009/2012 at a price of £1,500 per £2,000 stock. Which of the following are correct statements concerning this issue?

A   The latest date at which the stock can be redeemed is 2009.
B   The latest date at which the stock can be redeemed is 2012.
C   The redemption price will be in the range £2,009 - £2,012.
D   Annual interest payments on £2,000 stock will be £150.

10   A company has made an issue of 8% convertible loan stock with a par value of £100. The stock can be redeemed in four years time at £130, or converted into shares at the rate of 40 shares per £100 loan stock. At which of the following share prices would an investor not opt for redemption?

A   £2.00
B   £2.50
C   £3.00
D   £3.50

Total Marks = 20

15   **OBJECTIVE TEST QUESTIONS: LONG-TERM FINANCE VI**   *36 mins*

1   A company is to make a rights issue of one share at £1.60 for every three existing shares. There is a current dividend payment due of 4p per share, but the new shares will not qualify for this. The current price per share just prior to the rights issue is £2.12 cum dividend.

What is the theoretical ex rights price per share?

A   £1.95
B   £1.96
C   £1.99
D   £2.00

2   Which one of the following best describes the term 'coupon rate' as applied to debenture stock?

A   The annual interest received on the face value of the units of the stock

B   The annual interest received divided by the current ex-interest market price of the stock

C   The total rate of return on a stock, taking into account capital repayment as well as interest payments

D   The minimum rate of interest required to maintain the market value of the stock at or above par value

3   At 1 January, the equity share of Rick Pool plc had a market value of 80p each. There are 40 million share in issue.

The summary P&L account for the year to 31 December is as follows.

	£'000	£'000
Profit after tax		8,000
Ordinary dividend - interim paid	800	
- final proposed	2,400	
		3,200
Retained profits		4,800

During the year, a final dividend of 5.5p per share from the previous year was paid. At 31 December, the equity share price was 85p.

What was the return for equity shareholders in the year to 31 December, based on the start-of-year share value?

A   15.6%
B   16.3%
C   23.1%
D   31.3%

4   A company's irredeemable loan stock has a coupon rate of 10% and pays interest of £5 per £100 nominal stock on both 1 January and 1 July each year. If the cum interest price on 31 December is £92, what is the annual cost of the loan capital to the company? Ignore taxation.

A   10.9%
B   11.2%
C   11.5%
D   11.8%

5   The ordinary share price of Kroll plc is currently 200p. Dividend is paid once a year and has very recently been paid for the previous year. The net dividend for the year was 5p and a 20% annual growth rate in perpetuity is expected for future dividend payments.

Using the dividend growth model, what is the cost of capital of Kroll plc's equity?

A   22.5%
B   23.0%
C   23.1%
D   23.3%

6   The ordinary shares of Dribb plc have a market value of 125 pence each cum div. The annual dividend for the year, which is about to be paid, is 5 pence per share. The expected annual growth rate in dividends is 10% per annum into the foreseeable future, so that the dividend payable at the end of next year is expected to be 5.5. pence, and so on.

The cost of capital for Dribb plc's ordinary shares, using the dividend growth model, is

A   14.2%
B   14.4%
C   14.6%
D   15.0%

7   Elbo plc has just paid an annual ordinary dividend of 20p per share. The dividend is expected to rise by 10% per annum (compound). The cost of equity is 15%.

According to the dividend valuation model, what should be the market value per share ex div in one year's time?

A   440p
B   464p
C   484p
D   506p

8   The following data relate to an all-equity financed company.

Dividend just paid	£180,000
Earnings retained and invested	60%
Return on investments	15%
Cost of equity	20%

What, according to the theory of share values, should be the market value of the company (to the nearest £1,000)?

A   £900,000
B   £1,363,000
C   £1,636,000
D   £1,784,000

9   There are limits to the amount of debt capital that a company will be able to raise. Which of the following items will *not* act as such as limit?

A   High interest rates on extra borrowing
B   Limits imposed by covenants made on debentures already in issue
C   Insufficient assets to provide security for an extra loan
D   Borrowing restrictions in the company's Articles of Association

10   Suppose that, for a given level of activity, a firm's ratio of variable costs to fixed costs were lower and, at the same time, its ratio of debt to equity fell. What would be the impact on the firm's financial risk and operating risk?

	Financial risk would	*Operating risk would*
A	Increase	Increase
B	Decrease	Increase
C	Increase	Decrease
D	Decrease	Decrease

Total Marks = 20

16   OBJECTIVE TEST QUESTIONS: LONG-TERM FINANCE VII   *36 mins*

1   A company has 14% irredeemable loan stock in issue. Investors require a gross yield of 12% on this stock. The corporate tax rate is 35% and the basic rate of income tax is 25%. What is the cost of the loan stock to the company?

A   7.80%
B   9.00%
C   9.10%
D   10.50%

2   Pepper plc issued its 12% irredeemable debentures at 102. The current market price is 95. The company is paying corporation tax at a rate of 40%.

The current cost of capital to the company of these debentures is

A   7.1%
B   7.2%

C   7.6%

D   12.6%

3   Sandy Beech plc has announced a 1 for 4 rights issue at a subscription price of £2.50. The current cum rights price per share is £4.10.

What is the theoretical value of the fight per existing share?

A   8p

B   32p

C   40p

D   £1.28

4   At the present moment, the yield on index-linked gilts is 2%, the yield on long-dated government stocks is about 7% and the rate of inflation for the foreseeable future is about 6% per annum.

Approximately how much per annum would the government have to pay in interest per £100 of index-linked gilts?

A   £2

B   £4

C   £7

D   £8

5   The results of a company for the year ended 31 March 20X2 were as follows.

	£
Profit on ordinary activities after tax	2,500,000
Extraordinary profit after tax	400,000
Profit after tax for the financial year	2,900,000
Preference dividend	200,000
Ordinary dividend (paid and proposed)	1,200,000
Retained profits for the year	1,500,000

What is the dividend cover?

A   1.92 times

B   2.07 times

C   2.08 times

D   2.25 times

6   Ardour plc is a small public company with 10,000,000 5p ordinary shares in issue. Its results for the year just ended are as follows.

	£	£
Profits on ordinary activities after tax		800,000
Extraordinary losses net of tax		(100,000)
		700,000
Dividends: interim (paid)	100,000	
final (proposed)	300,000	
		400,000
Retained profits		300,000

The market price per share is currently 80p cum div. What is the P/E ratio?

A   9.5

B   9.6

C   10.0

D   11.0

7   The following data relates to shares of Gowan plc at the end of the day on 28 May 20X2.

PUBLISHING

22

Share price

		Closing prices, 27 May		
High for year	*Low for year*	*Buying price*	*Mid-market price*	*Selling price*
240p	190p	210p	220p	230p

The earnings per share for the year to 31 December 20X1 were 15p.

What is the P/E ratio for the company that would be reported in the financial press on 28 May 20X2?

A   14.0
B   14.3
C   14.7
D   15.3

8   The systematic risk of a project's return is the result of uncertainties in the return caused by

A   Factors unique to the project
B   Factors unique to the firm undertaking the project
C   Factors unique to the industry to which the project belongs
D   Nationwide economic factors

9   The beta coefficient of a security measures

A   The correlation between the return on the market index and the return on the security

B   The covariance between the return on the market index and the return on the security divided by the variance of the return on the market index

C   The variance of the return on the security divided by the variance of the return on the market index

D   The standard deviation of the return on the security divided by the standard deviation of the return on the market index

10   For which of the following reasons might a company that is perceived as 'risky' have a lower beta factor than an equivalent company that is perceived as less risky?

A   The risky company has a lower financial gearing level.

B   Inaccuracies in the estimation of beta factors from linear regression analysis or the company's returns over time.

C   The risky company has lower systematic risk but higher unsystematic risk.

D   The risky company is larger in size.

Total Marks = 20

If you struggled with these objective test questions, go back to your BPP Study Text for Paper 4 and revise Chapters 5 to 11 before you tackle the longer questions on sources of long-term finance.

If you would like a bank of objective test questions which covers a range of syllabus topics, order our MCQ cards using the order form at the back of this Kit.

---

17   BARDSEY PLC   *36 mins*

It is currently June 20X7. Bardsey plc operates a chain of city centre furniture stores, specialising in high quality items. It is 60% owned by the original family founders. Its sales over the past decade have never grown faster than 5% in any one year, even falling during a recent recession. No growth is expected from existing operations in the next few years despite continuing to offer generous credit to customers.

In order to achieve faster growth, it is considering the development of a number of 'out of town' sites, adjacent to giant supermarkets and DIY stores. During 20X7, this would involve a capital outlay of £50m plus additional working capital requirements of £20m in order to finance stock-building. In recent years, Bardsey's capital expenditure, mainly store refurbishments and vehicle replacements, and averaging around £10m per annum, has been financed entirely from cash flow. This category of investment will continue at about the same level in 20X7. Bardsey's fixed assets were revalued two years ago.

Bardsey's accounting statements for the last financial year are summarised in Exhibit A, and Exhibit B gives information on key financial indicators for the stores sector as a whole (listed companies only).

Bardsey's debentures currently sell on the stock market at £130 per £100 nominal. The current bank base rate is 8%, and economists expect interest rates in general to fall over the next few years. The stock market currently applies a price:earnings ratio of 11:1 to Bardsey's shares.

Exhibit A: Bardsey's financial statements

PROFIT AND LOSS ACCOUNT
FOR THE YEAR ENDED 31 DECEMBER 20X6

	£m
Turnover	150.0
Cost of sales*	(90.0)
Operating profit	60.0
Interest charges	(15.0)
Pre tax profit	45.0
Corporation tax	(12.0)
Profits after tax	33.0
Dividends proposed	(20.0)
Retained earnings	130.0

* This includes depreciation of £8m.

BALANCE SHEET AS AT 31 DECEMBER 20X6

	£m	£m	£m
Assets employed			
Fixed (net):			
Land and premises	200		
Fixtures and fittings	50		
Vehicles	50		
			300
Current:			
Stock	60		
Debtors	100		
Cash	40		
		200	
Current liabilities:			
Trade creditors	(85)		
Dividends payable	(20)		
Tax payable	(12)		
		(117)	
Net current assets			83
Total asset less current liabilities			383
15% Debentures 2010-12			(100)
Net assets			283
Financed by			
Issued share capital (par value 25p)			100
Revaluation reserve			60
Profit and loss account			123
Shareholders' funds			283

Exhibit B: Selected ratios for the stores sector

Return on (long-term) capital employed	14.3% (pre tax)
Return on equity	15.3% (post tax)
Operating profit margin	26.2%
Fixed asset turnover (sales/fixed assets)	1.2 times
Stock period	180 days
Debtor days	132 days
Gearing (total debt/equity)	42%
Interest cover	3.2 times
Dividend cover	2.1 times
P/E ratio	15:1

Required

As Bardsey's chief accountant, you are instructed to:

(a) Calculate Bardsey's expected net cash flow in 20X7 without the investment, assuming no change in the level of net working capital   **5 Marks**

(*Note.* A statement in FRS 1 format is not required.)

(b) Prepare a report, containing suitable reservations about the use of ratio analysis, which compares Bardsey's financial performance and health with the stores sector as a whole

15 Marks

Total Marks = 20

18   S PLC   *36 mins*

S plc issues a debenture at par carrying a 9% coupon. The debenture is redeemable in five years and each unit of £100 is convertible into 20 ordinary shares at any time prior to redemption. At the date of issue the yield on comparable nonconvertible debentures is 12% and the company's shares are quoted at 400p.

Required

(a) Calculate the conversion premium on the debenture at the date of issue and explain in general terms the relationship between the conversion premium and the coupon rate on convertible debentures.   **5 Marks**

(b) Assuming a 10% annual growth rate in share price, calculate the conversion value of the debenture three years after issue and explain why the debenture's market value is likely to exceed this figure.   **5 Marks**

(c) Explain why the market value of a convertible debenture is likely to be affected by the dividend policy of the issuing company.   **5 Marks**

(d) Explain what strategy a company might be pursuing when raising capital in the form of a convertible as distinct from raising straight debt or straight equity.   **5 Marks**

Total Marks = 20

19   Z PLC   *36 mins*

Z plc is a long-established company with interests mainly in retailing and property development. Its current market capitalisation is £750 million. The company trades almost exclusively in the UK but it is planning to expand overseas either by acquisition or joint venture within the next two years. The company has built up a portfolio of investments in UK equities and corporate and government debt. The aim of developing this investment portfolio is to provide a source of funds for its overseas expansion programme. It is currently 1 December 20X7. Summary information on the portfolio is given below.

Type of security	Value £ million	Average % return over last 12 months
UK equities	23.2	15.0
US securities	9.4	13.5
UK corporate debt	5.3	8.2
Long-term government debt	11.4	7.4
3-month Treasury bonds	3.2	6.0

Approximately 25% of the UK equities are in small companies' shares, some of them trading on the Alternative Investment Market. The average return on all UK equities over the past 12 months has been 12%. On US equities it has been 12.5%.

Ignore taxation throughout this question.

Required

(a) Discuss the advantages and disadvantages of holding such a portfolio of investments in the circumstances of Z plc. **10 Marks**

(b) One of Z plc's corporate debt investments is £50,000 nominal in a convertible loan stock 20X7/X9, currently selling at £106.50 per £100 of stock. The coupon rate is 6%. If not converted, it is repayable on 31 December 20X9 at par. Interest is payable annually and has just been paid for 20X7. Bonds of similar risk without a conversion feature are currently selling to return 7%.

The 20X7 date for conversion is 31 December 20X7 at a conversion ratio of 20 shares per £100 of stock. The ratio applicable for conversion in 20X8 is 18 shares per £100 of stock. The market price of the ordinary shares is 540 pence. At the time the bonds were purchased by Z plc in 20X6, the equity share price was 480 pence. Assume that interest rates have remained unchanged since the bonds were purchased.

Required

(i) Explain what is meant by the terms *conversion premium* and *conversion discount*.

(ii) Advise the company's treasurer about the factors to consider before deciding whether to convert the loan stock in 20X7 or 20X8. Include all relevant calculations in your advice. **10 Marks**

Total Marks = 20

20   **NEWSAM PLC**   *36 mins*

It is now December 20X4. Newsam plc is a quoted company which produces a range of branded products all of which are well-established in their respective markets, although overall sales have grown by an average of only 2% per annum over the past decade. The board of directors is currently concerned about the company's level of financial gearing, which although not high by industry standards, is near to breaching the covenants attaching to its 15% debenture issue, made in 20W2 at a time of high market interest rates. Issued in order to finance the acquisition of the premises on which it is secured, the debenture is repayable at par value of £100 per unit of stock at any time during the period 20X4-X7.

There are two covenants attaching to the debenture, which state:

'At no time shall the ratio of debt capital to shareholders' fund exceed 50%. The company shall also maintain a prudent level of liquidity, defined as a current ratio at no time outside the range of the industry average (as published by the corporate credit analysts, Creditex), plus or minus 20%.'

Newsam's most recent set of accounts is shown in summarised form below. The buildings have been depreciated since 20W2 at 4% per annum, and most of the machinery is only two or three years old, having been purchased mainly via a bank overdraft. The interest rate payable on the bank overdraft is currently 9%. The finance director argues that Newsam should take advantage of historically low interest rates on the European money markets by issuing a medium-term Eurodollar bond at 5%. The dollar is currently selling at a premium of about 1% on the three-month forward market.

Newsam's ordinary shares currently sell at a P/E ratio of 14, and look unattractive compared to comparable companies in the sector which exhibit an average P/E ratio of 18. According to the latest published credit assessment by Creditex, the average current ratio for the industry is 1.35. The debentures currently sell in the market at £15 above par.

Summarised financial accounts for Newsam plc for the year ended 30 June 20X4

BALANCE SHEET AS AT 30 JUNE 20X4

Assets employed	£m	£m	£m
Fixed (net):			
Land			5.0
Premises			4.0
Machinery and vehicles			11.0
			20.0
Current:			
Stocks	2.5		
Debtors	4.0		
Cash	0.5		
		7.0	
Current liabilities:			
Creditors	(4.0)		
Bank overdraft	(3.0)		
		(7.0)	
Net current assets			0.0
Total assets less current liabilities			20.0
Long-term creditors:			
15% Debentures 20X4-X7			(5.0)
Net assets			15.0

	£m
Financed by:	
Ordinary shares (25p par value)	5.0
Reserves	10.0
Shareholders' funds	15.0

PROFIT AND LOSS ACCOUNT EXTRACTS FOR THE YEAR ENDED 30 JUNE 20X4

	£m
Sales	28.00
Operating profit	3.00
Interest payable	(1.00)
Profit before tax	2.00
Taxation	(0.66)
Profit after tax	1.34
Dividend	(0.70)
Retained profit	0.64

Required

(a) Calculate appropriate gearing ratios for Newsam plc using:

    (i)   Book values

    (ii)   Market values **3 Marks**

(b) Assess how close Newsam plc is to breaching the debenture covenants. **3 Marks**

(c) Discuss whether Newsam plc's gearing is in any sense 'dangerous'. **4 Marks**

(d) Discuss what financial policies Newsam plc might adopt:

    (i)   In order to lower its capital gearing, and

    (ii)   To improve its interest cover **10 Marks**

Total Marks = 20

21   **MRF** *36 mins*

MRF is a charitable organisation and exempt from all taxes. It is about to acquire some new capital equipment for a special project. The President of the charity has been advised that it might be advantageous to acquire the equipment with a finance lease. The cost to the charity of the equipment, if it were purchased outright, would be £22.5 million. However, the leasing company would be able to negotiate a 20% discount on this price because of its long-term commercial relationship with suppliers of the type of equipment being purchased. This discount would not be available to the charity if it purchased the equipment with a bank loan.

The leasing company is nearing its year end and is keen to obtain the tax advantages denied to MRF because of its charitable status. It has therefore offered what it considers to be very favourable terms. Payments by MRF would be £7.5 million per annum for 6 years, payable at the end of each year of the lease contract.

Writing down allowances are available to the leasing company at 25 per cent on a reducing balance basis. At the end of year 6, it is estimated that the second-hand value of the equipment would be £4 million. Insurance and maintenance would be the responsibility of the charity, whether it leases or purchases the equipment.

The cost of a bank loan to the charity would be 12 per cent. The opportunity cost of capital for the leasing company would be 14 per cent.

Assume no time lag in tax payments or refunds.

You should work to two decimal places throughout.

Required

(a) Assume you are MRF's treasurer. Evaluate the financial aspects of the lease and recommend to the President whether the charity should purchase with a bank loan or use a finance lease. You should state the reasons for your recommendation and any assumptions you make in arriving at your decision. **8 Marks**

(b) Now assume that you are an account negotiator for the leasing company. You have been informed that MRF has decided to buy the equipment with a bank loan at 12 per cent interest. Your boss, Helen, has asked you to advise her whether the lease terms could be reduced so as to be competitive with the bank loan. The leasing company pays tax at the marginal rate of 33 per cent. Assume that the lease receipts from MRF are fully taxable.

Required

Write a short report advising Helen of:

(i)   The annual lease payments required for the charity to be indifferent between the bank and the leasing company

(ii)   The effect on the leasing company's evaluation if the lease payments were reduced to the amount calculated above (if you are unable to calculate a figure, assume £5 million per annum)

(iii)   Other actions which the company could take to rescue the deal

Supporting calculations should provided where appropriate.   **12 Marks**

Total Marks = 20

22   ABC PLC   *36 mins*

ABC plc is classified as a small company for corporation tax purposes and is liable to tax at 21%. The company is considering the purchase of a new computer system. The Chief Executive has been advised that it might be advantageous to lease the computer system rather than buy with a secured bank loan. The before-tax cost of a bank loan to ABC plc would be 11½%. Apart from the possible financial benefits which might arise, he has been told that leasing provides a hedge against obsolescence.

The capital cost of the computer would be £50,000. The leasing company, which is not the supplier or manufacturer of the equipment, has offered what it considers to be very favourable terms for the lease of the computer. Payments would be £15,000 per annum for five years. The first payment would be made at the beginning of the lease contract. This would be followed by four further payments at the beginning of each of the next four years. Insurance and maintenance of the computer would be the responsibility of the lessee. At the end of year 5, the second-hand value of the computer is expected to be £5,000.

The leasing company pays tax at the marginal rate of 31%. Writing down allowances are available on the computer at 25% on a reducing balance basis. The company's required rate of return on equity is 15% and it considers this deal to be of about the average risk of its commercial ventures. The lessor will be able to finance the purchase of the computer from retained earnings.

Required

(a)   Evaluate the financial decision concerning the lease from the point of view of both the lessee and the lessor.   **8 Marks**

(b)   Write a report to the Chief Executive of ABC plc explaining the purpose and conclusions of your evaluation. Include in your report an explanation of the claim that leasing provides a hedge against obsolescence.   **8 Marks**

(c)   The Chief Executive of ABC plc claims that the evaluation is basically a capital budgeting exercise and that the company's weighted average cost of capital is a more appropriate rate to use as a discount rate.

Discuss the validity of the Chief Executive's comments.   **4 Marks**

Total Marks = 20

23   ARMADA   *36 mins*

Armada Leisure Industries plc is already highly geared by industry standards, but wishes to raise external capital to finance the development of a new bowling alley in Plymouth. The

29

stock market has recently reached a record level but economic forecasters are expressing doubts about the future prospects for the UK economy.

Required

(a) Assess the arguments for and against a rights issue by Armada. **10 Marks**

(b) Examine the relative merits of leasing versus hire purchase as means of acquiring capital assets. **10 Marks**

Total Marks = 20

24 **RISK AND MARKET EFFICIENCY** *36 mins*

(a) You are the company accountant with a medium-sized privately owned company. The company has surplus funds which it does not believe it will be able to invest in company operations for at least five years. The majority shareholders are also the directors of the company and they do not wish the surplus funds to be distributed as dividends. A board meeting has therefore been called to discuss the proposal that the funds be invested in a portfolio of medium to long-term securities.

Three of the directors have recently attended a short course at the local university on 'Investment and the Management of Risk'. They make the following comments at the meeting, based on their interpretations of what they have learnt on the course.

'If we hold a portfolio of stocks, we need only consider the systematic risk of the securities.'

'As a cautious investor we must always consider total risk.'

'We should not buy anything if the expected return is less than that on the market as a whole, and certainly not if it is below the return on the risk-free asset.'

Required

(i) Explain to the members of the board the meaning of systematic, unsystematic and total risk and advise them, briefly, how all three types of risk can be measured.

(ii) Discuss the directors' comment. **12 Marks**

(b) The following two comments were drawn from separate articles in a highly respected financial newspaper.

'Market efficiency does not mean that share prices can be forecast with accuracy.'

'The research department of a large firm of stockbrokers has developed a multiple regression model, based on data collected between 1964 and 1994, which is claimed to give statistically significant results for predicting share prices.'

Required

Discuss these comments and explain why they are not contradictory. **8 Marks**

Total Marks = 20

25 **COST OF CAPITAL** *36 mins*

(a) Explain what is meant by 'cost of capital' and why it is an important figure for businesses. **6 Marks**

(b) Explain and discuss how each of the following factors are likely to separately affect a company's cost of capital.

    (i)   A high level of gearing

    (ii)   A volatile share price

    (iii) A low dividend payout

14 Marks

Total Marks = 20

26 LEISURE INTERNATIONAL PLC

36 mins

The following is an extract from the balance sheet of Leisure International plc at 30 June 20X2.

	£'000
Ordinary shares of 50p each	5,200
Reserves	4,850
9% preference shares of £1 each	4,500
14% debentures	5,000
Total long-term funds	19,550

The ordinary shares are quoted at 80p. Assume that the market estimate of the next ordinary dividend is 4p, growing thereafter at 12% per annum indefinitely. The preference shares, which are irredeemable, are quoted at 72p and the debentures are quoted at par. Corporation tax is 33%.

Required

(a) Use the relevant data above to estimate the company's weighted average cost of capital (WACC), ie the return required by the providers of the three types of capital, using the respective market values as weighting factors.   **7 Marks**

(b) Explain how the capital asset pricing model would be used as an alternative method of estimating the cost of equity, indicating what information would be required and how it would be obtained.   **7 Marks**

(c) Assume that the debentures have recently been issued specifically to fund the company's expansion programme under which a number of projects are being considered. It has been suggested at a project appraisal meeting that because these projects are to be financed by the debentures, the cutoff rate for project acceptance should be the after-tax interest rate on the debentures rather than the WACC. Comment on this suggestion.   **6 Marks**

Total Marks = 20

27 CRAZY GAMES PLC

36 mins

You are an accountant with a practice which includes a large proportion of individual clients, who often ask for information about traded investments. It is now December 20X8. You have extracted the following data from a leading financial newspaper.

(i)

Stock	Price	P/E ratio	Dividend yield (% gross)
Buntam plc	160p	20	5
Zellus plc	270p	15	3.33

(ii) Earnings and dividend data for Crazy Games plc are given below.

Year	20X3	20X4	20X5	20X6	20X7
EPS	5p	6p	7p	10p	12p
Dividend per share (gross)	3p	3p	3.5p	5p	5.5p

The estimated before tax return on equity required by investors in Crazy Games plc is 20%.

(iii) The gross yield to redemption on gilts are as follows.

Treasury 8.5% 20Y0	7.00%
Exchequer 10.5% 20Y5	6.70%
Treasury 8% 20Z5	6.53%

Required

Draft a report for circulation to your private clients which explains:

(a) The meaning and the relevance to the investor of each of the following:

   (i)   Gross dividend (pence per share)

   (ii)   EPS

   (iii)   Dividend cover

Your answer should include calculation of, and comment upon, the gross dividends, EPS and dividend cover for Buntam plc and Zellus plc, based on the information given above. **10 Marks**

(b) How to estimate the market value of a share.

Illustrate your answer by reference to the data in (ii) on Crazy Games plc, using the information to calculate the market value of 1,000 shares in the company. **6 Marks**

(c) The shape of the yield curve for gilts, based upon the information given in (iii) above, which you should use to construct the curve. **4 Marks**

Total Marks = 20

28   **JERONIMO PLC**   *36 mins*

Jeronimo plc currently has 5 million ordinary shares in issue, which have a market value of £1.60 each. The company wishes to raise finance for a major investment project by means of a rights issue, and is proposing to issue shares on the basis of 1 for 5 at a price of £1.30 each.

James Brown currently owns 10,000 shares in Jeronimo plc and is seeking advice on whether to not to take up the proposed rights.

Required

(a) Explain the difference between a rights issue and a scrip issue. Your answer should include comment on the reasons why companies make such issues and the effect of the issues on private investors. **6 Marks**

(b) Calculate:

   (i)   The theoretical value of James Brown's shareholding if he takes up his rights

   (ii)   The theoretical value of James Brown's rights if he chooses to sell them

4 Marks

(c) Using only the information given below, and applying the dividend growth model formula, calculate the required return on equity for an investor in Jeronimo plc.

Jeronimo plc
Current share price: £1.60
Number of shares in issue: 5 million
Current earnings: £1.5 million
Dividend paid (pence per share)
20X5: 8
20X6: 9
20X7: 11
20X8: 11
20X9: 12

4 Marks

(d) If the stock market is believed to operate with a strong level of efficiency, what effect might this have on the behaviour of the finance directors of publicly quoted companies?

6 Marks

Total Marks = 20

SOURCES OF SHORT-TERM FINANCE

Questions 29 to 37 cover sources of short-term finance, the subject of Part C of the BPP Study Text for Paper 4.

29   OBJECTIVE TEST QUESTIONS: SHORT-TERM FINANCE I   *36 mins*

1   An amount of £10,000 is invested at a fixed rate of 10% per annum. What will be the value of the investment in three years' time if the interest is compounded every six months?

    A   £11,576

    B   £13,310

    C   £13,400

    D   £17,716

2   Which of the following could a company not use as a source of short-term credit?

    A   Trade credit from suppliers

    B   Bank overdraft

    C   Factoring of trade debts

    D   Mortgage on property

3   Which of the following statements is not a feature of an overdraft facility?

    A   Interest is paid on the full facility.

    B   Legal documentation is minimal in comparison with other types of loan.

    C   Repayable on demand.

    D   Assets are normally required as security.

4   Of what is the following statement a definition?

'A document issued by a bank on behalf of a customer authorising a person to draw money to a specified amount from its branches or correspondents, usually in another country, when the conditions set out in the document have been met.'

    A   Bill of exchange

    B   Export guarantee

    C   Banker's draft

    D   Letter of credit

5   Which of the following factors would a bank be least likely to take into account when deciding whether to lend money to a company?

    A   The purpose of the loan

    B   The amount of the loan

    C   The duration of the loan

    D   The currency in which the loan is denominated

6   Kenyon plc is awaiting the go-ahead to start its new building programme. This is likely to take place within the next 90 days, but the precise start date and timing of the cash flows are still uncertain. The company has £150,000 available in cash in anticipation of the investment. Which of the following is the least appropriate use of the funds in the interim period?

A   Investment in equities
B   Treasury bills
C   Bank deposits
D   Local authority deposits

7   Which of the following services would not normally be offered by a factoring company?

A   Provision of finance by advancing, say 80% of invoice value immediately, and the remainder on settlement of the debt by the customer.

B   Taking over responsibility for administration of the client's sales ledger.

C   Issuing invoices to customers on behalf of the client.

D   Non-recourse finance, ie take over responsibility for bad debts.

8   Which of the following is the least important consideration when assessing how to invest a short-term cash surplus?

A   Length of time for which the funds are available
B   Maximising the return generated by the funds
C   Ease of realisation
D   Risk associated with calling in the investment early

9   Which of the following theories could not be used to explain the term structure of interest rates?

A   Expectations theory
B   Miller-Orr model
C   Liquidity preference theory
D   Market segmentation

10   What is the value of a five year annuity of £100, assuming interest rates are 8%?

A   £400
B   £500
C   £850
D   £1,250

Total Marks = 20

30   OBJECTIVE TEST QUESTIONS: SHORT-TERM FINANCE II   *36 mins*

1   A company with large amounts of surplus cash may decide to invest it in short-term money market instruments. Which of the following money market investments would carry the *lowest* interest rate?

A   Sterling certificates of deposit (CDs)
B   Treasury bills
C   Finance house deposits
D   Local authority deposits

2   An organisation invests £14,000 at an interest rate of 6% per annum, compounded monthly.

How much will be available in two years' time?

A   £14,840
B   £15,680
C   £15,730
D   £15,780

BPP PUBLISHING

3   A manufacturer of china commemorating the Olympic Games is facing a short-term liquidity shortage. Which of the following assets could it sell in order to make good the cash shortfall while doing the minimum damage to its core activities?

    A   10% of its fleet of delivery vehicles

    B   The pigment blending plant

    C   The patent on a new design of china pouring device intended to commemorate the Olympic Games

    D   Its 60% equity stake in the company that supplies its gold leaf

4   A person wishes to have £10,000 in savings in three years' time. She plans to make regular monthly payments into a saving account which offers monthly interest of 0.5% (compounded monthly).

How much should the monthly payments be, to the nearest £1?

    A   £278
    B   £304
    C   £369
    D   £428

5   Which of the following investments would not be appropriate for a company with a temporary cash surplus of approximately one week?

    A   Local authority deposits
    B   Money market lending arranged directly
    C   Treasury bills
    D   Convertible loan stock

6   What is the value of £3,000 per year in perpetuity, when the interest rate is 12%?

    A   £8,333
    B   £25,000
    C   £36,000
    D   £75,000

7   An investor buys £11,000 (nominal value) of a bond with a coupon rate of 10%, for the current market value of £10,000. Average market returns are 12%. What is the interest yield to the nearest one percent?

    A   9%
    B   10%
    C   11%
    D   12%

8   A company with a large amount of surplus cash may decide to invest it in short-term money market instruments. Which of the following money market investments would carry the lowest interest rate?

    A   Sterling certificates of deposit (CDs)
    B   Treasury bills
    C   Finance house deposits
    D   Local authority deposits

9   Which of the following statements about inflation is untrue?

   A   Inflation introduces uncertainty into a company's financial projections.

   B   Inflation makes it more difficult to appraise company performance accurately.

   C   Because inflation erodes the capital value of amounts borrowed, it favours lenders at the expense of borrowers.

   D   With very low inflation, or deflation, negative interest rates are possible.

10   Suppose that the yield curve has been steeply inverted and, as a consequence of the persistently high short-term interest rates, the bond market eventually comes under pressure and bond prices start to fall. What is the likely consequence for equity share prices and equity yields?

   A   Equity prices will fall; equity yields will rise.
   B   Equity prices will fall; equity yields will fall.
   C   Equity prices will be unaffected; equity yields will be unaffected.
   D   Equity prices will rise; equity yields will fall.

Total Marks = 20

If you struggled with these objective test questions, go back to your BPP Study Text for Paper 4 and revise Chapters 12 to 15 before you tackle the longer questions on sources of short-term finance.

If you would like a bank of objective test questions which covers a range of syllabus topics, order our MCQ cards using the order form at the back of this Kit.

---

31   INTEREST RATES   *36 mins*

Towards the end of 1998 and into 1999 there was an increasing perception in the UK and around the world that interest rates would start to fall significantly.

(a)   What are the likely implications to a typical company of lower interest rates?   **8 Marks**

(b)   If you were the Financial Director of a company with a large investment programme and no capital gearing, explain what changes might result to both the investment programme and its financing as a result of falling interest rates.   **12 Marks**

Total Marks = 20

32   YIELD CURVE   *36 mins*

(a)   What is a yield curve?   **6 Marks**

(b)   To what extent does the shape of the yield curve depend on expectations about the future?   **14 Marks**

Total Marks = 20

33   EXCESS CASH AND MONEY MARKET INSTRUMENTS   *36 mins*

(a)   The treasurer of B plc has forecast that, over the next year, the company will generate cash flows in excess of its requirements. List four possible reasons for such a surplus, and explain the circumstances under which the board of directors might decide to keep the excess in liquid form.   **8 Marks**

(b) The following table of London money rates shows the relationship between maturity and interest rates for four types of short-term investment, as published in the financial press.

	One month	Three months	Six months	One year
Sterling certificates of deposit	$9^7/_8$	$10^1/_{16}$	$10^3/_{16}$	$10^5/_{16}$
Local authority bonds	$9^7/_8$	10	$10^1/_4$	$10^1/_2$
Finance house deposits	10	$10^1/_8$	$10^3/_8$	$10^9/_{16}$
Treasury bills (buy)	$9^{11}/_{16}$	$9^3/_4$	-	-

Explain:

(i) The nature of the instruments listed, and

(ii) The main reasons for the differences in interest rate between the instruments and over time

12 Marks

Total Marks = 20

34   4D PLC   *36 mins*

(a) Briefly explain the factors which a company's treasurer should consider before investing in marketable securities.

6 Marks

(b) 4D plc is a manufacturing company whose shares are listed on the London Stock Exchange. It is expecting to have surplus cash resources available for at least 12 months. The board has decided to develop an investment portfolio of marketable securities. The company's financial advisers have recommended four securities for the board to consider. These are as follows.

Security 1: Regularly traded shares in a medium-sized UK retailing company. The equity beta is quoted as 1.2.

Security 2: Shares in a relatively small but rapidly growing UK company in a high-technology industry. The shares have an equity beta of 1.6.

Security 3: Shares in an American bank which are listed on US stock exchanges but not in the UK. They are currently quoted at US$25.50. An equity beta is unavailable but 4D plc's stockbroker estimates that the required rate of return on the shares is 12% per annum.

Security 4: Short-dated government bonds.

The expected return on Treasury Bills is 5% per year, and that of the market is 12%.

4D plc's own equity beta is 0.8 and this is not expected to change in the foreseeable future.

The board can invest in one or more of these securities in any proportion.

Required

(i) Calculate the risk and expected return of the investment portfolio assuming 30% of available funds is invested in each of securities 1 and 2 and 20% in each of securities 3 and 4.

4 Marks

(ii) Write a report for the board advising which, if any, of the four securities listed above should be considered as suitable investments for a company such as 4D plc. Also comment on the types of marketable securities, other than those listed above which could be considered by 4D plc.   **10 Marks**

Total Marks = 20

35   RT PLC   *36 mins*

(a)   RT plc has forecast the following cash movements for the next six months.

Cash available now	£2,000,000
Inflow in two months	£4,000,000
Outflow in four months	£2,000,000
Outflow in six months	£4,000,000

Assume that all movements of cash take place on the last day of each two-month period.

The structure of short-term interest rates is as follows.

Current		*Expected in 2 months*		*Expected in 4 months*	
Maturity period	*Annual yield*	*Maturity period*	*Annual yield*	*Maturity period*	*Annual yield*
	%		%		%
2 months	7.3	2 months	8.0	2 months	8.3
4 months	7.4	4 months	8.1	4 months	8.4
6 months	7.5	6 months	8.2	6 months	8.3

The company invests surplus cash balances in marketable securities. Company policy is to hold such securities to maturity once they are purchased. Every purchase transaction of marketable securities costs £100.

Required

(i)   Calculate which securities should be purchased to maximise before-tax income.

(ii)   Discuss the criteria that would influence a company's procedure for selecting marketable securities.   **12 Marks**

(b)   *Required*

Comment on the following statements.

(i)   'Interest rates have a strong influence on the demand for liquidity and an apparently weak influence upon business investment.'

(ii)   'Cash management models sound a good idea in theory, but they are of no practical use to most companies.'   **8 Marks**

Total Marks = 20

36   EXPANDALOT LTD   *36 mins*

(a)   Explain the causes and symptoms of, and cures for, overtrading.   **10 Marks**

(b)   Expandalot Ltd is a manufacturing company whose latest accounts are as follows.

PROFIT AND LOSS ACCOUNTS FOR THE YEARS ENDING 31 MARCH

	20X4	*20X5*
	£	£
Sales	500,000	1,000,000
Gross profit	100,000	150,000
Net profit	25,000	30,000

BALANCE SHEETS AS AT 31 MARCH

	20X4		20X5	
	£	£	£	£
Fixed assets		100,000		120,000
Current assets				
Stock	40,000		100,000	
Debtors	34,000		90,000	
Cash	1,000		-	
		75,000		190,000
Less current liabilities				
Overdraft	15,000		50,000	
Trade creditors	25,000		100,000	
Other creditors	5,000		10,000	
		45,000		160,000
		130,000		150,000
Share capital		10,000		10,000
Profit and loss account		120,000		140,000
		130,000		150,000

You may assume an annual inflation rate of 5% during the period March 20X4 to March 20X5. The bank overdraft has recently been negotiated on the understanding that the limit of £50,000 must be reduced to £40,000 by March 20X6.

Evaluate whether Expandalot shows the symptoms of overtrading. **10 Marks**

Total Marks = 20

37   OVERDRAFT USAGE

36 mins

Official statistics show that over the past four to five years, overdraft usage has been falling by around 5% per annum and is being replaced by other forms of asset-based lending.

Required

(a) Explain the main uses of overdraft facilities as part of a company's working capital management policy   **9 Marks**

(b) Discuss the alternative sources of finance which are available   **11 Marks**

Total Marks = 20

WORKING CAPITAL MANAGEMENT

Questions 38 to 56 cover working capital management, the subject of Part D of the BPP Study Text for Paper 4.

38   OBJECTIVE TEST QUESTIONS: WORKING CAPITAL MANAGEMENT I *36 mins*

1   Hampden plc has decided to adopt a moderate working capital policy. It has fluctuating current assets of £1m, permanent current assets of £5m, and fixed assets of £9m. Which of the following mixes of finance is the company most likely to choose?

A   Short-term financing of £1m; permanent financing of £14m
B   Short-term financing of £0.5m; permanent financing of £14.5m
C   Short-term financing of £2m; permanent financing of £13m
D   Short-term financing of £4m; permanent financing of £11m

2   The following figures are taken from the balance sheet of Genus plc:

	£m
Stocks	2
Debtors	3
Cash	1
Creditors	3
5 year bank loan	3

What is the current ratio?

A   1.33
B   2.00
C   1.00
D   0.33

3   The following figures are taken from the accounts of Green Ltd:

	£
Stocks	400,000
Debtors	600,000
Cash	200,000
Creditors	800,000
Debenture	800,000

What is the quick ratio?

A   0.75
B   1.50
C   0.50
D   1.00

4   What is the typical ratio of debtors to total assets in UK companies?

A   15% - 20%
B   20% - 25%
C   25% - 30%
D   30% - 35%

5   Which of the following are not stages in the credit cycle?

A   Negotiation of the price of the goods
B   Receipt of the customer order
C   Credit screening and agreement of terms
D   Goods despatched with delivery note

6   The following figures have been extracted from the accounts of Winchendon plc:

	£
Total sales	200,000
Cash sales	20,000
Credit sales	180,000
Year end debtors	25,000
Bad debts	5,000

What is the average debt collection period in days (based on 365 days per year)?

A   50.7
B   60.8
C   54.8
D   45.6

7   Dent plc is considering whether to factor its sales ledger. It has been offered a 'without recourse' package by the factor at a cost of 2% sales, plus an administration fee of £5,000 per year. Annual sales are currently £1m, with bad debts of 1%. What is the annual cost of the package to Dent likely to be?

A   £5,000
B   £20,000
C   £24,800
D   £25,000

8   Gorman plc is considering changing its credit policy. It currently allows customers 90 days credit, but suffers bad debts amounting to 3% of its annual sales of £2m. It is proposing to reduce the credit period to 30 days, which should cause the bad debts to fall to 1% of turnover. However, it expects that this will result in a reduction in sales of 20%. This reduction will also be reflected in the level of purchases and stockholding. What will be the effect of this on the annual financing cost? Current figures are:

Stocks (raw materials and finished goods)	£500,000
Annual purchases	£360,000
Creditors	£30,000
Cost of capital	10%

A   Saving of £46,000
B   Increase of £46,000
C   Saving of £36,000
D   Increase of £36,000

9   Which of the following are not current assets?

A   Cash
B   Marketable securities
C   Dividend payments
D   Raw material stocks

10   Which of the following are not current liabilities?

   A   Trade creditors
   B   Taxation owed
   C   Dividend payments
   D   Interest due on marketable securities

Total Marks = 20

39   OBJECTIVE TEST QUESTIONS: WORKING CAPITAL MANAGEMENT II

36 mins

1   Which of the following costs should be excluded when preparing a cash budget?

   A   Taxation
   B   Finance lease payments
   C   Fixed asset purchases
   D   Depreciation

2   Dowton Ltd has average monthly sales of £100,000, of which 20% are cash sales. 30% of the credit sales are paid for at the end of the month following month of invoice. The remainder are settled in the second month following month of invoice. Bad debts amount to 2% of total turnover. What is the total receipts figure likely to be in a normal month?

   A   £100,000
   B   £98,000
   C   £90,000
   D   £88,000

3   Which of the following courses of action would be the least appropriate in reducing the size of a cash deficit?

   A   Delay major items of capital expenditure
   B   Increase the time taken to pay creditors
   C   Increase the stock level
   D   Seek an extension of the overdraft facility

4   Deere plc is starting up a new production line to make rocking horses. It expects to make 500 in January, 600 in February and 800 in March. The unit selling price is £100 per horse. Material costs amount to 30% of the selling price, and are purchased in the month prior to production. A 30 day credit period is taken. Direct labour costs are 20% of the selling price, and wages are paid weekly. Variable overheads are £10 per unit, and are paid in the month after they are incurred. What is the total cash outflow that Deere should include in its cash budget for March?

   A   £48,000
   B   £46,000
   C   £42,000
   D   £40,000

5   Lovett plc is preparing its cash budget for the coming year. Which of the following items in the profit and loss budget can be included directly into the cash budget without any adjustment?

   A   The sales forecast, which has no increase in the number of units sold, but includes a price increase in the second quarter.

   B   Corporation tax at 30% on the budgeted profit for the year.

   C   Depreciation, which is unchanged from the previous year.

   D   Wages, which are paid in the month in which they are incurred. A pay increase of 3.5% has been included from June.

6   Which of the following items is the most likely to cause 'float'?

   A   Cheque payments
   B   BACS payments
   C   Debit card payments
   D   Standing orders

7   Which of the following payment methods would be inappropriate for use by a medium sized company trading in the UK?

   A   BACS
   B   CHAPS
   C   Cheque
   D   VISA

8   Which of the following is a cash management model?

   A   The Baumol model
   B   The dividend valuation model
   C   The liquidity preference theory
   D   The EOQ model

9   Which of the following statements does not form a part of the Miller-Orr cash management model?

   A   Management should set upper and lower cash limits.
   B   There is a predetermined normal level, called the return point.
   C   It is assumed that cash is consumed at a constant rate.
   D   Cash inflows and outflows are random.

10   The payee, on receipt of a cheque or cash, might delay presenting the money to the bank. What is this delay known as?

   A   Transmission delay
   B   Lodgement delay
   C   Clearance delay
   D   Float

Total Marks = 20

40 OBJECTIVE TEST QUESTIONS: WORKING CAPITAL MANAGEMENT III

36 mins

1   Palmer Ltd has been offered credit terms of 2.5/10, net 60. If the company refuses the discount, what is the implied cost in interest per annum?

    A   15.2%
    B   15.6%
    C   18.7%
    D   30%

2   Which of the following payments would not normally be made by standing order?

    A   Hire purchase payments
    B   Insurance premiums
    C   Property rental payments
    D   Trade creditor payments

3   What is the main way in which a payment made by direct debit differs from one made by standing order?

    A   The person who makes the payment initiates each payment.

    B   The person who receives the payment initiates each payment.

    C   The payment is made at regular intervals.

    D   The payment goes directly from the customer's bank account to the supplier's bank account.

4   The economic order quantity (EOQ) formula is used to determine the optimal ordering quantity for an item of stock. Which of the following definitions of elements in the formula is incorrect?

    A D = the usage in units for one year (the demand)
    B C_o = the cost of placing orders for one year
    C C_h = the holding cost per unit of stock for one year
    D Q = the reorder quantity

5   Kennedy plc manufactures shopping trolleys. It produces 2,500 trolleys per year, each of which has four wheels. The wheels are purchased from a single supplier, and it costs £25 to place an order. The cost of holding a single wheel in stock for a year is 50p. How many wheels should be ordered each time to minimise stock costs (answer to the nearest 10)?

    A   350
    B   500
    C   710
    D   1,000

6   Kennedy plc manufactures shopping trolleys. It produces 2,500 trolleys per year, each of which has four wheels. The wheels are purchased from a single supplier, and it costs £25 to place an order. The cost of holding a single wheel in stock for a year is 50p. How many orders should be placed each year to minimise stock costs?

    A   3
    B   10
    C   14
    D   20

7   Kennedy plc manufactures shopping trolleys. It produces 2,500 trolleys per year, each of which has four wheels. The wheels are purchased from a single supplier, and it costs £25 to place an order. The cost of holding a single wheel in stock for a year is 50p. What is the length of the stock cycle?

A   2.6 weeks
B   3.7 weeks
C   5.2 weeks
D   17.3 weeks

8   Which of the following would not normally form part of the purchasing manager's responsibilities?

A   Liaising with the R & D department to find suppliers for materials which are to the specifications required by the designers.

B   Locating and selecting suppliers.

C   Agreeing prices, discounts and lead times with suppliers.

D   Issuing payments to suppliers.

9   Francine Ltd is a small restaurant business. It has just acquired a new van under a hire purchase agreement, and it must make a monthly payment to the HP company of £276.53. Which of the following payment methods is the most appropriate for Francine to use?

A   Cheque
B   Standing order
C   Direct debit
D   Banker's draft

10   At Your Service Ltd is a small domestic cleaning business. It has just acquired a new van for £12,750, which is needed urgently since the old one has been written off in an accident. The garage will not accept a company cheque on collection of the vehicle. Which of the following payment methods is the most appropriate for At Your Service to use?

A   Cash
B   Standing order
C   Direct debit
D   Banker's draft

Total Marks = 20

41   **OBJECTIVE TEST QUESTIONS: WORKING CAPITAL MANAGEMENT IV**

36 mins

1   Which of the following is associated with a lengthening in the operating cycle of a business?

A   A reduction in the trading cycle
B   An increased investment in working capital
C   An increase in the payment period to creditors
D   A reduction in the time taken to produce the goods in the factory

2   Which of the following might be symptoms of overtrading?

A   There is a rapid fall in turnover.
B   The business has an excess of current liabilities over current assets.
C   The payment period to creditors gets shorter.
D   The quick ratio rises.

3   Bearing in mind the Miller-Orr model, which of the following statements about cash management is untrue?

    A   If transaction costs in buying and selling securities increase, control limits should be made narrower

    B   If the variation in cash balances is high, then wide control limits should be set

    C   The Miller-Orr model assumes that short-term cash movements change in a random way

    D   If rates of interest are high, then relatively narrow control limits should be set

4   Panweb plc has cash outgoing of £2,450,000, spread evenly through the year. Selling Treasury bills carries a transaction cost of £25. The annual interest rate on Treasury bills is currently 7 per cent.

    The company treasurer wishes to use the Baumol cash management model to find the optimal amount of Treasury bills that should be sold each time there is a replenishment of cash.

    What is this optimal amount?

    A   £6,860
    B   £41,833
    C   £98,000
    D   £171,500

5   Which of the following could be causes of overtrading?

    A   A loan is repaid and replaced with another source of long-term finance.
    B   Turnover is decreasing fast with an unchanged long-term capital structure.
    C   There is a period of low inflation.
    D   A tranche of redeemable preference shares are repaid from existing funds.

6   Delicious Foods plc is considering whether to increase its normal period of credit to customers. Which of the following factors is not relevant to this decision?

    A   The overall level of additional sales that would be generated and the effect on profitability

    B   The required rate of return on the investment in additional debtors

    C   The average period of credit taken from suppliers

    D   The average period of credit offered by competitors

7   Apply the Miller-Orr cash management model to find the maximum cash holding for the company to which the following data apply.

    Minimum cash holding £2,500
    Variance of daily cash flows £2,000,000
    Transaction cost for sale/purchase of Treasury bills £25
    Interest rate: 0.020 per cent per day

    A   £2,657
    B   £5,157
    C   £7,970
    D   £10,470

8   A company is considering the terms of credit to offer to a customer. Which of the following is not relevant to this decision?

     A   The bargaining power of customer and supplier

     B   The financial soundness of the customer

     C   Accepted norms within the industry

     D   All of A, B and C

9   Which of the following will result in a lengthening stock turnover period?

     A   An increase in sales

     B   A slowdown in trading

     C   A decrease in finished goods stocks

     D   A reduction in the operating cycle

10   The Treasurer of a supplier of hand-baked cakes to retailers is surprised to discover that the average cash balance has risen significantly despite a month of low sales. The majority of employees are paid on a piecework basis; sales are on credit. Which of the following facts could not have contributed to this situation?

     A   The low sales figure for the month

     B   The price increase that was implemented two months ago

     C   Five workers having been made redundant this month

     D   Work having fallen behind on the new packaging line

Total Marks = 20

42   OBJECTIVE TEST QUESTIONS: WORKING CAPITAL MANAGEMENT V

36 mins

1   Which of the following facts might not suggest that a company is over-capitalised with respect to working capital?

     A   A current ratio in excess of 4:1

     B   An increasing rate of stock turnover

     C   An average period of credit taken from suppliers that is short and reducing

     D   A ratio of sales:working capital lower than that for comparable companies

2   A number of factors will be considered by managers responsible for the cash management of a large company. Which of the following factors will make managers prefer long-term to short-term debt?

     A   Exposure to interest rate movements

     B   Inaccurate cash flow forecasts

     C   Risk of a deteriorating credit rating

     D   Exposure to exchange rate fluctuations

3   Which of the following statements is incorrect?

     A   Knowing the size of their usable cash balances can help companies to increase their profits.

     B   Companies should be able to ascertain the size of their usable cash balances from their cash book.

     C   The Miller-Orr model for cash management assumes that cash inflows and outflows for the next period, usually one month, cannot be predicted.

     D   The term 'float' refers to the amount of money tied up between the time when a payment is initiated and the time when the funds become available for use in the recipient's bank account.

4   When a company starts to expand too rapidly, it might start overtrading. Which of the following is not a symptom of overtrading?

   A   A high ratio of current assets to current liabilities
   B   A high ratio of current assets to proprietors' capital
   C   A low ratio of current assets to current liabilities
   D   Longer creditors turnover period

5   Which of the following decisions is a financing decision?

   A   Whether to purchase a competitor's business
   B   Whether to lease assets, as opposed to outright purchase
   C   Whether to merge with another business
   D   Whether to sell a poorly performing subsidiary

6   The interest cover ratio, like the gearing ratio, is often used to assess the financial risk of a company, and an interest cover of less than 3 times would often be regarded as a sign of high risk.

   What is the interest cover of the company whose results are shown below?

   Pileup Ltd

	£'000
Profit before interest and tax	200
Interest	80
	120
Tax	40
	80
Preference dividend	40
Earnings	40

   A   1.0 times
   B   1.5 times
   C   2.0 times
   D   2.5 times

7   A company uses a computer model for financial planning, which produces a profit and loss account and balance sheet. Within the model, the following relationships hold:

Ratio of fixed assets to working capital	2.0
Current ratio	3.0

   The first run of the model uses a sales forecast of £240,000 and a sales:capital employed ratio of 0.5.

   What value will the first run produce for current assets?

   A   £160,000
   B   £240,000
   C   £320,000
   D   £360,000

8   Pipes Ltd uses a computerised financial model of its operations. by entering the sales forecast and values for parameters, the model will produce a profit and loss account and a balance sheet.

   Parameter values:

Net profit margin	25%
Return on capital employed	10%
Ratio of fixed asset to working capital	1:1
Current ratio	1.5:1

   The first trial run of the model will use a sales forecast of £960,000.

49

What value will the first trial run produce for current liabilities?

A   £480,000

B   £1,200,000

C   £1,800,000

D   £2,400,000

9   Most large retail organisations accept credit cards such as Visa and Access. Compared with payment by cheque, which of the following benefits is *not* obtained by retailers from the use of major credit cards?

A   More sales volume

B   Fewer bad debts

C   Quicker cleared funds

D   Lower bank/credit card company charges

10   Low Ltd needs to hold stock of material XYZ for resale to customer. Basic data about material XYZ are as follows.

Annual sales demand (50 week year)	3,000 units
cost of placing and processing a purchase order	£259
Cost of holding one unit of XYZ for a year	£27
Normal delay between placing an order and receiving goods	3 weeks

What is the economic order quantity (EOQ) for material XYZ, and what is the average frequency at which purchase orders should be placed?

	EOQ	*Frequency of orders*
A	170 units	3 weeks
B	170 units	6 weeks
C	240 units	4 weeks
D	240 units	7 weeks

Total Marks = 20

If you struggled with these objective test questions, go back to your BPP Study Text for Paper 4 and revise Chapters 16 to 23 before you tackle the longer questions on working capital management.

If you would like a bank of objective test questions which covers a range of syllabus topics, order our MCQ cards using the order form at the back of this Kit.

---

43   MORIBUND PLC   *36 mins*

(a)   Explain the term 'operating cycle'.   **6 Marks**

(b)   Calculate the operating cycle for Moribund plc for the years 20X1 and 20X2 on the basis of the following information.

	20X2	*20X1*
	£	*£*
Stock: Raw materials	150,000	130,000
Work in progress	60,000	50,000
Finished goods	200,000	150,000
Purchases	500,000	450,000
Debtors	230,000	180,000
Trade creditors	120,000	90,000
Sales	900,000	800,000
Cost of goods sold	750,000	650,000

8 Marks

(c)   Advise Moribund plc on the steps which might be taken in order to improve the operating cycle.   **6 Marks**

Total Marks = 20

44   RATIOS

36 mins

Among the financial ratios sometimes encountered in schemes of ratio analysis are the following.

(a)   Working capital: Total assets
(b)   Retained earnings : Total assets
(c)   Earnings before interest and tax : Interest charges plus annual repayment of loans

Required

(a)   (i)   Explain the purpose and meaning of each of these ratios.

(ii)   Use the data from the table below relating to X plc to illustrate how each ratio might be calculated for each of the four years.

(iii) Discuss briefly trends apparent from this ratio analysis.   **12 Marks**

(b)   Appraise the way in which X plc has financed its operations over the four-year period based on a comparison of years 1 and 4.   **8 Marks**

EXTRACTS FROM THE PUBLISHED ACCOUNTS OF X PLC

	Year 4 £	Year 3 £	Year 2 £	Year 1 £
Fixed assets				
Intangible	123,000	100,000	80,000	30,000
Tangible	1,179,500	1,036,000	1,030,000	1,027,000
Investments	10,000	10,000	-	-
	1,312,500	1,146,000	1,110,000	1,057,000
Current assets				
Stocks	479,000	454,000	432,000	375,500
Debtors	1,774,500	1,585,000	1,329,000	1,263,000
Cash and short-term investments	5,000	20,000	40,000	241,200
	2,258,500	2,059,000	1,801,000	1,879,700

	Year 4 £	Year 3 £	Year 2 £	Year 1 £
Current liabilities				
Trade creditors	956,500	767,000	714,000	679,000
Bank overdraft	504,000	274,500	24,700	-
Other	152,500	150,000	100,000	70,000
	1,613,000	1,191,500	838,700	749,000
Total assets less current liabilities	1,958,000	2,013,500	2,072,300	2,187,700
Less: Loans repayable after more				
than one year	124,000	248,000	372,000	496,000
Other liabilities	33,000	15,000	5,000	2,000
Net assets	1,801,000	1,750,500	1,695,300	1,689,700
Called up share capital	300,000	300,000	300,000	300,000
Profit and loss account				
Brought forward	1,450,500	1,395,300	1,389,700	1,324,400
Retained for year	50,500	55,200	5,600	65,300
	1,801,000	1,750,500	1,695,300	1,689,700
Turnover	6,660,000	6,343,000	6,041,000	5,492,000
Daily operating expenses excluding				
depreciation	17,644	16,534	15,852	14,338
Earnings before interest and tax	205,500	285,500	284,000	274,500
Interest charges	111,000	186,000	260,000	149,000

Total Marks = 20

51

45 YZPK PACKING CO LTD

36 mins

The YZPK Packing Co Ltd, a family-owned company, has now been trading for six years and has provided you with the following data relating to its last four trading years.

Extracts from its balance sheets

	20X3 £'000	20X4 £'000	20X5 £'000	20X6 £'000
Issued ordinary shares	26	75	75	255
Retained earnings	49	109	396	819
Bank overdraft (secured)	Nil	90	187	94

Extracts from its profit and loss accounts

	20X3 £'000	20X4 £'000	20X5 £'000	20X6 £'000
Turnover	725	1,335	2,496	4,608
Net profit (after tax)	18	48	212	334
Dividends proposed	Nil	Nil	Nil	51

All sales and purchases are made on credit.

Financial analysis

	Industry*	20X3	20X4	20X5	20X6
Current ratio	1.47	1.11	1.02	1.19	1.24
Acid test	0.85	1.03	0.90	0.94	0.95
Debtors, average collection period (days)	51	63	72	76	64
Creditors, period of credit taken (days)	72	103	146	121	118
Stockholding (days)	62	14	22	45	52
Net profit after tax to capital employed	21%	24%	26%	45%	31%

*The industry averages have been around this level for the whole of the four year period.

Required

(a) Comment on the company's growth in turnover and profits over the four years, and suggest possible problems which such rapid growth may cause. **5 Marks**

(b) Suggest reasons why the company's stockholding in days has been less than the industry average. **6 Marks**

(c) The board of directors is concerned about the cash flow position of the company. As chief accountant, write a memo to the board setting out various ways in which credit control could be improved and point out the potential threat caused by creditors. **9 Marks**

Total Marks = 20

46 IMPROVING CASH FLOW

36 mins

B Ltd is a wholly owned subsidiary of A plc and currently depends entirely on the parent company for any necessary finance. A plc, however, has its own cash flow problems and cannot permit B Ltd temporary loan facilities in excess of £50,000 at any time, even though the business of B Ltd is highly seasonal and is in a period of growth.

B Ltd has just prepared its cash budget for the year ahead, details of which are as follows. All figures are in thousands of pounds.

Month	1	2	3	4	5	6	7	8	9	10	11	12
Collections from customers	230	250	120	50	60	75	80	90	110	150	220	320
Dividend on investment							45					
Total inflows	230	250	120	50	60	75	125	90	110	150	220	320
Payments to suppliers		80		80		88		88		88		92
Wages and other expenses	102	77	58	103	79	59	105	80	62	108	83	63
Payments for fixed assets				70	10		15				5	
Dividend payable		80										
Corporation tax									120			
Total outflows	102	157	138	253	89	147	120	168	182	196	88	155
Net in or (out)	128	93	(18)	(203)	(29)	(72)	5	(78)	(72)	(46)	132	165
Bank balance/ (overdraft):												
Opening	30	158	251	233	30	1	(71)	(66)	(144)	(216)	(262)	(130)
Closing	158	251	233	30	1	(71)	(66)	(144)	(216)	(262)	(130)	35

The following supplementary information is provided.

(a) Two months credit on average is granted to customers.

(b) Production is scheduled evenly throughout the year. Year-end stocks of finished goods are forecast to be £114,000 higher than at the beginning of the year.

(c) Purchases of raw materials are made at two-monthly intervals. Three months' credit, on average, is taken from suppliers.

(d) The capital expenditure budget comprises:

New equipment for planned production	Month 4	£70,000
Routine replacement of motor vehicles	Month 5	£10,000
Progress payment on building extensions	Month 7	£15,000
Office furniture and equipment	Month 11	£5,000

Required

Review this information and advise the board of B Ltd on possible actions it might take to improve its budgeted cash flow for the year and to avoid any difficulties you can foresee.

Total Marks = 20

47　**PHOENIX PLC**　　　　　　　　　　　　　　　　　　　　　　　*36 mins*

It is currently December 20X7. Phoenix plc, which manufactures building products, experienced a sharp increase in profits before interest and tax from the £25m level in 20X5-X6 to £40m in 20X6-7 as the economy emerged from recession, and demand for new houses increased. The increase in profits has been entirely due to volume expansion, with margins remaining static. It still has substantial excess capacity and therefore no pressing need to invest, apart from routine replacements.

In the past, Phoenix has followed a rather conservative financial policy, with restricted dividend payouts and relatively low borrowing levels. It now faces the issue of how to utilise an unexpectedly sizeable cash surplus. Directors have made two main suggestions. One is to redeem the £10m secured loan stock issued to finance a capacity increase several years previously, the other is to increase the dividend payment by the same amount.

BPP PUBLISHING

Phoenix's present capital structure is shown below.

	£m
Issued share capital (25p par value)	70
Reserves	130
Creditors falling due after more than one year:	
7% secured loan stock 20Y7	10

Further information

(i)   Phoenix has not used an overdraft during the two years.

(ii) The rate of corporate tax is 33%.

(iii) The dividend paid by Phoenix in 20X5-6 was 1.50 pence per share.

(iv) Sector averages currently stand as follows.

Dividend cover	2.6 times
Gearing (long-term debt/equity)	45%
Interest cover	6.5 times

Required

(a)   Calculate the dividend payout ratios and dividend covers for *both* 20X5-6 *and* for the reporting year 20X6-7, if the dividend is raised as proposed.   **6 Marks**

(b)   You have recently been hired to work as a financial strategist for Phoenix, reporting to the finance director. Using the information provided, write a report to your superior, which identifies and discusses the relative merits of the two proposals for utilising the cash surplus.   **14 Marks**

Total Marks = 20

48   RIPLEY PLC   *36 mins*

(a)   The Treasurer of Ripley plc is contemplating a change in financial policy. At present, Ripley's balance sheet shows that fixed assets are of equal magnitude to the amount of long-term debt and equity financing. It is proposed to take advantage of a recent fall in interest rates by replacing the long-term debt capital with an overdraft. In addition, the Treasurer wants to speed up debtor collection by offering early payment discounts to customers and to slow down the rate of payment to creditors.

Required

As his assistant, write a brief memorandum to other Board members explaining the rationales of the old and new policies and pinpointing the factors to be considered in making such a switch of policy.   **6 Marks**

(b)   Bramham plc, which currently has negligible cash holdings, expects to have to make a series of cash payments of £1.5m over the forthcoming year. These will become due at a steady rate. It has two alternative ways of meeting this liability.

Firstly, it can make periodic sales from existing holdings of short-term securities. According to Bramham's financial advisers, the most likely average percentage rate of return on these securities is 12% over the forthcoming year, although this estimate is highly uncertain. Whenever Bramham sells securities it incurs a transaction fee of £25, and places the proceeds on short-term deposit at 5% per annum interest until needed.

The second policy involves taking a secured loan for the full £1.5m over one year at an interest rate of 14% based on the initial balance of the loan. The lender also imposes a

54

flat arrangement fee of £5,000, which could be met out of existing balances. The sum borrowed would be placed in a notice deposit account at 9% and drawn down at no cost as and when required.

Bramham's Treasurer believes that cash balances will be run down at an even rate throughout the year.

Required

Advise Bramham as to the most beneficial cash management policy. Ignore tax and the time value of money in your answer.   **9 Marks**

(c)   Discuss the limitations of the model of cash management used in part (b).   **5 Marks**

Total Marks = 20

49   RECENT RESEARCH   *36 mins*

(a)   Recent research has shown that a large percentage of small company failures were due to poor financial management skills and poor credit management.

Required

Explain the problems faced by small companies in respect of credit management, and discuss internal actions which they could take to minimise the effects of these problems.   **8 Marks**

(b)   A medium-sized manufacturing company is suffering a fall in sales of many of its product lines. It is reviewing its business strategy and the heads of all departments have been asked to review their activities. The accounting department has been asked to review specifically the company's credit control policy. At present the company offers its goods to customers on 30 days' credit (from date of invoice), subject to satisfactory trade references. It does not offer a discount for prompt payment.

Required

Assume you are a management accountant working in the company's credit control department. Write a report to the Credit Manager which:

(i)   Discusses the contribution that credit control policy can make to overall business strategy

(ii)   Assesses the advantages and disadvantages of introducing discounts for prompt payment. Include in your assessment a calculation and comment on the true cost of discounts. For the sake of your discussion you should assume a 1% discount for payment within 10 days if the normal credit period allowed continues at 30 days.   **12 Marks**

Total Marks = 20

50   WHICHFORD PLC   *36 mins*

The £25,000,000 annual credit sales of Whichford plc are spread evenly over the weeks of the working year. Sales within each week are also spread evenly over the five working days.

Although Whichford operates from 19 separate locations, all invoicing of credit sales is carried out by the central head office. Sales documentation is sent by post daily from each location to the head office, and from these details invoices are prepared. Postal delays affecting the receipt of documentation by the head office, delays in processing at head office, together with the non-working weekend period all contribute to the considerable delay in despatching invoices. As a result of these delays only some of the sales made on Monday

55

and Tuesday of each week are invoiced that same week; the remainder of sales made on Monday and Tuesday and all sales made between Wednesday and Friday are not invoiced until the following week.

An analysis of the delay in invoicing, measured by the delay between the day of sale and the date of despatch of the invoice, indicated the following typical pattern.

Delay in invoicing	*Sales subject to this delay*
Days	%
3	20
4	6
5	40
6	22
7	12

A further analysis indicated that debtors take, on average, 35 days credit before paying. This period is measured from the day of despatch of the invoice.

It is proposed to hire a number of microcomputers to undertake invoicing at each of the 19 sales locations. The use of computers would ensure that all invoices were despatched either on the day of sale or on the next working day. The revised delay in invoicing would result in 50% of invoices being despatched with no delay, 40% subject to a delay of one day, and 10% subject to a delay of three days (because of the weekend).

A computer package, currently in the final stages of development, would assist the follow-up of debtors and, if used, is likely to reduce the number of days credit taken by customers to 30. Again this is measured from the day of despatch of the invoice.

Use of the microcomputers would save head office and postage costs of £48,000 a year spread evenly over the year. Whichford finances all working capital from a bank overdraft at an interest rate of 15% a year applied on a simple daily basis.

Required

Ignoring tax, determine the maximum monthly rental that Whichford should consider paying for the hire of the computers if they can be used:

(a) Only to speed the invoicing function   **8 Marks**

(b) To speed invoicing and reduce the period of credit taken from 35 to 30 days following the despatch of an invoice   **4 Marks**

(c) 'Effective management of working policy can improve a business's cash flow and profitability.'

   What issues should be considered by management when a policy for credit control is formulated?   **8 Marks**

Total Marks = 20

51   DISCOUNT   *36 mins*

(a) A company offers its goods to customers on 30 days credit, subject to satisfactory trade references. It also offers a 2% discount if payment is made within 10 days of the date of invoice.

   Required

   (i)   Calculate the cost to the company of offering the discount, assuming a 365-day year.

   (ii) Compare offering discounts to customers to encourage early settlement of bills with using debt factors.   **10 Marks**

(b) Two aspects of working capital policy which require managerial decisions are the level of current assets and the manner in which they are financed.

Required

Discuss aggressive, moderate and conservative policies in these areas.   **10 Marks**

Total Marks = 20

---

52   **MP LTD**   *36 mins*

MP Limited is a manufacturing company which trades with a large number of suppliers of raw materials and components. The company's financial manager has asked you, her assistant, to review the terms of trade and their associated costs. As part of the exercise, you randomly choose three regular suppliers of one particular component. They have the following terms:

Supplier A   charges a fixed penalty of 2% of invoice value for late payment

Supplier B   charges compound interest at 2% per 30-day period after the due date of payment

Supplier C   offers a 2% discount if payment is made within 10 days of invoice date but charges simple interest at 10% per annum on the invoice value if payment is after the due date

Assume that the due date for payment in each case is 30 days but that MP Limited's current credit control policy is to take an average of 90 days to pay these suppliers' invoices.

To simplify your calculations, assume also that MP Limited purchases £1,000 worth of goods from each supplier every month.

Required

Write a report to the financial manager which includes:

(a) A calculation of the annualised interest rate (ie percent per annum) for each of the three suppliers   **8 Marks**

(b) A discussion of the arguments for and against using trade credit as a source of funds, in general and from MP Limited's point of view, given their current credit policy
     8 Marks

(c) A discussion of the advantages and disadvantages to MP Limited of introducing standard terms of trade with which all suppliers will have to conform   **4 Marks**

Total Marks = 20

---

53   **OVERDRAFT**   *36 mins*

XYZ plc is an unlisted company which has been trading for almost 10 years. The board of directors is concerned about the cost and level of the company's overdraft which have been increasing over the past two years. The company's financial manager estimates the deterioration will continue into next year (20X5) and beyond unless action is taken. The directors agree that the company should take action to improve its liquidity and debt collection procedures and, as a consequence, reduce the overdraft. The options available are as follows.

(a) Offer a cash discount to all credit customers of 1.5% for payment within 10 days. The normal terms of trade allow for 60 days although many customers regularly exceed this limit. Approximately 70% of sales are on credit and all credit customers trade regularly up to their maximum credit limit. If this scheme is introduced, approximately half of all credit customers are expected to take advantage. Bad debts are expected to fall by 50%.

(b) Employ a debt factoring company. The factor has agreed to accept 90% of XYZ plc's credit customers and will charge a commission of 2% of acceptable debtors' value. Finance charges will be 11%, which is 5% over base rate. XYZ plc will take the maximum finance available and use it to turn the overdraft into a cash balance. The use of a debt factor is expected to result in a saving of £65,000 on XYZ plc's in-company credit management costs.

XYZ plc pays overdraft interest at 4% over base rate. Its opportunity cost of capital is 12%. Summary financial information is as follows.

	20X5 Forecast £'000
Turnover	4,850
Cost of sales	2,862
Bad debts	48
Profit after tax	325
Stock	455
Trade debtors	850
Total current assets	1,305
Trade creditors	550
Overdraft	565
Total current liabilities	1,115
Net current assets	190
Shareholders' funds	1,575
Director's loan (13% unsecured 20Y0)	450

Required

Evaluate for *each* of the *two* options:

(a) The net financial benefit to the company
(b) The effect on current ratios and debtors' days

and recommend, with reasons, which should be chosen to meet the directors' objectives.

Total Marks = 20

54 **KESWICK PLC** *36 mins*

(a) Discuss:

(i) The significance of trade creditors in a firm's working capital cycle **4 Marks**

(ii) The dangers of over-reliance on trade credit as a source of finance **4 Marks**

(b) Keswick plc traditionally follows a highly aggressive working capital policy, with no long-term borrowing. Key details from its recently compiled accounts appear below.

	£m
Sales (all on credit)	10.00
Earnings before interest and tax (EBIT)	2.00
Interest payments for the year	0.50
Shareholders' funds (comprising £1m issued share capital, par value 25p, and £1m revenue reserves)	2.00
Debtors	0.40
Stocks	0.70
Trade creditors	1.50
Bank overdraft	3.00

A major supplier, which accounts for 50% of Keswick's cost of sales, is highly concerned about Keswick's policy of taking extended trade credit. The supplier offers Keswick the opportunity to pay for supplies within 15 days in return for a discount of 5% on the invoiced value.

Keswick holds no cash balances but is able to borrow on overdraft from its bank at 12%. Tax on corporate profit is paid at 31%.

Required

Determine the costs and benefits to Keswick of making this arrangement with its supplier, and recommend whether Keswick should accept the offer.

Your answer should include the effects on:

- the working capital cycle
- interest cover
- profits after tax
- earnings per share
- return on equity
- capital gearing

12 Marks

Total Marks = 20

55   **FENTON SECURITY PLC**   *36 mins*

Fenton Security plc are manufacturers and wholesalers of locks and household security fittings. Over the last twelve months the company has encountered increasing problems with late payment of debtors.

The last twelve months of credit sales of £67.5 million show an increase of 10% over the previous year, but the company's overdraft, on which it is charged 12% p.a. has also increased (by £1.8 million) over the last year. The company is concerned to reduce its working capital requirements by reducing the debtor collection period.

Fenton's management accountant has extracted an aged debtors profile which is shown below:

% of Total debtor payments (by value)	Average Collection Period
5	30
28	45
10	60
30	75
16	90
11	120

Bad debts currently stand at £2 million per annum.

Fenton is considering the introduction of early settlement discounts. The current invoicing terms require payment to be made within 30 days of the date of issue of the invoice. The management accountant has suggested that a 1% discount be offered to all customers who comply with these payment terms, and he estimates that 50% of total payments (by value) would be on these terms (an average settlement period of 30 days for these payments can be assumed). The discount scheme would be expected to be taken up by customers who already pay in 75 days or less.

As an alternative way of reducing the debtors figure, Fenton could use a with recourse debt collection service, which has quoted a price of 1% sales receipts. It is estimated that using the service will have the effect of reducing debtor days by 20 and eliminating 50% of bad debts.

59

Required

(a) Calculate the change in working capital requirements and bad debts which would result from:

(i)   The introduction of the early settlement discounts

(ii)   The use of the debt collection service

and recommend which (if either) policy should be adopted by Fenton. Your answer should clearly show all workings.   **10 Marks**

(b) There are a number of methods that can be adopted to assess the creditworthiness of a potential credit customer. Describe and comment upon two such methods that Fenton could adopt to help reduce the current level of bad debts.   **5 Marks**

(c) Explain the term 'invoice discounting' and the pros and cons of its use as a way of improving cash flow.   **5 Marks**

Total Marks = 20

Answers

1   OBJECTIVE TEST QUESTIONS: THE FINANCE FUNCTION I

1   A   Although the treasurer may be involved in the preparation of the cash budget, he will not be primarily responsible for producing and monitoring the company's budgets, since this is a financial control function.

2   C   The wealth of the shareholders comes from dividends received and from the market value of the shares.

3   D

4   A   Earnings is a measure of absolute income. Value for money is concerned with the relationship of service levels to the resources used in achieving them.

5   D   Agency refers to the relationship that exists between the owners and managers of a business.

Investors and shareholders are specific examples of the wider group of stakeholders.

6   A   This makes it more difficult for the management to decide upon an appropriate policy for dividends and retentions.

7   D   Financial intermediary is the general term for anyone who carries out this function. Business angels, merchant bankers and venture capitalists may all act as financial intermediaries.

8   D   The AIM and the Stock Exchange are both examples of capital markets.

9   A   This is the UK central bank, and not an institutional investor.

10   C   Venture capital is generally most appropriate for new investments with above average risk. Renovation of an existing facility is a part of the ongoing activity of the business, and is unlikely to have much impact on the overall level of returns. It is therefore unlikely to be appropriate for a venture capital investment.

2   OBJECTIVE TEST QUESTIONS: THE FINANCE FUNCTION II

1   D   No new shares are issued in an introduction (A) and so there is no need to underwrite.

An offer for sale by tender would not normally need underwriting since the issue price reflects the value of the shares as perceived by the market. Underwriting would only be necessary if there is a risk that there will be under-subscription even at the minimum price.

It is unnecessary to underwrite a placing since a purchaser for the shares is arranged in the issue process.

Although a rights issue should not need underwriting in theory, since all the shares are being offered to existing shareholders, in practice it will usually be underwritten. This is to ensure that sufficient funds are raised from the issue, even if the rights are not fully exercised.

2   A   A financial intermediary is a party that brings together providers and users of finance, either as broker or principal. Although the DTI may provide information on sources of finance and opportunities for investment, it will not normally broker a specific relationship.

National Savings (Option B in the question) takes deposits from savers, which are then invested in government activities. It is therefore active in bringing together providers and users of finance.

Pension funds (C) hold deposits on behalf of pension scheme members and invest them so as to provide funds to pay for their future pensions. They are therefore providing a link between the providers and users of finance.

Clearing banks (D) take deposits from savers, which are used to lend to other parties so as to produce a satisfactory rate of return. They are therefore linking together surplus units with deficit units in the economy.

3   C

4   D   If the market is efficient, then share prices should move in a rational way, not in a random way.

Option A is not correct as the key to market efficiency is the availability and processing of information. If all relevant information is easily available to all investors, and investors respond to information in a rational way, then share prices will move quickly to reflect this information in a logical manner.

Option B is not correct as the transaction costs of buying and selling should not be so high as to discourage trading significantly.

Option C is not correct as the market should be large enough so that no one individual can, by his actions, affect the movement of the market.

5   D   A stock market provides liquidity (B), a source of long-term capital (C) and a means of allocating capital (A). D would apply only if markets are perfectly efficient, which in practice they are not.

6   D   Specialist information refers to the type of information that is only available to professional investors such as fund managers. Under the semi-strong form of the hypothesis, such information is not expected to influence share prices.

Past share price movements (A) affect the share price as investors seek to identify and interpret trends in price movements.

Option B includes things such as the newly published annual accounts, or a published earnings forecast. Prices will be expected to respond to this type of information.

C is a form of publicly available information.

7   D   Over-the-counter markets are free from Stock Exchange regulations, but OTC dealers will be members of a Self Regulatory Organisation and are subject to the Financial Services Act.

8   D   Listing makes a company more vulnerable to takeover since the shares are made available to a wider number of investors and the company has no control over who can buy and sell its shares.

Option A is not correct as a stock market listing widens the number of potential investors, and may also improve the company's credit rating, making debt finance easier and cheaper to obtain.

Option B is not correct as shares traded on the stock market can be bought and sold in relatively small quantities at any time. This means that it is easier for investors to realise a part of their holding.

Option C is not correct as quoted companies are commonly believed to be more financially stable.

9   D   The minimum number of shares should be issued at the highest possible price to raise the sum required. Option A would use a range of prices, which is

unacceptable, and it would also mean that more shares were issued than is necessary.

In case B, the principle of issuing at the highest possible price is correct, but shares can only be issued at one price and not at a range of prices.

Although C would minimise the number of shares issued and maximise the share price, unfortunately the issue would not succeed because not enough investors are prepared to pay £3.00 for the shares.

D is the correct option because 800,000 investors are prepared to pay £2.50 or more for the shares, and this would raise the required amount of money.

10   A   The efficient market hypothesis concerns the extent to which prices reflect relevant information under different degrees of information-processing efficiency.

In the context of capital markets, operational efficiency can be taken to reflect the level of transaction costs, including the spread between buying and selling prices for stocks.

Allocative efficiency can be taken as referring to the success with which a market directs resources to their most productive users.

X-inefficiency refers to a tendency of monopolistic enterprises to be lax about the control of costs, in the absence of competitive pressure on profit margins.

3   OBJECTIVE TEST QUESTIONS: THE FINANCE FUNCTION III

1   C

2   D   When shares are issued at a deep discount to their current market price it becomes much more likely that existing shareholders will exercise their rights to realise the value of their rights. This avoids the need to have the issue underwritten. Share issues at a deep discount are fairly rare.

3   B   An example of deferred equity, defined in answer B, is convertible loan stock. The term 'deferred equity' is not used to describe different classes of shares (answers A and C).

Confusingly, however, 'deferred ordinary shares' are a class of ordinary shares which are not entitled to dividend unless profits rise above a certain level, or until after a certain period of time has elapsed. Deferred ordinary shares may be held by founders of the company. However, this class of shares is *not* what is meant by the term 'deferred equity'.

A golden share is a share with special voting rights or power attached, and a golden share in a company that has been privatised might be held by the government, with the right perhaps to prevent an unwelcome takeover of the company by a foreign multinational.

4   A   Retained earnings are a more significant finance source than share issues (B). Investment trusts are able to 'gear' themselves through debt (C). Earning profits does not necessarily produce more cash (D): more cash might be tied up in debtors, for example.

5   A   Flotation costs (eg the fees of accountants, solicitors and market makers / sponsors, printing and advertising costs, and Stock Exchange fees) are written off against reserves and not through the profit and loss account.

Option B is not correct. Flotation puts the company under public scrutiny and will make it subject to the expectations of the investment community.

Option C is not correct. Although flotation may provide an opportunity for founder owners to realise part of their investment, as a result their control will diluted by the admission of new shareholders.

Stock exchange regulations (D) exist to protect the shareholder.

6 C Overvaluation of the shares by investors does not mean the company will gain from going private. Shares in public hands would then be relatively expensive to buy up.

Option A is not correct. The Board may be disillusioned with pressures from investors for 'short-term' results.

Option B is not correct. Going private might avoid the risk of an unwelcome takeover bid.

Option D is not correct. If the Board believes that the shares are significantly undervalued, the company may gain by going private.

7 D Prudential control refers to the monitoring of banks and other financial institutions by the central bank or other authority.

Option A is not correct. Financial intermediaries provide advice and information to investors on available investment opportunities and their associated risks and returns.

Intermediaries reduce investment risks (B) for individuals by creating an investment portfolio.

Maturity transformation (C) overcomes the problem of matching the time periods for which a company or individual needs funds with the time periods over which investors wish to invest.

8 C Credit control will normally be dealt with by a separate credit control department.

9 B When shareholders take up a rights issue they will have to subscribe additional money for new ordinary shares. They are thus putting additional equity funds into the company.

When shareholders take a dividend payment (A) they are taking funds out of the company, not putting them into the company.

A share buy-back (C) will not bring in new funds. The company pays shareholders for their shares and cancels them.

If shareholders subscribe to a debenture issue (D), although they are putting additional funds into the company, these are not equity funds. Debentures are a form of fixed interest loan stock which do not confer the rights of ownership and control that are associated with equity shares.

10 A

4 FINANCIAL MANAGEMENT

The statement at first sight appears straightforward. However, some of the terms used are ambiguous, and it is helpful to address these as a means of setting this objective into the context of the **stakeholder theory of the firm.**

(a)   What does 'to maximise' mean, and what are the implications of pursuing policies aimed at value maximisation?

(b)   What is meant by **value** and how is it measured?

(c)   Is value maximisation the only objective of the firm? If not, then what are the **other objectives** and what inter-relationships exist?

Maximisation implies that the management will seek the **best possible outcome from a given set of circumstances,** rather than settling for a merely satisfactory outcome (or **satisficing**). This statement therefore carries with it assumptions about the company's attitude to risk in making business and financial decisions. If it is perceived that unacceptably risky projects are being accepted by the management with the aim of earning the highest possible profits and maximising their personal short-term returns through bonus schemes and so on, this may well have the effect of depressing the share price and thereby reducing the wealth of the ordinary shareholders.

One way in which the value of a firm can be defined is by calculating the **present value of expected future dividends.** This involves making assumptions about the future, many of which will be subjective, and there will be varying degrees of forecast error. Such an approach involves looking at the firm from the point of view of its shareholders.

Alternatively, value could be defined in the context of other stakeholders such as employees or customers. In the former case, value could be defined in terms of expected future remuneration flows, and value maximisation would then imply that remuneration should be at as high a sustainable level as possible. Customers on the other hand might hope for the highest possible level of product quality and innovation for the lowest possible price. Neither of these groups are directly interested in the maximisation of profits and dividends.

Increasingly today, firms operate within a matrix of different objectives and constraints, both **financial** and **non-financial**. Other financial objectives could include targets for **operating profitability**: for example management may require divisions to produce a minimum of 20% return on capital employed. There may also be policies on the maximum level of **gearing** that will be allowed. The problem is that although these targets may be formulated with the aim of helping the firm to maximise its financial performance, they are usually measured over a short-term period (typically one year). As a result they may conflict with the aim of maximising value in the long term.

Non-financial objectives could include:

(a)   Maintaining good relationships with customers and suppliers and acting ethically in all circumstances

(b)   Making training and career development a priority

(c)   Acting as a responsible member of the community within which the firm operates. Many companies now act within the framework of a clearly defined environmental policy which is regulated by a separate supervisory board.

Such non-financial objectives are not in direct opposition to the aim of maximising financial value, and may even contribute to it by improving the image and popularity of the firm. However, in the short term at least they are likely to act as constraints on value maximisation.

In conclusion, the statement is a starting point from which to examine a firm's objectives. However it does not provide a complete definition of a firm's aims and must be set in the context of the various stakeholders in the firm, and evaluated over different timescales.

5   **STAKEHOLDERS**

> **Pass marks.** Here you need to identify and to discuss the concept of maximising shareholder wealth as the assumed primary financial good.

(a)   One of the principles of the market economy is that if the owners of businesses attempt to achieve **maximum profitability** this will help to **increase the wealth of society**. As a result, it is usually assumed that a proper objective for private sector organisations is profit maximisation. This view is substantially correct. In general, the market economy has out-performed planned economies in most places in the world. Two key objectives of financial managers must therefore be the effective management of shareholders' funds and the provision of financial information which will help to increase shareholder wealth.

However, profit-seeking organisations can also cause problems for society. For example, monopolists are able to earn large returns which are disproportionate to the benefits they bring to society. The costs of pollution fall on society rather than on the company which is causing it. A company may increase profitability by making some of its work-force redundant but the costs of unemployed people fall on society through the social security system.

The question that then follows is 'Should individual companies be concerned with these market imperfections?'

Two opposing viewpoints

(i)   It can be argued that companies should only be concerned with maximisation of shareholders' wealth. It is the role of government to pick up the problems of market imperfections (eg by breaking up monopolies, by fining polluters and by paying social security benefits).

(ii)   A company is a **coalition of different stakeholder groups:** shareholders, lenders, managers, employees, customers, suppliers, government and society as a whole. The objectives of all these groups, which are often in conflict, need to be considered by company managers when making decisions. From this viewpoint, financial managers cannot be content with meeting the needs of shareholders only.

The truth is somewhere in between. The over-riding objective of companies is to create long-term wealth for shareholders. But this can only be done if we consider the likely behaviour of other stakeholders. For example, if we create extra short- term profits by cutting employee benefits or delaying payments to creditors there are likely to be repercussions which reduce longer term shareholder wealth. Or if we fail to motivate managers and employees adequately, the costs of the resulting inefficiencies will ultimately be borne by shareholders.

Summary

The financial manager is concerned with managing the company's funds on behalf of shareholders, and producing information which shows the likely effect of management decisions on shareholder wealth. But management decisions will be made after also considering other stakeholder groups and a good financial manager will be aware that financial information is only one input to the final decision.

(b)

> **Pass marks.** Only two of the situations need be addressed in your answer.

(i)   **A private company converting into a public company**

When a private company converts into a public company, some of the existing shareholder/managers will sell their shares to outside investors. In addition, new shares may be issued. The dilution of ownership might cause loss of control by the existing management.

The stakeholders involved in potential conflicts are as follows.

(1)   **Existing shareholder/managers.** They will want to sell some of their shareholding at as high a price as possible. This may motivate them to overstate their company's prospects. Those shareholder/managers who wish to retire from the business may be in conflict with those who wish to stay in control – the latter may oppose the conversion into a public company.

(2)   **New outside shareholders.** Most of these will hold minority stakes in the company and will receive their rewards as dividends only. This may put them in conflict with the existing shareholder/managers who receive rewards as salaries as well as dividends. On conversion to a public company there should be clear policies on dividends and directors' remuneration.

(3)   **Employees, including managers who are not shareholders.** Part of the reason for the success of the company will be the efforts made by employees. They may feel that they should benefit when the company goes public. One way of organising this is to create employee share options or other bonus schemes.

(ii)   **A highly geared company attempting to restructure its capital finance**

The major conflict here is between **shareholders** and **lenders**. If a company is very highly geared, the shareholders may be tempted to take very high risks. If the gamble fails, they have limited liability and can only lose the value of their shares. If they are lucky, they may make returns many times the value of their shares. The problem is that the shareholders are effectively gambling with money provided by lenders, but those lenders will get no extra return to compensate for the risk.

In restructuring the company, something must be done either to shift risk away from the lenders or to reward the lenders for taking a risk.

Risk can be shifted away from lenders by taking security on previously unsecured loans or by writing restrictive covenants into loan agreements (e.g. the company agrees to set a ceiling to dividend pay-outs until gearing is reduced, and to confine its business to agreed activities).

Lenders can be compensated for taking risks by either negotiating increased interest rates or by the issue of 'sweeteners' with the loans, such as share warrants or the issue of convertible loan stock.

Other stakeholders who will be interested in the arrangements include **trade creditors** (who will be interested that loan creditors do not improve their position at the expense of themselves) and **managers,** who are likely to be more risk averse than shareholders if their livelihood depends on the company's continuing existence.

(iii)   **A public company offering to run the UK lottery on a not-for-profit basis**

The stakeholders who will gain will be:

(1)   Lottery winners

(2)   Charities and other beneficiaries of lottery money

(3) The government (which can claim that the lottery is not 'tainted' by the profit motive)

The losers will be shareholders who will receive no apparent return for investing their money.

The problem with this sort of arrangement is that the company will probably charge for its services on a full-cost basis. If the company does nothing other than run the lottery, there is no real incentive to control or reduce the costs. However, if the lottery is an 'add-on' to the company's main business, the full cost charge will be higher than the incremental cost of running the lottery and a profit will be made, even if not specifically disclosed.

6   POLICY DECISIONS

> **Pass marks.** This question deals with some of the basics of financial management, both in general terms, and in relation to different elements of the finance function. The questions asked are quite specific, and you should be careful to address the issues as requested, and not merely to write all you know about the topics involved.

(a) Maximising the wealth of the ordinary shareholders generally implies aiming to maximise profits in a way that is consistent with long-term stability. On occasion this means that short-term gains must be sacrificed in the interests of the long-term profitability of the company. There are three major types of decisions that must be faced in the context of this overall financial objective.

Investment decisions

Investment decisions involve committing funds to:

(i) **Internal investment** projects (and being prepared to withdraw funds from these projects in the event of their proving to be unprofitable)

(ii) **External investment** decisions that involve the takeover of another company or a merger

(iii) **Disinvestment decisions,** which involve selling or liquidating an unwanted part of the business such as an unprofitable subsidiary

The outcome of investment decisions directly affects the level of earnings that the firm makes, and this is thus a major determinant of the value of the firm where this is defined as the present value of projected cash flows.

Investment decisions involve the commitment of funds in various ways. The ways in which these funds are raised, and the form in which they are held, form the basis of the second type of major policy decision:

Financing decisions

The assets of a company will be financed by a combination of:

- Share capital
- Reserves
- Long-term liabilities
- Short-term liabilities

The choice of the appropriate mix of finance involves balancing the following factors.

- The relative cost and ease of sourcing additional funds of different types
- The effects on the net worth of the business of using a particular source of funds

- The effect on the overall financial risk of the business of using a particular source of funds

- Maintaining an appropriate level of liquidity

Financial management is concerned with obtaining funds for investment, and investing those funds profitably so as to maximise the value of the firm. It is not enough to invest at a profit – the company must be able to pay its investors at least the rate of return that they require, otherwise they will take their funds elsewhere. Investments must therefore earn at least the **opportunity cost of finance**.

Dividend decisions

Dividends must be paid out of earnings, and the level of earnings is directly related to the outcome of the investment decisions made by the company. At the same time, the value of a company's shares will be related to the amount of dividends that the company has been paying, and also to the expectations of future dividends. Thus dividends themselves also have an impact on the value of the firm. The level of dividends is also further related to financing decisions since retained earnings are one of the most important sources of new funds for companies.

(b) **Treasury**

A definition of **treasurership** is 'the function concerned with the provision and use of finance. It includes provision of capital, short-term borrowing, foreign currency management, banking, collections and money market investment' *(CIMA)*. Thus, of the three types of policy decision discussed above, the treasury department is primarily concerned with financing policy at a high level within the organisation. The department is likely to be involved both in the determination of policy in this area, and in the achievement of the related financial objectives. While the treasurer may have an input to investment policy, this will not be one of his key roles.

Treasury will also be involved to some extent in the determination and implementation of **dividend policy** since, as explained above, this is closely related to both short-term and long-term financing decisions.

The **functions of the treasury department** may include the following.

(i)   Input to the determination and implementation of financial aims, strategies and policies

(ii)   Implementation of the appropriate financial and treasury systems

(iii)   Undertaking liquidity management to ensure that the company has the liquid funds it needs, and that it invests any surplus funds, even for very short terms

(iv)   Banking relationships and arrangements, and the day to day management of money

(v)   Arranging the best mix of debt finance, including leasing and factoring agreements

(vi)   Management of foreign currency operations, including exposure policies and procedures, exchange dealing, international monetary economics and exchange regulations

(vii)   Corporate finance in relation to equity capital management, business acquisitions and divestments, project finance and joint ventures

(viii) Corporate taxation

(ix)   Risk management and insurance

(x)   Pension fund investment management.

Financial control

Financial management can be defined as the management of the finances of an organisation in order to achieve the financial objectives of the organisation. In general terms, there are two aspects to financial management:

•   Financial planning
•   Financial control

The financial control function is concerned with monitoring performance to determine the extent to which the various activities of the organisation are meeting their financial objectives. This involves the use of existing budgets, actual results and financial forecasts to evaluate performance.

The financial control department is therefore primarily concerned with the area of investment policy, although it may also deal with financing policy in evaluating the way in which funds are being raised and used, and the relative costs of finance. The direct input of this department to **policy determination** is relatively low, but it does make an important contribution to the **achievement of policy**.

Good financial control will mean:

•   Mistakes may be made once, but not repeated

•   Investments that are not achieving their objectives are identified and action taken to remedy the situation

•   Forthcoming problems are identified quickly and dealt with appropriately

7   MERCHANT BANK

> **Pass marks.** Take care to avoid confusion as to the support services that might be provided by the merchant bank itself or by its associates (for example, underwriting).

(a)   If the management of a company is to bring the company successfully to the capital market by obtaining a listing on a stock exchange, it will generally need to call upon the expertise of a merchant bank to supplement the skills and knowledge already available within the management team.

The role of merchant banks in the **issue of new share and loan capital** is a major element of merchant banking. The banks do not just provide advice but also assist in the organisation of capital issues. Capital issues business is not the exclusive preserve of merchant banks, however, and organisations other than merchant banks also undertake capital issues work.

The merchant bank can be expected to **advise on the need for other advisors** such as lawyers and public relations consultants. It will also be expected to advise on **compliance** with stock exchange and other regulations, and **the law**, although specialist legal matters may need to be dealt with by company lawyers.

Advice will also be given on the **form of capital** which is to be made available, for example any split between preference and ordinary capital, and the possibility of convertible shares. The merchant bank should also advise on how much stock is to be issued.

Whenever an issuing house sponsors a capital issue, its reputation is at stake. It must therefore satisfy itself as to the **integrity of the company** and its **long-term business stability and strength.** It must be satisfied in particular that the accounting

72

information about the company, prepared by a firm of reporting accountants, is satisfactory. It must also advise the company carefully about the offer price of the shares, balancing the different interests of existing holders of stock with those of new holders. Future dividend policy will need to be considered as part of this process.

As an insurance against under-subscription for offered shares, an issuing house will usually arrange for the issue to be **underwritten** by a syndicate of merchant banks, discount houses and other financial institutions. The underwriters agree to take and pay for any shares which are not subscribed for by the public, and in return they receive an underwriting commission which is related to the total value of the issue.

The merchant bank will assist with the **promotion** of the introduction, which may include a programme of press advertising and presentations to potential major institutional investors.

(b) The **process of deregulation** in recent years has encouraged businesses from various different segments of the financial services sector to come together within a single financial services organisation. This process has been claimed by some to enable a more convenient all-round service to be provided to corporate clients, who would have less need to turn to a multiplicity of advisors. However, the changes have inevitably led to increasing conflicts of interest.

Such conflicts have led to a number of well-publicised problems in the capital markets concerning the conduct of different parties to transactions. It is open to speculation how many other problems of conflict of interest have arisen which have not come to light.

A financial services company may be involved in advising a corporate client about a new share issue, an acquisition or a bid defence. The same company may hold a significant amount of shares in the same company as a **marketmaker** in those shares. It could also be involved in advising investors about whether the shares should be bought, sold or held.

Among publicised cases in which conflicts of interest have arisen were those of Guinness and Blue Arrow. In the case of Blue Arrow, companies in the same group as the financial advisor involved took up undisclosed positions in the shares, thus concealing the failure of the launch from investors.

The firms which provide a variety of services in departments between which conflicts of interest could arise have attempted to reassure clients that rules operated within the organisation inhibit the development of conflicts, for example by ensuring that the departments are managed separately with little communication between them. Such rules would be necessary, for example, to ensure that marketmakers do not have access to price- sensitive information.

A compliance officer may be appointed to ensure that the rules are obeyed. However, as the cases which have come to law have shown, it is sometimes questionable whether the so-called **Chinese walls** which the firms claim to have set up are more than paper-thin. It would be surprising if cases similar to the Guinness and Blue Arrow cases did not continue to come to light in the future.

8   MARKET EFFICIENCY

> **Pass marks.** When discussing the issues in part (b) you should consider them in relation to the efficient markets hypothesis, and not simply write as much as possible about the given topic. You do not need an exhaustive knowledge of, for example, penny shares, to be able to make a reasoned answer to this question.

(a) It is often argued that the UK and US stock markets are **efficient capital markets,** in which:

(i) The prices at which securities are traded reflect all the relevant information that is available to buyers and sellers, meaning that prices change quickly to reflect all new information about future prospects

(ii) No individual dominates the market

(iii) Transaction costs are not so high as to impact significantly on the level of trading activity

If the market is efficient, then share prices should vary in a rational way.

The main forms of market efficiency are usually defined in relation to the varying degrees of efficiency with which the market processes information, and are as follows.

Weak form. This form of the hypothesis contends that share prices only change when new information about a company and its profits have become available. Share prices do not change in anticipation of new information being announced. Since new information arrives unexpectedly, it follows that share prices should be expected to change in a random manner and therefore that definable trends in share prices should not exist.

Semi-strong form. This form of the hypothesis contends that share prices reflect both all relevant information about past price movements and their implications, and all knowledge that is publicly available. This means that it will be expected that share prices can anticipate the formal announcement of new information. For example, if two companies plan a merger, their share prices will inevitably change once the merger plans are formally announced.

The market would show semi-strong efficiency if it were able to anticipate such an announcement, so that share prices of the two companies would change in advance of the merger plans being confirmed. Research in the UK and the US suggests that this does happen in practice, with the conclusion being drawn that the stock markets in these countries do demonstrate semi-strong form efficiency.

Strong form. If the market displays strong form efficiency, it would react in both the ways described above, but in addition, prices would also reflect information from insider knowledge available only to experts such as investment managers. If this is the case, then it would follow that managers should not need to worry overmuch about the presentation of information in one years accounts provided that they are taking decisions aimed at maximising the net worth of the firm in the long term. This does not seem to be borne out by the short-term nature of much decision making in quoted companies.

In addition, an expert such as an investment manager should be able to use his privileged access to additional information about companies to earn a higher rate of return than an ordinary investor. However, if unit trust results do out-perform the market, the excess returns would seem to be absorbed by management charges, since there is no evidence that such funds to consistently beat the market.

(b) (i) The **fundamental theory of share values** is based on the theory that the 'realistic' market price of a share can be derived from a valuation of estimated future dividends. If this theory is correct, the price of any share will be predictable, provided that all investors have the same information about a company's expected future profits and dividends, and a known cost of capital.

The evidence supports the theory in general terms, and thus supports the efficient markets hypothesis in relating the price of the shares to available information. However, in practice, share price movements are also affected by day to day fluctuations reflecting supply and demand, confidence, interest rate movements etc.

Technical analysis attempts to predict share price movements by assuming that past price patterns will be repeated. It has no particular theoretical underpinning, but has shown to be successful in practice. It can therefore be used in conjunction with fundamental analysis to predict some of the smaller scale day to day movements in prices.

Both theories are therefore consistent with the efficient markets hypothesis, and both also play an important role in creating an efficient stock market. This is because an efficient market depends on the widespread availability of cheap information about companies and market conditions, and the use of these techniques by the financial institutions on behalf of their clients is important in disseminating this information throughout the market.

(ii) It is illegal to deal in shares on the basis of **privileged information** that has been obtained by virtue of working for the company or for one of its professional advisers. Since the shares would be traded on the basis of information that is not available to the market, the occurrence of this practice could be described as demonstrating an 'extra-strong form' of market efficiency. The expectation would be that the individual would be able to make excess profits as a result of the use of privileged information.

The Stock Exchange maintains a surveillance group whose purpose is to scrutinise all unusual transactions. This group is effectively using the efficient markets hypothesis to help it to define what is a 'normal' transaction and therefore to identify cases where excess profits have been made on the basis of insider information.

(iii) The development of **index tracking funds** recognises the implications of the semi-strong form of the efficient markets hypothesis. It accepts the fact that it should not be possible to outperform the market on a consistent basis, and offers individuals the opportunity to allow their investment to 'track' one or other of the market indices, such as the FTSE 100 index. This allows the investor to take some of the excess risk out of equity investment by linking returns to the overall performance of the market, which in the long-term has significantly out-performed many other investment sectors.

(iv) Creative accounting involves the distortion of reported financial performance to enhance the image of the company, or to divert attention from hitherto unperceived problems. It has been argued that the market displays sufficient efficiency under the semi-strong form of the hypothesis for investors to see through such ploys.

In practice, however, this is questionable. There are numerous examples of companies that managed to convince the market of the plausibility of their accounting manipulations for a considerable period, before the problems were exposed in full. Examples of this include Polly Peck in the 1980s, and more recently, the failure of Powerscreen, a company that had a notable penchant for the capitalisation of development expenditure.

9   TREASURY DEPARTMENT

> **Pass marks**. In your discussion of the treasury function you should relate it as far as possible to the service based multinational in question.

(a)   The official CIMA and Association of Corporate Treasurers definition of treasury management is 'the corporate handling of all financial matters, the generation of external and internal funds for business, the management of currencies and cash flows, and the complex strategies, policies and procedures of corporate finance'.

Main treasury responsibilities in a service-based multinational company

(i)   It will make a significant contribution to the definition of corporate financial objectives, including strategies, policies and systems.

(ii)   It will be responsible for liquidity management, ensuring that the company has the liquid funds it needs and that it invests any surplus funds, even for the very short term. This will involve:

   (1)   Managing working capital and the transmission of funds within the group

   (2)   Maintaining banking relationships and arrangements for short-term borrowings and investments

   (3)   Money management

(iii) It will carry out funding management, including funding policies and procedures, and the sources and types of funds to be used. This involves the negotiation of all forms of borrowing and alternative sources of funds such as leasing.

(iv)   In a multinational company, currency management will be a very important role. This includes:

   (1)   Exposure policies and procedures
   (2)   Exchange dealing, including futures, options and derivative products
   (3)   International monetary economics and exchange regulations

(v)   The department will have an input to corporate finance decisions including items such as:

   (1)   Equity capital management - the form in which further equity should be raised

   (2)   Dividend policy

   (3)   Financial information for management

   (4)   Mergers, acquisitions and divestments

   (5)   Project finance and joint ventures

   (6)   Corporate taxation

   (7)   Risk management and insurance

   (8)   Pension fund investment management

(vi)   It will be responsible for liaising with the management of associated companies on treasurership matters.

Although treasury functions are currently the responsibility of the Chief Accountant, it is not clear whether these functions are carried out in a centralised or a decentralised manner. For the purposes of this discussion it will be assumed that much of the responsibility currently lies with the operating units.

Benefits of a separate centralised treasury function

(i)   Liquidity management can be improved by allowing bulk cash flows and therefore lower bank charges, and by avoiding the proliferation of small local surpluses and overdrafts.

(ii)   The centralisation of cash surpluses means that larger amounts are available for short-term investment thus giving better investment opportunities.

(iii)   Borrowings can be arranged in bulk at lower interest rates than for smaller amounts.

(iv)   Foreign currency risk management is likely to be improved since it will be possible to match receipts and payments made in a given currency across all the subsidiaries. This means that the need for more expensive hedging methods such as forward rate agreements is minimised.

(v)   A specialist department can employ experts with knowledge and experience of corporate treasurership, derivative products and so on.

(vi)   The centralised precautionary balance is likely to be lower than the sum of the local precautionary balances.

(vii)   It is easier to measure the performance of the treasury team in financial terms, for example by way of the net interest cost.

(viii) Multilateral netting between subsidiaries may be possible, depending on the regulations of the countries concerned. This should result in reduced transaction costs because there will be a reduced level of transfers between different currencies.

(b)   **Advantages of operating a profit centre treasury department**

(i)   Some companies, particularly those with a high level of foreign exchange transactions, are able to make significant profits from their treasury activities. Treating such departments as profit centres recognises the fact that some activities may earn revenues for the company and may as a result make treasury staff more motivated.

(ii)   Recognition of the department as a profit centre may allow the company to introduce an element of performance related pay should it wish to do so.

Disadvantages of operating a profit centre treasury department

(i)   Operating the department as a profit centre may encourage a **more aggressive attitude to risk** which may be difficult to reconcile with the directors' requirements. In addition it means that a good system of controls must be in place to prevent speculation.

(ii)   If it is a true profit centre, then **market prices should be charged** for the treasury service to other departments. It may be difficult to put realistic prices on some services such as the arrangement of finance or general financial advice. If the charges are viewed as too high by the subsidiaries they may be tempted to seek outside advice instead and thus the advantages of a centralised treasury function will be lost.

(iii)   Even with a profit centre approach it may be difficult to measure the success of a treasury department because successful treasury activities sometimes involve **avoiding the incurring of costs.** For example, a successful currency hedge during a period of strong currency movements may prevent the company from incurring a substantial loss.

77

10 MULTIPLE CHOICE QUESTIONS: LONG-TERM FINANCE I

1 C A rights issue involves the offer of shares to the existing shareholders. It therefore cannot be used to offer shares to the public for the first time.

2 B A placing involves the issue of new shares to institutions, while share splits and scrip issues are not means of gaining a Stock Exchange quotation.

3 A Earnings per share is defined as the net profit attributable to ordinary shareholders (ie profit after interest and tax) divided by the number of shares in issue. In this case: £500,000 ÷ 250,000 = £2

4 C The price/earnings ratio is the market price per share divided by the earnings per share. In this case, £20/£2.

5 D Dividend yield is the dividend per share divided by the market price per share expressed as a percentage. In this case: (£500,000 × 60% ÷ 250,000)/£20 = 6%

6 B The dividend cover is calculated as the earnings (after interest and tax) per share divided by the dividend per share. It measures the ability of the company to maintain the existing level of dividend. In this case: (£500,000/250,000) ÷ (£300,000/250,000) = 5/3 = 1.67.

7 C The theoretical ex rights price can be calculated as follows.

Assume that a shareholder holds 4 shares in Dukes plc. He will receive one new share at a price of £4. His new holding can be summarised as:

	£
4 shares at £5.00	20.00
1 share at £4.00	4.00
	24.00

The theoretical ex rights price is therefore £24 ÷ 5 = £4.80 per share.

8 B The value of the right will be the theoretical ex rights price, minus the issue price. In this case £4.80 – £4.00.

9 C The theoretical ex rights price can be calculated as follows.

Assume a shareholder holds 4 shares in Dukes plc. He will receive one new share at a price of £4. This will yield at a higher rate than the existing holding:

	£
4 shares at £5.00	20.00
1 share at £4.00 × 12.5/10	5.00
	25.00

The theoretical ex rights price is therefore £25 ÷ 5 = £5.00 per share.

10 D Although preference shareholders are paid a fixed percentage of the profits, these shares carry part-ownership of the business, and the payments are not therefore tax deductible.

11   MULTIPLE CHOICE QUESTIONS: LONG-TERM FINANCE II

1   C   This is a completely different class of stock with different levels of risk and return. Although its price may be affected by similar factors to those that affect the price of the convertible stock, it is unlikely to have any **direct** effect on the market price of the latter.

2   A   Under a finance lease, the risks and rewards of ownership are transferred to the lessee, who will therefore normally be responsible for maintenance.

3   B   If the proportion of the value of the asset in the contract is less than 90% the lease would be classed as an operating lease.

4   D   This is a type of fraud similar to pyramid selling. The others are all Government schemes that provide funds to small businesses for:

    A   Investment in regions that qualify for selective assistance
    B   Support of innovative technology in businesses with less than 50 staff
    C   Subsidised employment of graduates in small businesses

5   C   The gearing ratio based on book values is the ratio of prior charge capital to prior charge capital plus equity (including reserves) = £0.5m/£2m. It would be equally correct to calculate the ratio as prior charge capital to equity, excluding prior charge capital from the denominator. In this case, the answer would be 33%.

6   D   The ratio is calculated as prior charge capital divided by prior charge capital plus equity plus equity. Each element is calculated using market prices, and reserves are excluded. In this case, the calculation is (£0.2m + £0.3m)/(£1.875m + £0.5m) = 21%.

7   C   The market value of equity should be *ex div*, ie excluding dividend due.

8   B   The cost of capital can be found using the CAPM:

$$k_e = R_f + (R_m - R_f)\beta$$

where k_e = cost of equity
    β = beta value
    R_f = risk free rate of return
    R_m = market rate of return

In this case:

$$k_e = 10\% + 1.2(15\% - 10\%)$$
$$k_e = 16\%$$

9   B   The cost can be found using the following expression:

$$k_d = \frac{i(1-t)}{P_o}$$

where k_d = cost of debt (after tax)
    i = annual interest
    t = rate of corporation tax
    P_o = market value of debt (ex interest)

In this case:

$$k_d = \frac{10(1-0.30)}{90-10}$$
$$k_d = 8.8\%$$

10   D   Provided that the new investment has a similar risk profile to the existing operations, the nature of the new business area is irrelevant.

12 **MULTIPLE CHOICE QUESTIONS: LONG-TERM FINANCE III**

1 A Option A describes the source of finance that the majority of companies prefer traditionally. This is because it is simple, no recourse has to be made to the shareholders, and the control structure of the company is unaffected.

New share issues (B) are expensive and risky. They are normally only undertaken when large amounts of new capital are required.

Rights issues (C) are cheaper and easier to arrange than new share issues. However they must be priced attractively to ensure that enough shareholders will exercise their rights to make the issue a success.

Bank borrowings (D) are a major source of finance since debt finance is generally cheaper and easier to arrange than equity, but it lacks the simplicity of using cash from retained earnings.

2 D

Dividend cover   = EPS/Dividend per share

Dividend per share = EPS/Dividend cover
       = 42/2.1 = 20p

Dividend yield   = DPS/Share price

Share price   = DPS/Dividend yield
       = 20/0.16 = 1250p

Miscalculations may have led you to choose other answers.

3 A B, C and D are all different terms for the same thing.

4 A Finance from retained earnings has the same cost as the rest of the equity capital. However their use does not incur transaction costs.

If the shareholders wish to make a capital profit (B) then they will prefer their income in the form of capital growth rather than dividends. Thus they will be in favour of the company operating a policy of high retentions.

Option C is not correct. Since no change is made to the structure of the ownership of the business, the use of retentions does avoid the possibility of a change in control.

Option D is not correct. In this situation the directors will not have to go to the general meeting to obtain permission for a further capital issue to finance new projects. The use of retained earnings therefore allows them greater autonomy in their decisions.

5 D

	£
Equity: 1,000,000 × 240 pence	2,400,000
Preference shares: 400,000 × 75 pence	300,000
Loan stock: 250,000 × 80/100	200,000
	2,900,000

Answer A is the total book value for the securities.

If you took there to be 100,000 shares, you might have reached the incorrect answer B.

If you showed the loan stock at book value, you might have reached answer C.

6 C C is a completely different class of stock with different levels of risk and return. Although its price may be affected by similar factors to those that affect the price of the convertible stock, it is unlikely to have any **direct** effect on the market price of the latter.

A is the minimum price at which the stock should be traded. If the market price falls to this level it means that the market attaches no value to the conversion rights.

B will affect the price of the stock because the expected future value of the equity will determine the market valuation of the conversion rights.

The length of time to conversion (D) will affect the price since the longer the period, the greater the risk of volatility in performance and interest rates. Expectations of changes that could occur during this period will therefore impact upon the price of the stock.

7   B   The price at which the shares will be purchased on the exercise date is fixed by the company at the date the warrants are issued.

Option A is not correct. The warrant will normally be quoted at a premium in these circumstances because the share price will be rising due to the expectation of future growth in earnings.

Option C is not correct. Warrants make loan stock more attractive because they give investors the opportunity to buy equity in the future at a price that is likely to be at a reasonable discount to the current market price of the shares.

Option D is not correct. An investor who buys loan stock will also obtain warrants allowing him to subscribe for new shares in the future. Unsecured loan stock is often unattractive due to the risks attached and this is one method of making the stock more attractive at no immediate cost to the company.

8   C   An operating lease is a short-term contract which may not last for the full life of the asset. The lessor owns the asset.

9   A   The price/earnings (P/E) ratio measures the relationship between the market price of the equity and the earnings attributable to equity. It therefore provides a measure of how the market views the performance of the company. Although the level of financial risk may have some impact on this ratio, it is not the principal determining factor.

Option B is not correct. Although there is more than one method of calculating the financial gearing of a company, each approach provides a measure of the relationship between shareholders' capital plus reserves, and prior charge capital and/or borrowings. It is this relationship that determines the level of financial risk of the company.

Option C is not correct. The debt ratio (also known as the debt/equity ratio) is the ratio of a company's total debts, short-term and long-term, to its total assets, net fixed assets plus total current assets. It is a measure of the overall level of debt in the capital structure – the higher the level of debt, the higher the financial risk of the company.

Option D is not correct. Interest cover is a measure of financial risk that is designed to show the risks in terms of profit rather than in terms of capital value. It is calculated as the number of times that the profit before interest and tax can be divided by the total interest charge. Generally an interest cover of less than three times is considered low.

10   D $k_e = R_f + (R_m - R_f)\beta$
$k_e = 7 + 9 \times 1.25 = 18.25\%$

Note that the market risk premium is the excess of the expected return on the market above the risk-free rate.

13   MULTIPLE CHOICE QUESTIONS: LONG-TERM FINANCE IV

1   A   A company is said to be 'low geared' when there is less debt than equity in the capital structure. A ratio of 25% means that only 25% of the capital is in the form of debt, and so this is the correct answer.

2   D   A gearing ratio of 150% means that there is one and a half times as much debt as equity in the capital structure. Since the level of debt exceeds the level of equity, this is an example of high gearing.

3   B   Systematic risk is present in a diversified portfolio of shares.

4   C   Interest cover is the number of times the interest charge can be divided into the level of profits before interest and tax. As the gearing rises, the interest also rises, and therefore the interest cover is likely to fall rather than to rise.

5   D   Ordinary shares rank last for repayment in the event of liquidation, and the dividends are only paid out of distributable profits after all other liabilities have been paid. They therefore carry the highest level of risk.

A bank overdraft (A) will be repayable on demand and is likely to be secured against specific assets. The risk of the bank not getting its money back is therefore relatively low.

Although a mortgage (B) is for a long period, the debt will be secured against the property itself and therefore the risk to the bank is low.

Preference shares (C) rank after debt but before equity in the event of liquidation. Therefore the level of risk is higher than for the overdraft and the mortgage, but lower than for the ordinary shares.

6   B   Interest is treated as an expense under most tax regimes, while dividends are not.

7   C   The cost of capital is estimated from the returns required by investors, as reflected in the relationship between the level of dividends and the market price of the shares. Although it may be affected by average market returns, this is not a key determining factor.

8   A   The primary period covers the expected economic life of the asset, while the secondary period allows the lessee continued use of the equipment, usually at a nominal cost.

Option B is not correct. It is a financial reporting requirement to show the capital value of the asset n the lessor's balance sheet.

Option C is not correct. The risks and rewards of ownership are transferred to the lessee who will therefore normally be responsible for maintenance.

Option D is not correct. The lessor is normally a finance house, which buys the equipment from the manufacturer and leases it to the user.

9   C   *Using market values*

	£m
Equity (10m shares × £3,60)	36
Debt	8
	44

WACC = (15% × 36/44) + (7% × 8/44) = 12.27 + 1.27 = 13.5%

Using book values

Equity: £5m + £10m = £15m
Debt: £8m

WACC = 15% × 15/23 + 7% × 8/23 = 9.78 + 2.43 = 12.2%

If you forgot that the cost of debt should be net of tax, you may have got answers B or D.

10   A   This can be useful since the gearing ratio is unchanged, and hence the perceived risk of the company is not altered.

The lessee is able to update equipment more readily than if it were owned outright (B).

C: this means that, all other things being equal, the lease is more expensive than other forms of debt.

D is irrelevant to the position of the lessee.

14   MULTIPLE CHOICE QUESTIONS: LONG-TERM FINANCE V

1   A   Vendor credit involves the buyer obtaining goods on credit and agreeing to pay the vendor by instalments. Hire purchase is an example of vendor credit.

Lender credit involves the buyer borrowing money and using the money to purchase goods outright.

Acceptance credits are a source of finance from banks for large companies. They have nothing to do with hire purchase.

A finance lease is an agreement between the lessee and the lessor for the majority of the asset's useful life. However, ownership of the asset is retained by the lessor.

2   D $$\begin{aligned} \text{Total value} &= \text{Coupon value} + \text{Terminal value} \\ &= £6 \times 4.111 + £100 \times 0.507 \\ &= £24.67 + £50.70 \\ &= £75.37 \end{aligned}$$

Answers A and C include only one of the two elements of the total value. You might have chosen answer B if you took discount factors at 6% instead of 12%.

3   B   Assuming that there is no change in the earnings performance of the company, price B would avoid a drop in the share price after the issue. However, it would be unlikely to succeed because there is no incentive for shareholders to take up their rights.

A is the value of the rights attaching to one share at an offer price of £2.00, not the price at which the new shares should be offered.

C and D are above the current market price and are therefore inappropriate.

4   D   A scrip (or bonus) issue is a means of converting equity reserves into issued share capital. No cash movement takes place.

Option A is the nominal value of Mr Norman's existing holding. It is irrelevant to the scrip issue.

Option B is the market value of the new shares that would be issued to Mr Norman and Option C is the nominal value of the new shares that would be issued to Mr Norman. However, no payment is made for a scrip issue by existing shareholders.

5   D   A stock split involves splitting the issued shares into smaller units with a proportionately smaller nominal value. The purpose is to create cheaper shares with greater marketability. There will be no effect on reserves.

6   B   The dividend cover is the maximum possible equity dividend that could be paid out of profits after tax / actual dividend. In this case, it is the profit after tax for the year that should be used.

Option A uses the profits before tax in the calculation and is incorrect. Option C uses the profits after dividend in the calculation and is incorrect. Option D uses the reserves figure in the calculation and is incorrect.

7   C   Earnings per share is calculated as the profit attributable to equity (ie profit after tax) for the period (in this case the profit after tax) divided by the number of equity shares in issue and ranking for dividend.

Option A uses the correct profit figure, but uses the book value of the equity as the denominator rather than the number of shares in issue. Option B is incorrect because it uses the retained profit figure in the calculation instead of the profit available for distribution (ie, the profit after tax). Option D uses the profit before tax in the calculation and is therefore incorrect.

8   D   While the level of other creditors will impact upon the cash forecast for the company, and therefore the liquidity position, it is not a factor that will normally have a direct influence on the directors' decision.

Option A is not correct. The directors must comply with the law to ensure that only profits available for distribution are paid out as dividends.

Option B is not correct. Investors usually expect a consistent dividend policy from the company, with stable dividends each year or, even better, steady growth in dividends.

Option C is not correct. Dividends are a cash payment, and a company must have enough cash to pay the dividend it declares.

9   B   The stock can be redeemed between 2009 and 2012. 2012 is therefore the latest possible redemption date.

Option C is not correct. No information is given concerning the redemption price.

Option D is not correct. Annual interest payments of 10% will be based on the nominal price of the stock, not the issue price.

10   D   The minimum share price at which an investor would opt to convert is £3.25, since this is the price at which the value of the shares received would match the cash received on redemption. £3.50 is above this price and therefore the stock would be converted rather than redeemed. The other options (A, B and C) are below this price and therefore the stock would be redeemed rather than converted in those cases.

15   **MULTIPLE CHOICE QUESTIONS: LONG-TERM FINANCE VI**

1   B

	£
Three current shares have an ex div value of ($\times$ 2.08)	6.24
One new share – subscription price	1.60
Theoretical ex rights value of four shares	7.84
Theoretical ex rights price per share ($\div$ 4)	£1.96

2   A

3   A   Return = Dividend received + Capital gain (or minus capital loss)

	pence
Final dividend from previous year received	5.5
Interim dividend	2.0
Capital gain (85 – 80)	5.0
Return	12.5

Return based on start-of-year values $= \dfrac{12.5}{80} = 15.6\%$.

4   D

Ex interest price = £92 – 5   = £87 per £100 nominal stock

Interest per £100 nominal stock   = £5 per half year

Cost of stock per half year $= \dfrac{5}{87} = 0.05747$

Cost of stock per year $= (1.05747)^2 - 1$
$= 0.118 = 11.8\%$

5   B $r = \dfrac{d_0(1+g)}{MV \text{ ex div}} + g = \dfrac{5(1.20)}{200} + 0.20 = 0.23$ or 23%

6   C $r = \dfrac{d_0(1+g)}{MV \text{ ex div}} + g = \dfrac{5(1.10)}{120} + 0.10 = 14.6\%$

7   C   At the end of the year:

(1)   The current dividend will be 22p (+ 10%)
(2)   The expected growth rate in dividends will still be 10%

$MV = \dfrac{22(1.10)}{(0.15-0.10)} = 484p$

8   D   The growth rate in dividends, g, is assumed to be (a) the proportion of total earnings that are retained in the business for re-investing to produce higher profits and dividend growth, multiplied by (b) the return on these re-investments, R. Thus g = bR.

Here   g = $0.60 \times 0.15 = 0.09$

$MV = \dfrac{180,000(1.09)}{(0.20-0.09)} = £1,783,636$, say £1,784,000

9   A   High interest rates might deter a company from borrowing, but will not limit how much it *is able* to borrow. In certain circumstances, items B, C and D might impose such a limit. Debentures might be issued with a covenant whereby the company agrees not to borrow beyond certain limits until the debentures have been (Option B). A bank might refuse to lend if security is insufficient (Option C). Some companies have an item in their Articles of Association (Option D) restricting the borrowing powers of its directors (for example, stating that without the sanction of ordinary shareholders, the directors cannot allow total borrowing to exceed the value of equity plus reserves).

10 B   Financial risk is the risk that operating profits might be insufficient to cover interest costs of debt capital and leave a reasonable return for equity shareholders. Financial risk therefore increases as gearing rises, and (as in this case) decreases when gearing falls.

Operating risk is the risk that contribution (sales minus variable costs of sales) will be insufficient to cover fixed costs and earn a profit unless a sufficient volume of output and sales is achieved. Higher fixed costs, which are implied in this situation, cause operating risk to increase.

16   MULTIPLE CHOICE QUESTIONS: LONG-TERM FINANCE VII

1   A $12\% \times (1 - 0.35) = 7.8\%$

The market value of the loan stock will be $\frac{12}{14} \times £100 = £85.71$ per £100 nominal stock.

2   C   Cost $= \frac{12}{95} \times (100 - 40)\%$

$= 7.6\%$ (after tax)

3   B
	£
Current value of shares (× £4.10)	16.40
Subscription price for 1 share	2.50
Theoretical value of 5 shares ex rights	18.90

	£
Theoretical ex rights price (£18.90 ÷ 5)	3.78
Subscription price	2.50
Theoretical gain on 4 current shares	1.28
Theoretical value of right per existing share (÷ 4)	32p

4   D   Index-linked gilts are government stocks in which the annual return for investors is set at a 'real' level in excess of the rate of inflation, which is here 6% per annum, giving a yield of (approximately) 8% per annum or £8 per £100 of stock.

5   D
	£'000
Total profit after tax	2,900
Preference dividend	200
Profits available for distribution to ordinary shareholders	2,700
Actual dividend to ordinary shareholders	1,200

Dividend cover (2,700 ÷ 1,200) = 2.25 times

6   B
Profit on ordinary activities after tax	£800,000
Number of shares	10 million
EPS	8p

		£	
Market price ex div:	price cum div	0.80	
less	Dividend proposed/payable	0.03	
	Price ex div		0.77p

P/E ratio = 77p ÷ 8p = 9.625, say 9.6.

7   C   Mid-market price ÷ EPS = 220p ÷ 15p = 14.7

8   D   Factors A, B and C are all caused by unsystematic risk which an investor can avoid by diversifying his investment.

9   B   The beta factor for a company's shares can be calculated as:

$$\beta = \frac{cov(s,m)}{var(m)}$$

where   m   is the market rate of return
        cov(s,m)   is the covariance between the return on the company's shares (s) and the market rate of return
        var(m)   is the variance of the market return

(Candidates for several examinations are expected to now this formula.)

10   C   Financial gearing and size influence the perceived risk of companies in such a way that their beta factors will be affected. Differences in risk suggested by items A and D should therefore both be reflected in existing betas. Some estimating errors will occur (item B) in the mathematical techniques for calculating betas, but these will influence the perceived risk of companies: a higher beta factor, even if inaccurately calculated, will indicate higher perceived risk.

Answer C is correct. Some companies might have a low systematic risk with share prices responding in only a relatively small way to change in conditions affecting the rest of the market. However, their specified individual risk (unsystematic risk) might be very high, subjecting the company to sharp fluctuations in returns/share price. Firms of commodity dealers might be examples.

17   BARDSEY PLC

> **Pass marks**. This question contains some easy computations but what will pass or fail you is your performance on the discussion topics, which account for about 75% of the marks and a lot greater percentage of the effort and understanding.
>
> *Other points*. All of the discussions in this question are of the utmost importance for the financial management part of this paper. Only a minority of candidates really understand the principles properly, so give yourself a competitive advantage by working through this solution carefully!

(a) *Net cash flow in 20X7*

Assuming no change in sales, no cost increases, £10 million of replacement investment and no change in net working capital, the company's **net cash flow** in 20X7 can be calculated as follows:

Source of funds	£m	£m
Operating profit		60
Add back depreciation		8
Less: applications:		68
Interest paid for 20X7	15	
Tax (20X6 charge paid)	12	
20X6 dividend paid	20	
Reinvestment in fixed assets	10	
		57
Net cash flow		11

> *Other points*. The same figure could have been reached quickly as: Retained earnings 13 add Depreciation 8 less Reinvestment 10, giving 11, which is a pretty easy five marks!

(b)

To: The Board of Directors
From: Financial Manager

Report on the financial performance and financial health of Bardsey plc

I have compared **key financial ratios** taken from Bardsey's 20X6 accounts with figures for the stores sector average. These are shown in the appendix to this report. When comparing Bardsey, a specialist furniture retailer, with the stores sector as a whole, allowances must be made for the specific nature of our trade. Various other reservations on the interpretation of financial ratios are given at the end of this report. That said, the following comments can be made.

Profitability

Our company shows a **return on capital employed** (ROCE) higher than the sector average which at first sight seems good news considering the high space requirements of displaying furniture and the fact that our fixed assets were revalued to realistic figures only two years ago.

ROCE is the return earned on total equity and debt funding the company. If the debenture were to be repurchased on the market and refinanced by a loan at market rate, this would cost £130 million. The ROCE would then reduce to 14.5% (60/413), which is about average.

Looking at how our profit is earned we can see clearly that our company earns high profit margins but has a low fixed asset turnover. This indicates our high price policy which results in a lower turnover, but further investigation compared with other furniture retailers is needed before firm conclusions can be drawn.

Return to shareholders

When we look at the return on equity shareholders' funds it is significantly worse than the sector average. The probable reasons are:

(i)   The interest rate on our debentures is now well above the market rate. Refinancing could improve this ratio but would not necessarily improve available cash flows and is therefore open to debate.

(ii)   Our gearing is below the sector average. High gearing increases the return on equity, but is not necessarily recommended as it increases shareholders' risk.

Growth

Our dividend cover is lower than average, indicating that the proportion of funds which we are reinvesting for growth is lower than for most companies in our sector. This is borne out by our zero growth forecasts for existing operations and the low P/E ratio which probably indicates low market expectations of **growth**.

Liquidity

Our **liquidity ratios** (current ratio and quick ratio) are quite high for a retailing company, indicating sound liquidity but inefficiency in the use of working capital (see below). Again, comparison with other furniture retailers is required.

Gearing

Our **gearing** is fairly low compared with the sector average as shown by the low debt/equity ratio and the high interest cover. Increasing the gearing would improve shareholders' returns because debt is cheap compared with equity finance, especially when the cost after corporation tax relief on interest is considered. However, increasing debt by too much will make the shareholders' position more risky and may not be desirable.

Utilisation of working capital

This is an area that needs careful investigation. On the face of it we are significantly '**over-capitalised**' with regard to working capital.

We are giving very long payment periods to some debtors. We need to determine whether this is because of policy or lax credit management. Our furniture stays in stock for a long period compared with other companies. The stock period needs to be compared with other furniture retailers and our high selling price policy needs to be taken into consideration.

We are also holding a high cash balance which may be questioned by shareholders if it is not distributed or reinvested.

Reservations on the ratio analysis

In addition to the fact that **comparative data** on other furniture retailers is unavailable, the following reservations can be made about the analysis:

(i)   The ratios should be examined over a period of years, to allow for short-term fluctuations.

(ii)   Results should be examined at other times of year besides the year end. Our business can be seasonal.

(iii)   Our accounting policies should be compared with those of other companies and any material differences taken into account.

(iv)   To evaluate performance properly we should also consider a range of non-financial measures, covering in particular customer satisfaction, market share, quality, resource utilisation and innovation.

Conclusion

Our company appears reasonably **profitable** and has sound **liquidity**. There is no immediate financial problem. However, in order to survive, we probably need to reinvest for growth. The company's existing plans for growth appear exciting but clear strategies must be formulated especially for image, pricing policy and distribution policy if we are attempting to attract a wider cross-section of the market.

If the 'out of town' strategy is successful, it may give us an opportunity to sell some of our city centre sights releasing cash for investment in more productive assets.

Appendix

		Bardsey	*Stores sector average*
Return on capital employed	= 60/383	15.7%	14.3%
Return on equity	= 33/283	11.7%	15.3%
Operating profit margin	= 60/150	40.0%	26.2%
Fixed asset turnover (sales/fixed assets)	= 150/300	0.5 times	1.2 times
Stock period	= 60/90 × 365	243 days	180 days
Debtor days	= 100/150 × 365	243 days	132 days
Gearing (total debt/equity)	= 100/283	35%	42%
Interest cover	= 60/15	4.0 times	3.2 times
Dividend cover	= 33/20	1.65 times	2.1 times
Current ratio	= 200/117	1.71	Not given
Quick ratio ('acid test')	= (200 – 60)/117	1.20	Not given
P/E ratio		11	15

18 S PLC

> **Pass marks**. This question required only very simple calculations to be made. In approaching the discussion of the relationships between convertible debenture values and share prices and dividends it is helpful to view the convertible as a form of delayed equity rather than as loan stock.

(a) At the date of issue, the market value of each share to be received is 400p. Therefore to convert the debenture to 20 shares would mean that the value of the shares received would be 20 × 400p = £80.00. Since the debenture price was £100.00, this implies a **conversion premium** of £20.00 (£100 – £80), or 25% (100 × 20 ÷ 80).

The fact that a conversion premium exists, and that the **coupon rate** on convertibles is frequently less than that on irredeemable stocks reflects expectations of share price movements. It is expected that the share price will increase between the date of issue of the stock and the date of conversion in such a way as to mean that conversion on the due date will allow the debenture holder to obtain shares at a discount to the prevailing market price.

(b) If the market price of the shares grows at 10% per annum, then the price after three years will be 532.4p (400p × 1.1 × 1.1 × 1.1). If the debenture is converted at that date, then the value of the shares received will be £106.48 (532.4p × 20).

It is likely that the market value of the debenture will exceed this because investors will be expecting to see continued growth in the price of the shares, in excess of the cost of the funds tied up in the debenture, and therefore the terminal value of the debenture will be considerably higher. The debentures will reflect these expectations by trading at a higher price than the current conversion value.

(c) Dividend policy is one of the major factors which determines the share price. Under the **dividend valuation model**, the share price is held to be directly related both to the current dividend and to the expected future growth in dividends:

$$p_0 = \frac{d_0(1+g)}{(k_e - g)}$$

where:

p_0	=	market price of shares
d_0	=	current level of dividend
k_e	=	required rate of return
g	=	expected annual growth in dividend

Thus it can be seen that dividend growth is important in determining the likely market value of the shares. As has already been discussed above, the market value of the shares is very important in determining the price of convertibles, and therefore the dividend policy of the company will have an important effect on the value of convertible stock.

(d)   Companies normally issue convertibles in the expectation that the **holders will exercise their options**. Convertibles can therefore be seen as a form of **delayed equity**. They are attractive to the firm when the price of the ordinary shares is abnormally low at the date of issue, and at times when to issue a further tranche of equity would result in a significant drop in earnings per share. However they also carry the risk that the share price will not rise in line with expectations at the time of issue and that holders will not therefore convert. If the debentures are dated, then the company must have funds in place to allow redemption on the due date. Convertibles also have a short term benefit in that interest payments are allowable against tax.

Convertibles therefore may form part of the strategy of a company whose objective is to raise new equity, but which for various reasons does not wish to go directly to the market in the short term. They are often preferable to straight loan stock since they **do not commit the company indefinitely** to the payment of large interest bills. They further allow the company to **widen the investment base** by attracting investors looking for a guaranteed short term income plus the possibility of a capital gain at a later date. They have also recently formed a part of the strategy of companies that wished to manipulate their reported gearing and earnings per share, since they could choose whether to show them as equity or debt. However, this loophole has now been closed.

19   Z PLC

> **Pass marks**. Be sure that you understand the meaning of conversion premium and conversion discount.

(a)   Z plc wishes to build up a fund for foreign investment which will be spent within the next two years. There are **two main points** to consider.

   (i)   The rate of return from invested funds must always be reviewed against the risk of the investment. In the long term, equity investments show a higher rate of return than government securities and corporate debt but they suffer from the risk that in the short term the stock market might fall, severely reducing the funds available for investment.

   (ii)   Ideally the funds should be accumulated in the currency of the country where they will eventually be spent.

   Below, we expand on these points in relation to Z plc's case.

   Z plc has investments in UK and US equities. At the time of writing, both of these stock markets have been performing well, but to maintain more than 60% of the fund in equities is taking a risk of over-reliance on equities.

   The portfolios of UK and US equities have shown higher rates of return than the stock market average for these countries. This is very good news but it probably indicates that the portfolios have an above-average proportion of high-beta shares. Such shares will tend to do very well when the stock market is rising but are likely to fall more than average if there is a stock market collapse. A similar point can be made about the small companies' shares which can be very volatile.

Because of the principle of **liquidity preference**, long-term debt instruments tend to show a higher average rate of return than short-term bonds. However the long-term government bonds suffer from the same problem as equities: there is a risk that they might have to be sold at a point when their value is low. The 3-month Treasury Bonds do not suffer from this risk.

The investment in UK corporate debt shows a higher rate of return than the UK government debt. However there is higher default risk on corporate debt.

On balance then, Z plc's portfolio is a long way from being risk-free. With less than two years to go before the money is spent, it is probably wise to transfer some of the money out of equities into low-risk deposits. The proportion in deposits can be gradually increased as the date gets nearer.

As a hedge against currency risk, investments or deposits should now be made in the currencies in which the eventual investment will take place. With the pound at a high level against most currencies in the world, now is probably a good time to effect this change.

(b)

> **Pass marks**. Convertible loan stock is an interesting investment, having the return and risk characteristics of an option. This is a good question, except that the convertible is trading at a discount below the underlying share price, which is unrealistic in the scenario given. The decision maker must choose between selling now, converting now, converting after one year, or holding to redemption.

(i) The **conversion premium** is the difference between:

- The current market price of the convertible loan stock, and
- The current market value of the equivalent shares if the conversion was made

In other words, a premium indicates that the value of the stock is higher than that of the underlying shares. This is because the convertible loan stock is normally a better investment than the underlying shares. It will enable the holder to gain from any increase in the share price but protects against a collapse in share price by having a minimum value as loan stock.

If, however, the market price of the convertible is less than that of the equivalent shares, there is a **conversion discount**.

(ii) The treasurer has four options:

- Sell the stock now at £106.50 (31 December 20X7)
- Convert now (31 December 20X7)
- Convert in one year's time (31 December 20X8)
- Hold the stock to redemption (31 December 20X9)

Option 1: Selling the stock now will give cash of 50,000/100 × £106.50 = £53,250.

Option 2: Converting now will give 50,000/100 × 20 = 10,000 shares with a current value of £54,000.

Option 4: Holding to redemption will give 6% interest for 2 years and a redemption value of £50,000. Discounting at 7%, the appropriate rate for debt of this risk:

Year		£	7% factor	Present value £
1-2	6% interest	3,000	1.808	5,424
2	Redemption	50,000	0.873	43,650
				49,024

The present value of holding to redemption is £49,074.

Looking at these three options, the stock is at a discount to the value of the equivalent shares which means that **converting now** (option 2) gives the best value, £54,000.

Option 3 will give interest after one year of £3,000 and $50,000 \times 18/100$ shares, ie 9,000 shares. The present value of the interest at 7% is £2,805.

So, if option 3 is to be better than option 2, the present value of the share value in one year's time must be more than £54,000 – £2,805 = £51,195, which is £5.69 per share.

£5.69 is 5.4% higher than the current share price.

On the basis of the figures, therefore, and ignoring brokerage fees, the decision is to convert the loan stock to shares now, receiving £54,000, unless it is expected that the present value of the share price in one year's time will be more than £5.69, which would require a growth in the share price of 5.4% above the cost of equity capital.

The decision cannot be made purely on the basis of these figures, however, because the different options have different levels of risk attached to them. If the loan stock is converted now and the shares are held, they might collapse in value over the next two years. If, on the other hand, the shares are sold for cash, the opportunity of share price growth is lost. If the convertible is held until the last date for conversion it provides a protection against share price collapse and the opportunity of gaining from a share price increase. The decision is ultimately a subjective one, based on the Treasurer's attitude to risk.

> **Pass marks**. As already mentioned, the idea that the convertible stock can be at a discount on a conversion day, as in this question, is unrealistic! The best decision would in fact be to convert the stock to shares, immediately sell them for £54,000 cash and buy more convertible stock for £53,250, making a risk free gain of £750 (1.4%). This arbitrage process could be repeated until the cost of the stock rose sufficiently so that transaction costs prevented any further gains.

20   NEWSAM PLC

> **Pass marks**. The question does not specify the ways in which the gearing has been calculated. You should therefore define clearly your basis of calculation of gearing and explain the reasons for your choice. In the final part of the question do not limit your discussion to the options suggested in the question but consider what other appropriate sources of funds might be available to Newsam.
>
> This question offered a substantial amount of accounting information to enable you to illustrate their answers numerically but more importantly, to allow an opportunity to show your expertise in interpreting accounting statements.

(a) **Capital gearing** is concerned with a company's long-term capital structure. The covenants attaching to the debenture do not define clearly what they mean by capital gearing in this context, in particular whether the bank overdraft should be included as long-term debt capital. However, since it appears that the overdraft has been used principally to finance fixed assets in the form of machinery rather than as a source of working capital, it is probably reasonable to argue that it should be included as part of the prior charge capital. The **gearing ratio** can thus be defined as:

$$\frac{\text{Prior charge capital}}{\text{Shareholders' funds}} = \frac{\text{Debentures} + \text{overdraft}}{\text{Ordinary shares} + \text{reserves}}$$

The gearing ratios can now be calculated.

(i) Book values: $\dfrac{£5.0\text{m} + £3.0\text{m}}{£5.0 + £10.0\text{m}} = 53.3\%$

(ii) *Market values*

Market value of debentures:

£5.0m × 115% = £5.75m

Market price of shares = P/E ratio × Earnings per share

  = P/E × $\dfrac{\text{Profit after tax}}{\text{Number of shares}}$

  = 14 × £1.34m/20m = 93.8p

Market value of equity = Market price × number of shares

  = 93.8p × 20m = £18.76m

Gearing ratio = $\dfrac{£5.75\text{m} + £3.0\text{m}}{£18.76\text{m}} = 46.6\%$

(b) It appears from the calculations above that if calculated on the basis of **book values**, Newsam has already breached the covenant relating to the gearing level. If the gearing is calculated using **market values**, then Newsam has not yet breached this covenant, but with a gearing of 46.6% is very close to doing so. If short-term creditors were included, the gearing measures would be increased.

The required liquidity range for the current ratio is 1.08 (£1.35 × 80%) to 1.62 (1.35 × 120%). Newsam's current ratio (current assets: current liabilities) is 1.0 (£7.0m:£7.0m). The company is therefore in breach of the covenant with respect to liquidity.

(c) A **high gearing level** only constitutes a danger when the level and volatility of earnings is such that the company is at risk of being unable to meet the interest payments as they fall due. If this situation arises the company could be forced to liquidate assets to meet the demands of its creditors, and this in turn could jeopardise its operating viability. It follows that the absolute level of gearing cannot be used to assess the financial risk faced by the company. It is more helpful to assess the level of interest cover in the light of the degree of volatility in earnings.

Interest cover can be calculated as the rate of operating profit: interest payable. In Newsam's case, the cover is currently 3.0 times (£3.0m:£1.0m). There is little evidence available on which to assess earnings stability, but the fact that sales growth has been steady rather than spectacular may be taken to imply that earnings are not especially volatile. If this is the case then the existing level of gearing does not appear to be dangerous.

A further factor to take into account is the **quality of the asset backing** since this will influence the attitude of its lenders if Newsam faces problems in repaying its debt. Land and buildings currently appear in the accounts at £9.0m, and it is of crucial importance to know how this relates to current market valuations. If this figure is conservative then the creditors' security could be fairly good.

Land and buildings at £9m represent 75% of the value of total creditors (including trade creditors). It is unlikely that anything close to the book valuation of plant and machinery and stock could be realised in the event of a forced sale; however, it is to be hoped that the major part of the debtors figures is collectable. Thus, in summary, the company appears to have adequate asset backing in the event of a forced restructuring or liquidation.

The factors discussed above, when taken together, suggest that the level of gearing is not particularly dangerous. However, if the company is actually in breach of its debenture covenants, the courses of action available to the debenture holders and their attitude towards the situation will be of key importance in determining the true dangers of the company's position.

(d) (i) If the company is to **lower its capital gearing** it needs either to increase the value of its issued share capital and reserves or to decrease the size of its borrowings. Since growth is low and cash resources relatively small it seems unlikely the company will be able to repay much of the debt in the short-term future from operational funds. However, one option might be to convert some of the owned plant and vehicles onto operating leases and thus reduce the size of the bank overdraft.

Similarly the company might be able to raise funds through a sale and leaseback of property which could be used to reduce the level of debt. There may also be some scope to reduce the level of working capital through improving stock and debtor turnovers and increasing the amount of credit taken from suppliers. However, the opportunities are likely to be limited: for example, the average debt collection period could probably not be reduced much below the current level of 52 days.

Policies that could be used to increase the size of shareholders' funds include the following.

(1) **Fixed asset revaluation**. It is implied that land and buildings have not been revalued since their acquisition twelve years ago. Despite a slump in the property market it is possible that land and buildings may be undervalued, and a revaluation could result in a strengthening of reserves and hence an improvement in the capital gearing.

(2) **Rights issue**. The reaction of the market to a rights issue will depend on the rating of the company and the purpose for which the issue is being made. In this case, growth has been slow, the P/E ratio is low in relation to the sector average implying a low rating, and the purpose of the issue is not to finance new growth opportunities but to reduce the level of debt. Taking these facts together, and given a relatively flat market, investors are unlikely to view such an issue positively. As a result the issue would need to be priced at a relatively large discount to make it attractive; this in turn would increase the earnings dilution and impact badly upon the share price.

(3) **Placing**. The company may find it easier to make a placing with the institutions. However, it might need to gain the agreement of the shareholders to forgo their pre-emptive rights in this situation.

(4) **Brand capitalisation**. The appearance of the balance sheet could be improved by this method, but investors and creditors may not place much weight on such a valuation.

(ii) In order to improve the level of interest cover, Newsam will need to **reduce the level of its interest charges**. Options available include the following.

(1) Redeem the debentures and replace with additional overdraft. This would reduce the interest cost as follows.

£5m × (15% – 9%) = £0.3m

The interest cover would then become:

£3m ÷ (£1.0m – £0.3m) = 4.3 times

(2) Redeem the debentures and replace with a medium-term Eurodollar bond. This would reduce the interest cost:

£5m × (15% – 5%) = £0.5m

The interest cover would become:

£3m ÷ (£1.0m – £0.5m) = 6 times

The improvement in interest cover makes this appear an attractive option. However if the dollar continues to strengthen in the manner suggested by the forward rates, at 4% per annum, this would effectively wipe out the benefit by the end of the first year.

(3) Redeem the debentures and replace by another or of medium to long-term debt such as a medium-term bank loan.

Although probably more expensive than the overdraft or eurodollar bond, this would be free from the risk of foreign currency movements and would offer more security than the use of short-term finance which is repayable on demand.

It is therefore suggested that, unless Newsam has significant dollar incomes, it should investigate the possibility of a medium-term sterling loan.

21 MRF

> **Pass marks**. You should state clearly the reasons for your choice of discount rates, and your assumptions as to the tax position of the rates chosen. In the final part of the question you should consider other methods of making the deal attractive to MRF. It is helpful to draw attention to the effect of the different tax positions of the two organisations on the calculations.

(a)
REPORT

To: MRF President
From: MRF Treasurer   Date: 19 November 20X6
Subject: Financial evaluation of project financing

The purpose of this paper is to evaluate the alternatives of buying the new capital equipment using a bank loan and acquiring the equipment under a finance lease. Since MRF has charitable status, no writing down allowances are available if the equipment is purchased, and no tax relief will be available on payments made to the leasing company. Since the cost of the bank loan would be 12%, it is proposed to **evaluate the alternatives** at this rate since this is effectively the **marginal cost of capital** for the project.

Purchase using bank loan

If the equipment is purchased, there are two relevant cash flows that arise. These are the payment for the equipment at the start of the project, and the receipt on the sale of the equipment at the end of year 6:

		£
Year 0	(£22.5m × 1.000)	22.50m
Year 6	(£4.0m × 0.507)	(2.03m)
Net cost of project		20.47m

Finance lease alternative

In this case, MRF would make annual payments of £7.5m at the end of each of the years one to six. The PV cost of this can therefore be found by applying a six year annuity at 12% to the annual cost:

£7.5m × 4.111   £30.83m

Conclusions

On financial grounds, purchase of the equipment using the bank loan has a much lower PV cost over the life of the project. Insurance and maintenance costs will be unaffected by this decision.

Signed: Treasurer

(b) REPORT

To: Account Manager
From: Account Negotiator   Date: 19 November 20X6
Subject: MRF leasing proposal

The purpose of this report is to evaluate the options available to us in order to gain the MRF business. This will include the calculation of the **annual lease payments** that we would need to offer in order to gain the business, the effect of such a **reduction** in leasing payments on our evaluation of the project, and a discussion of other options that we could consider in order to rescue the deal.

Annual lease payments required by MRF

For the charity to be indifferent between the bank and the leasing company, the annual payments would need to be reduced to the point where the PV cost of the payments over six years at 12% was the same as the PV cost of purchase using the bank loan. This can be found using the following expression, where 'a' = the annual lease payment made by MRF:

$$a \times 4.111 = £20.47m$$
$$a = £4.98m$$

This represents a reduction in the annual payment of £2.52m.

Financial implications of the reduction in payments

The calculation of the effect of this reduction in payments on the position of the leasing company is contained in the Appendix to this report. For the purposes of the evaluation it is assumed that the opportunity cost of capital of 14% is a net of tax figure, and the figure to be used in the evaluation. It is further assumed that the **writing down allowances** (WDAs) will be claimed from year 1, and that the balancing charge will be incurred in year 6. Tax payments are assumed to be made in the year in which the revenue/expenditure arises.

The figures show that the NPV of the lease on this basis is £0.17m, in other words, about breakeven.

Other factors to be considered

It has been shown that offering the equipment to MRF at an annual leasing figure of £4.98m offers little financial benefit. However, it may be possible to offer other

97

incentives to MRF in conjunction with a higher lease cost. These include the following.

(i) We may be able to structure a deal that offers a beneficial maintenance contract to MRF.

(ii) It is not clear what MRF's intentions are at the end of the six year period. The calculations assume that the equipment is disposed of. However, it may be beneficial for MRF to continue to use the equipment which could then be offered at a lower cost for a secondary period.

(iii) It may be possible to structure the annual payments in such a way as to offer MRF other cash flow benefits.

The **opportunity cost of capital** of 14% has been used, but it may be that a lower rate could be more appropriate to the specific risks associated with this project. If this is the case, then there may be more flexibility that the figures suggest in the MRF proposal.

Conclusions

It will be difficult for us to put together a package that is both attractive to MRF and financially beneficial to ourselves due to the different tax positions of the two organisations, even taking into account the discount available to us from the supplier. However, it has been shown that there are a number of other options that could be considered should we decide to pursue the deal.

APPENDIX

The first step is to calculate the net-of-tax cash flows.

Year	0	1	2	3	4	5	6
	£m	£m	£m	£m	£m	£m	£m
Capital expenditure	(18.00)						4.00
WDA		4.50	3.38	2.53	1.90	1.42	0.27
33% tax on WDA		1.49	1.12	0.83	0.63	0.47	0.09
Income from MRF		4.98	4.98	4.98	4.98	4.98	4.98
Net of tax income		3.34	3.34	3.34	3.34	3.34	3.34

The annual cash flow can now be calculated and discounted at 14% to find the present value of the lease.

Year	0	1	2	3	4	5	6
	£m	£m	£m	£m	£m	£m	£m
Capital expenditure	(18.00)						4.00
33% tax on WDA		1.49	1.12	0.83	0.63	0.47	0.09
Net income		3.34	3.34	3.34	3.34	3.34	3.34
Cash flow	(18.00)	4.83	4.46	4.17	3.97	3.81	7.43
Discount factor	1.000	0.877	0.769	0.675	0.592	0.519	0.456
PV cash flow	(18.00)	4.24	3.43	2.81	2.35	1.98	3.39
Cumulative PV	(18.00)	(13.76)	(10.33)	(7.52)	(5.17)	(3.19)	0.20

An annual lease revenue from MRF of £4.98m therefore yields a net present value of £200,000 for the lease as a whole.

22 ABC PLC

> **Pass marks**. The calculations for part (a) are quite simple, but make sure you state clearly the assumptions made about the discount rate used in the evaluation and the timing of the tax payments. Your answer to part (b) should be in the form of a report with an introduction, main section(s) and conclusion. If necessary, refer to the calculations made in part (a).
>
> *Other points*. Part (c) offers the chance to demonstrate an understanding of the two-stage nature of some capital investment decisions.

(a) The discount rate to be used is 9% which is the approximate **after tax cost of borrowing** at 11½%. It is assumed that tax is paid one period after that in which it arises. It is also assumed, in the absence of information about depreciation policies, that the **lease payments** are allowable in full for tax purposes.

Lease

Year	Lease payments £	Tax at 21% £	Cash flow £	Discount at 9%	PV cost £
0	(15,000)		(15,000)	1.000	(15,000)
1	(15,000)	3,150	(11,850)	0.917	(10,866)
2	(15,000)	3,150	(11,850)	0.842	(9,978)
3	(15,000)	3,150	(11,850)	0.772	(9,148)
4	(15,000)	3,150	(11,850)	0.708	(8,390)
5		3,150	3,150	0.650	2,048
NPV cost of leasing					(51,334)

The NPV cost of leasing exceeds £50,000. Because of writing down allowances, the NPV for the purchase option will be less than £50,000. On financial grounds leasing is therefore the preferred option.

The situation from the point of view of the leasing company is as follows.

Year	Revenue £	Capital costs £	Tax £	Net cash flow £	Discount at 15%	PV £
0	15,000	(50,000)		(35,000)	1.000	(35,000)
1	15,000		(775)	14,225	0.870	12,376
2	15,000		(1,744)	13,256	0.756	10,002
3	15,000		(2,470)	12,530	0.658	8,245
4	15,000		(3,015)	11,985	0.572	6,855
5		5,000	(3,424)	1,576	0.497	783
6			2,128	2,128	0.432	919
NPV of leasing agreement						(4,200)

Working: tax computation

Year	Revenue £	WDA £	Taxable £	31% tax £	Year of tax flow
0	15,000	(12,500)	2,500	775	1
1	15,000	(9,375)	5,625	1,744	2
2	15,000	(7,031)	7,969	2,470	3
3	15,000	(5,273)	9,727	3,015	4
4	15,000	(3,955)	11,045	3,424	5
5		(6,866)	(6,866)	(2,128)	6

The leasing company makes a net gain on the deal of £4,820 in present value terms. This is much less than the savings that ABC plc could make if it purchased rather than leased the equipment.

(b)
REPORT

To: Chief Executive
From: Management Accountant   Date: 12 May 20X4
Subject: Computer system financing options

Introduction

This report deals with the **relative merits of buying and leasing** the new computer system. Detailed supporting calculations can be found attached [see (a)].

Financial position

The calculations show that purchase of the equipment is a much **more financially advantageous** option than leasing. This assumes that it will continue to be possible to borrow at 11½% to finance the purchase. If we feel that it is likely that interest rates will rise, then the possibility of taking out a fixed rate loan should be considered. Alternatively it may be possible to hedge through a mechanism such as an interest rate swap or by the use of futures.

Other factors

Although, if the system is leased, the leasing company will be responsible for insurance and maintenance, we are effectively **locked into the deal** for the duration of the lease. We are therefore exposed to the risk that the equipment becomes obsolete during this period. To terminate the lease and to switch to new equipment is likely to carry heavy financial penalties. This sort of flexibility could only be found by taking out an operating lease, and this is almost certain to be even more expensive than a finance lease. A further alternative would be a turnkey operation involving facilities management, but this too would be very expensive.

Conclusions

The calculations show that the **relative financial loss** to us in the leasing situation is very great when compared with the financial gain that would be made by the leasing company. There is therefore little point in trying to negotiate a better deal. The discrepancy arises due to the different tax position of the two companies and our ability to use all our capital allowances. It is therefore recommended that the system should be purchased outright although we may need to do further work to identify the best way to finance the transaction.

Signed: Management Accountant

(c) It is important to appreciate that there are effectively two stages in the decision making process.

    (i)   The first step is to **evaluate the benefit to the company** of acquiring the system. This involves calculating the marginal cash flows that will result from the use of the system and then discounting these at the weighted average cost of capital.

    (ii)   Once the fact that the investment in the system should be undertaken has been established, the next step is to **evaluate the alternative methods of financing the acquisition**. This involves calculating the relative costs of the different methods of finance which are available.

In the calculations above, it is taken as given that the system will add value to the business and should be acquired. It is the second stage of the process that is being undertaken, and therefore it is the relative costs of finance which are important and not the weighted average cost of capital.

23   ARMADA

(a) The benefits of a rights issue to Armada are as follows.

    (i)   The company is highly geared and a rights issue would therefore serve to **reduce the level of gearing**, and thus the level of financial risk faced by the company would fall. It may be possible to replace some of the debt with the proceeds of the issue and thus further reduce the ratio. A reduction in gearing may also help Armada to avoid breaching any loan covenants and to achieve greater security from its creditors.

(ii) The market has been rising and rights issues are easier to accomplish on a **rising market**.

(iii) Since the market is high, Armada should be able to achieve the issue at a relatively **low cost** since less shares will need to be issued.

(iv) If **underwriters** are used, then the amount of finance that will be raised is known and guaranteed.

(v) If the issue is successful, it will not significantly change the **voting structure**.

The drawbacks to such an issue include the following.

(i) The issue will need to be priced at a discount to the current share price in order to make it attractive to investors. This will result in a **dilution in earnings** and a **drop in the share price**.

(ii) Since the economic outlook is poor, it is unlikely that the market will rise much further and thus Armada may be too late to take advantage of the benefits of issuing on a rising market.

(iii) If the issue is not successful, a significant number of shares will be taken up by underwriters. This may **alter the voting structure and control** of the company.

(iv) **Administration and underwriting costs** are high.

(v) It could be difficult to **convince the markets** of the need for the issue - it may be assumed that Armada is facing a cash crisis. If the issue fails then this problem will be compounded and it will be harder for Armada to achieve a successful issue in the future.

(vi) Shareholders may be unable or **unwilling to increase their investment** in Armada.

(b) A **lease** is an agreement between two parties pertaining to the use of an asset. The owner of the asset (the **lessor**) allows the **lessee** to use the asset in return for periodic payments. A lease is not in itself a means of acquiring ownership of the asset, although many leases do allow the lessee the option to purchase the asset at a nominal cost at the end of the lease period. **Hire purchase** is similar to leasing in that periodic payments are made in return for the use of the asset; however ownership of the asset is automatically transferred to the lessee at the end of the rental period.

The **advantages of leasing** are as follows.

(i) Leasing reduces the amount of capital needed to operate the company, as compared with purchasing the asset which requires a capital outlay. Hire purchase also normally requires a down payment to be made at the start of the contract.

(ii) When the asset is being used to generate additional business, the use of the a lease allows costs and revenues to be matched as the income from the use of the asset can be applied to pay the lease premiums.

(iii) Lease finance can be arranged relatively cheaply, quickly and easily.

(iv) Cash budgeting is facilitated since the timing and amount of the premiums are known at the outset.

(v) The use of a short-term lease rather than outright purchase allows the company to retain flexibility and to avoid the risk of obsolescence.

(vi) Lease premiums or, under UK Finance Act 1991 rules, a combination of depreciation and interest, are allowable against tax.

(vii) If the lease is an operating lease as opposed to a finance lease, it does not have to be disclosed on the balance sheet and therefore the true level of the company's gearing is not immediately apparent. However details of the lease commitments must be contained in a note to the accounts.

The **advantages of hire purchase** include the following.

(i) Unlike leasing, hire purchase allows the user of the asset to obtain ownership at the end of the agreement period.

(ii) The user can claim capital allowances on the purchase price of the asset. This is helpful if he is able to use them fully; if he is not then leasing may be a more attractive option.

(iii) The interest element of the payments is allowable against tax.

24   RISK AND MARKET EFFICIENCY

> **Pass marks**. Part (a) demands an understanding of the different types of risk, how they are measured, and their implications for investment strategy. In part (b) it is helpful to consider the relationship of the statements to time: are they explaining the past, describing the present or predicting the future?
>
> *Other points.* This question aimed to examine candidates' knowledge and understanding of different types of risk, the relationship between them and how they can be measured. It further examined for an understanding of market efficiency and how historical information can be related to future periods.

(a)   MEMORANDUM

To: Board of Directors
From: Management Accountant   Date: 23 May 20X5
Subject: Portfolio risk

The purpose of this paper is to provide a definition of the different types of **portfolio risk** and an explanation of their measurement, and to relate them to the recent board discussions on this subject.

There are three elements to be considered in this context.
(a)   Systematic risk
(b)   Unsystematic risk
(c)   Total risk

Total risk

The total risk of an investment is the sum of the systematic and the unsystematic elements. It is measured by the standard deviation of the returns on the investment.

Systematic risk

This is that element of risk that cannot be avoided by **diversification**. It must therefore be accepted by the investor unless he invests entirely in risk-free investments. He will expect to earn a return which is higher than the return on a risk-free investment in return for accepting systematic risk. The amount of systematic risk in an investment varies between different types of investment. Some industries by their nature are more risky than others, for example compare the restaurant business with the retailing of basic foodstuffs. Similarly, some individual projects will be more risky than others: compare the building of the Channel Tunnel with the replacement of a fleet of car ferries, which can be sold for use on alternative routes if necessary.

The **capital asset pricing model** (CAPM) is concerned with the measurement of systematic risk. It seeks to relate the premium on returns required by investors to the systematic risk of the company via a measure known as the beta factor. A beta factor in excess of 1.0 indicates that the share carries a higher level of systematic risk than the average for the market and vice versa.

Unsystematic risk

This is that element of risk which it is possible to eliminate through diversification. Therefore if an investor holds a well diversified portfolio he will be able to avoid unsystematic risk. The simplest approach to quantifying the unsystematic risk is indirectly in relation to the total risk and the systematic risk of the portfolio. Since the total risk is defined as the sum of the systematic and the unsystematic risk, it follows that the unsystematic risk element can be found by subtraction.

Implications for investment strategy

Since unsystematic risk can effectively be removed from the portfolio through diversification, it is true to say that if the portfolio is fully diversified then only systematic risk needs to be considered. However, it would be dangerous to ignore the total risk insofar as this provides an indicator as to whether the portfolio is in fact sufficiently diversified.

It may be the case that the price of a share indicates a return that is below that of the market or even of the risk-free asset. In theory, if the beta is lower as a result, the lower return makes the share worth investing in because of lower uncertainty.

Signed: Management Accountant

(b) An **efficient market** can be defined in terms of **information processing** as one in which the prices of traded securities reflect all the relevant information which is available to participants, where no individual or group of individuals dominates the market, and where transaction costs are insignificant. Thus it will be supposed that share prices respond quickly to all new information about future prospects. Since it is postulated that prices already reflect all the available information, it follows that at any one point in time future price movements cannot be forecast, since future information is not known and therefore the corresponding price movement is not known. The efficient market hypothesis thus provides a means of explaining the current level of share prices and not of forecasting their future levels. The implication for investors is that it is not possible for an investor consistently to outperform the market.

Mathematical models which attempt to predict movements in share prices are generally, as in this particular case, based on the analysis of a large volume of data over a long period of time. However, they are only likely to be able to predict the future with accuracy if the economic, financial, corporate and political framework that governed the period in question remains stable into the future. In practice, such conditions are in a constant state of change and therefore the predictive value of such models degrades quickly over time thus rendering such models of limited value. However, in the short term they may in themselves become an influence on the market since if sufficient people have faith in them they may influence buying behaviour and hence become something of a self-fulfilling prophecy. In the longer term though, prices will adjust back to their 'underlying' or 'real' values and the utility of the models will decline.

Neither statement claims to be able to predict the price of a given security with significant accuracy for a given point in time, and therefore to this extent they are not contradictory. Similarly, both statements are in fact concerned more with the historical movements in share prices than with their prediction into the future.

25 COST OF CAPITAL

> **Pass marks.** This searching question on cost of capital covers a range of topics. Although it appears at first sight to be fairly straightforward, a number of the topics raised have given rise to decades of debate and are still unresolved. To produce adequate answers requires an ability to summarise arguments concisely.

(a) In order to attract finance, a business must offer to pay a **return on the capital provided.** The cost of capital is the minimum rate of return which must be paid in order to encourage the supply of capital. Conversely, it is the minimum rate of return which the investor expects on the funds provided.

Higher returns are demanded for high risk investments than for those of lower risk. An investor providing equity share capital (ie, subscribing for ordinary share capital) suffers the risk of the business in which the investment is made and therefore demands a higher average rate of return than a lender, whose returns are subject to clear rules agreed in advance and are independent of business risk. The cost of equity capital is therefore higher than the cost of debt capital.

Further, the cost of equity capital will vary significantly between one business and another because of the difference in risk between the businesses. The cost of debt will also vary, depending on the investor's perception of the company's ability to meet the service payments and its willingness to offer security for the loan.

The overall cost of capital of a business is the weighted average cost of all the funds in use. It is important for a business to know its cost of capital because investments made by the business must generate after-tax returns sufficient to cover the cost of capital. If discounted cash flow analysis is used, the cost of capital can be used as a discount rate for appraising new investments.

(b) (i) If a company **increases its borrowings** there are two opposing effects on the weighted average cost of capital (WACC). Firstly, increased borrowing makes the surplus profits available to shareholders more volatile, resulting in increased risk and an increased cost of equity capital. By itself, this effect would increase the WACC. Secondly, the proportion of cheaper debt capital in the firm increases, and this works towards reducing the WACC. The overall effect is subject to debate but it is likely that, at reasonable levels of gearing, a company's overall cost of capital will fall when it increases borrowing, provided it can take advantage of tax savings on debt interest.

However, if gearing is increased to very high levels, there is an increased risk of the firm's bankruptcy, resulting in both equity and debt holders demanding higher rates of return and significantly increased costs of short term cash flow and working capital management. The WACC at high gearing can be damagingly high and firms are advised to avoid this scenario.

(ii) A **volatile share price** (ie one which moves rapidly up and down over time) may be caused by the company's sensitivity to general economic factors (systematic risk) or factors specific to the company (unsystematic risk). Only volatility caused by systematic risk will have an effect on the company's cost of equity capital.

For many companies a volatile share price is caused by high unsystematic risk. For example, the success of a new internet stock depends on its ability to take advantage of new discoveries and ideas on a daily basis. A shareholder who has a diversified portfolio of internet stocks is unconcerned by this form of unsystematic risk, because what is a failure for one company is likely to be good for another one, and the overall result on the portfolio is neutral. For such companies, therefore, there is no increase in the cost of capital, even though they carry high unsystematic risk.

However, companies which are highly sensitive to general fluctuations in the economy (such as motor manufacturers) will have a higher cost of capital, because this systematic risk cannot be diversified away when the share is held in a portfolio.

(iii)   A company which generates cash surpluses may choose to pay these out to shareholders as **dividends** or to reinvest within the business in order to increase future profits, cash flows and dividends. In theory, provided that the funds are invested wisely, a low dividend payout ratio should not affect the cost of equity capital, because shareholders will understand that a reduction in cash today will generate larger cash surpluses in the future. For a quoted company, the reduction in dividend should be immediately compensated by a corresponding increase in share price, because share prices are a reflection of future dividends.

However, a company's cost of equity capital is affected by the **amount of information given to the market** about its underlying level of profitability and the viability of its strategic direction and plans. If a company wishes to switch from high to low dividend payouts, care should be taken to accompany this with proper explanations, otherwise the market may assume that it is suffering from financial difficulties.

This situation is complicated by the fact that **some shareholders prefer capital growth** (eg those who prefer to take cash in the form of capital gains for tax purposes) whereas others prefer high dividends because they need to pay out a steady stream of cash disbursements (such as pension funds). A company may have already attracted a 'clientele' of shareholders preferring high dividends. If it suddenly switches to a policy of low payouts and high reinvestment, it may cause confusion, resulting in a drop in share price and an increase in the cost of capital.

26   LEISURE INTERNATIONAL PLC

Pass marks. This generally well answered question is testing your knowledge of the different theories relating to the cost of capital, as well as testing your ability to calculate the cost of capital correctly taking into account the effects of taxation.

In part (c) you are required to demonstrate the way in which the cost of capital should be used by the company in assessing individual projects. It may be helpful to approach this from the point of view of the effect of the new funding and investments on the overall capital structure of the firm, and the implications of this for raising finance in the future.

(a)   It is assumed that the market prices of the shares and debentures are quoted excluding dividend and interest. Since the WACC is to be calculated based on market values, the cost of reserves can be ignored.

Cost of equity. The dividend valuation model taking into account growth will be used.

$$k_e = \frac{d_1}{p_0} + g$$

where:

k_e	=	cost of equity
d_1	=	annual level of dividends
g	=	annual rate of growth in dividends
p_0	=	market price of shares (ex div)

In this case: k_e = 4/80 + 0.12

= 17.0%

Cost of preference shares

$$k_{pref} = d/p_o$$

where: k_{pref} = cost of preference shares

d_1 = preference dividend (9p)

p_o = market price of shares (72p)

k_{pref} = 9 / 72

= 12.5%

Cost of debentures. It is assumed that the debentures are irredeemable. The after tax cost to the company will be calculated.

$$k_d = \frac{i(1-t_c)}{p_o}$$

where: k_d = cost of debentures

i = annual interest payment (14p)

P_o = market price of debentures (100p)

t_c = rate of corporation tax (33%)

$$k_d = \frac{14(1-0.33)}{100}$$

= 9.4%

Weighted average cost of capital (WACC)

	No in issue £	Market price £	Market value £	Cost %	Weighted cost
Equity	10,400,000	0.80	8,320,000	17.0	141,440
Preference shares	4,500,000	0.72	3,240,000	12.5	405,000
Debentures	5,000,000	1.00	5,000,000	9.4	470,000
			16,560,000		2,289,400

WACC (2,289,400 / 16,560,000)   13.82%

(b) The **capital asset pricing model** (CAPM) provides an alternative to the dividend valuation model in calculating the cost of equity. Unlike the dividend valuation model, the CAPM seeks to differentiate between the various types of risk faced by a firm and to allow for the fact that new projects undertaken may carry a different level of risk from the existing business.

The model focuses on the level of **systematic risk** attaching to the firm, in other words, that element of risk which is common to all investments and which cannot be avoided by diversification. The model uses the **beta factor** as a measure of an individual share's volatility of expected returns as against the market average. A beta factor of less than 1.0 indicates that the expected volatility is less than that of the market as a whole, and vice versa.

The model can be formulated as follows:

$$k_e = R_f + [R_m - R_f] \beta$$

where: k_e = cost of equity capital

β = beta factor for the firm

R_m = market rate of return

R_f = risk free rate of return

Thus the additional information that would be required is as follows.

Beta factor. This can be calculated statistically from historical records of:

(i)   The returns earned by the share in terms of capital gains/losses and dividends

(ii)   The overall returns earned by the market

Market rate of return. The average annual rate of return on the securities market as a whole. This can be calculated from historical records.

Risk free rate of return. This is generally taken to be the rate of return on government stocks.

(c)   It is not usually correct to regard the **required rate of return** for an individual project as the cost of the actual source of funds that will be used to finance it, even where the funds can be traced directly. Debt is cheaper than equity only because there is an equity base which takes the risk - if the equity funds were not there then the company could not borrow. Each year some profits should be retained to increase the equity base, thus allowing further borrowing to take place. The borrowing is not independent of equity funds, and thus it is appropriate to combine the two in arriving at the cost of capital to be used in project appraisal.

The WACC reflects the company's long-term capital structure, and therefore capital costs. The capital structure generally changes only very slowly over time, and therefore the marginal cost of new capital should be approximately equal to the WACC. The **WACC** is therefore a more appropriate yardstick for the evaluation of new projects.

27   CRAZY GAMES PLC

> **Pass mark.** Your answer to this question must be presented in the form of a report to private clients. Presentation will be improved by the use of appropriate sub-headings for the different parts of the question, and you should also make the explanation clear enough for non-accountants to understand.

To: Private clients
From: Accountant
Date: 14 December 20X8
Subject: Purchase of traded investments

Introduction

In this report, we consider some terms commonly used in equity investment. We then look at how to estimate the market value of a share and the slope of the yield curve for gilt-edged securities

(a)   **Commonly used terms in equity investment**

Gross dividend (pence per share). At the end of the financial year, a company will announce the amount of profit that it has earned after paying interest to its providers of debt, and tax to the government. Of the remaining profits, a proportion may be retained for reinvestment in the business, and the rest will be paid out to the shareholders in the form of a dividend. The gross dividend per share is the amount that the shareholders will receive in respect of each of the ordinary shares held, *before* the deduction of income tax. It is a useful figure, particularly when quoted as the **dividend yield** (gross dividend as a percentage of the market price of the share) because it provides a method of comparison between the performance of different companies. The actual dividends for Buntam and Zellus are:

	Price	*Div yield*	*Div per share*	*Div payable*
Buntam	160p	5%	8p	6.4p
Zellus	270p	3.33%	9p	7.2p

The dividend payable is less than the dividend per share because the company must deduct income tax at the basic rate before making the dividend payment. However, this tax figure may be subject to adjustment when the investor completes his tax return, depending on his marginal rate of income tax. Although Zellus pays a higher level of dividends than does Buntam, the latter is to be preferred since the dividend yield is higher.

Earnings per share (EPS). This is the amount of profit after interest and tax that is attributable to each equity share, ie it is the profit available for dividends divided by the number of shares in issue. It is most useful to the shareholder when converted into a price/earnings (P/E) ratio, since this relates the absolute level of earnings to the market price of the shares. It can be found for Buntam and Zellus by dividing the share price by the P/E ratio.

	Price	*P/E*	*EPS*
Buntam	160p	20	8p
Zellus	270p	15	18p

When comparing investments, the P/E ratio is generally more important than the EPS. On this basis, Buntam would be a more attractive proposition than Zellus.

Dividend cover. This ratio compares the profit available for dividend with that actually paid. It therefore provides an indication of the probable ability of the company to sustain the current level of dividend payments. A very low level of dividend cover suggests that dividends may be more volatile. It also provides a measure of the proportion of profits retained for investment within the business. In general, the higher the level of retentions, the more likely there is to be a good level of capital appreciation. It is calculated as the EPS (net) divided by the dividend per share (net):

	EPS	*Div/share (net)*	*Div cover*
Buntam	8p	6.4p	1.25 times
Zellus	18p	7.2p	2.50 times

This suggests that Zellus has more potential for capital growth than Buntam, since the latter pays out almost all its earnings in the form of dividends and retains little for investment in new income generating projects.

(b) **How to estimate the market value of a share**

The key determinants of the price of a share are:

- The amount of dividends that a company pays

- The rate of growth of dividends

- The rate of return that shareholders require: this will vary with market conditions and the perceived level of risk associated with the company in question

These elements have been incorporated into a model of share valuation known as the **dividend growth model,** which discounts the expected dividend stream at the rate of return required by the investor. It can be expressed as:

$$P_0 = \frac{D(1+g)}{(k_e - g)}$$

where P_0 = market value of share (ex div)

D = current year's dividend

g = growth rate in earnings and dividends

k_e = shareholders' required rate of return

In the case of Crazy Games plc:

$$D = 5.5\text{p per share}$$
$$k_e = 20\%$$

The rate of dividend growth can be estimated as follows:

$$\text{Dividend in 20X3} \times (1 + g)^4 = \text{Dividend in 20X7}$$
$$(1 + g)^4 = \text{Dividend in 20X7} \div \text{Dividend in 20X3}$$
$$(1 + g)^4 = 5.5\text{p} \div 3\text{p}$$
$$(1 + g)^4 = 1.83$$
$$1 + g = \sqrt[4]{1.83}$$
$$g = 1.1636 - 1$$
$$g = 16.36\%$$

Substituting this into the formula:

$$P_o = \frac{5.5(1 + 0.1636)}{(0.20 - 0.1636)}$$

$$P_o = 175.8 \text{ pence per share}$$

This means that the market value of 1,000 shares would be £1,758.

(c) **The yield curve for gilts**

The yield curve plots the gross yield to redemption against the years to maturity of an investment. The current yield curve for gilts is as follows:

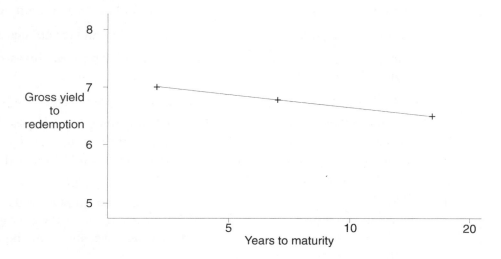

This particular curve is a **reverse yield curve,** ie it slopes in the opposite way to that which would normally be expected, given that investors generally require a higher rate of return to compensate for a longer investment period. The most common reason for a curve of this type is the general expectation that interest rates are entering a period of long-term decline.

BPP PUBLISHING

28 JERONIMO PLC

> **Pass marks.** In (c), two alternative methods are given to calculate the rate of dividend growth. However, the first method is superior if you can calculate fourth roots of numbers. In (d) good answers would define strong form market efficiency first. Points from the definition can then be used to support your reasons as to the possible effects of the hypothesis on managers' behaviour.

(a) **Rights issue**

A rights issue is a way of raising **new share capital** by means of an offer to existing shareholders enabling them to buy more shares, usually at a **price lower** than the **current market price**. Under a rights issue existing shareholders are invited to **subscribe cash** for new shares in proportion to their existing holdings.

A company may choose to make a rights issue for the following reasons:

(i) Rights issues are **cheaper** than offers for sale to the general public. This is because:

  (1) **No prospectus** is **required** (provided that the issue is for less than 10% of the class of shares concerned).

  (2) **Administration** is **simpler**.

  (3) The **costs** of **underwriting** will be **less**.

  The company will however need to **explain** clearly to shareholders the purpose for which the additional funds are required, and **demonstrate** that the **return on capital** will at least be **maintained**, and ideally enhanced as a result of the issue.

(ii) Relative **voting rights** are **unaffected** if shareholders all take up their rights.

(iii) Funds can be raised in this way for any type of **long term investment**, or to **reduce** the level of **capital gearing**.

The effects from the point of view of the **private investor** include:

(i) He must decide whether to **take up** or **sell** the rights. If the market is efficient, he should be **no worse off** whether he decides to take up the rights or to sell them. However, if he were to do nothing then he would **forego** the **financial benefits** of the issue.

(ii) If he decides to take up the rights he must have **additional funds** available to invest in the company. He must therefore decide if this is the **best use** of those funds, and also consider the effect of such an investment on the **risk/return profile** of his investment portfolio.

Scrip issue

A scrip issue (or bonus issue) is an issue of new shares to existing shareholders, by **converting equity reserves** into **issued share capital**. For example, a company with issued share capital of 10m £1 nominal value shares with a market price of £10 and reserves of £20m, could make a scrip issue of one for one. This would have the effect of doubling the number of shares in issue, and thus reducing the theoretical market price of the shares to £5.

The advantage to the company of a scrip issue is that it makes the **shares cheaper** and therefore **more marketable** on the Stock Exchange.

From the point of view of the investor, there should be **no change** as a result of a scrip issue. He is not required to subscribe additional capital, unlike the rights issue. Once the issue has taken place, he will own a **larger number of shares** in the company, but the overall value of his holding will be the same as it was before. However, in practice the **share price** may **rise slightly** as a result of improved marketability, and therefore he may experience a small capital gain.

(b) (i)

	£
5,000,000 shares have a 'cum rights' value of (× £1.60)	8,000,000
1,000,000 shares will be issued to raise (× £1.30)	1,300,000
The theoretical value of 6,000,000 shares is	9,300,000

The theoretical ex rights price is $\dfrac{9,300,000}{6,000,000}$ = £1.55 per share.

After the rights issue, James Brown will own 12,000 shares (10,000 + 2,000) at a price of £1.55. The theoretical value of his holding will therefore be £18,600.

(ii) Value of rights per share = Theoretical ex-rights price – Cost of taking up rights

= £1.55 – £1.30

= 25 pence per share

James Brown has the right to subscribe for an additional 2,000 shares. If he sells these rights he can expect to receive 2,000 × £0.25 = £500.

(c) The required return on equity using the dividend growth model:

$$k_e = \frac{D_0(1+g)}{P_0} + g$$

Where	D_0	=	Current level of dividends	=	12p per share
	g	=	Rate of growth in dividends (see below)		
	P_0	=	Market price of shares	=	£1.60 per share

'g' can be estimated over the four year period as $\sqrt[4]{12/8} - 1 = 0.1067$ ie 11%.

Alternatively, it can be approximated by finding the average annual rate of growth as follows:

Year	Div	Increase	Increase
	p	p	%
20X0	8		
20X1	9	1	12.5
20X2	11	2	22.2
20X3	11	0	0.0
20X4	12	2	9.1
			43.8

Over four years this gives an average rate of 11%.

The required rate of return can now be found:

$$k_e = \frac{12(1 + 0.11)}{160} + 0.11$$

$$k_e = 19.3\%$$

(d) An **efficient stock market** is one in which:

(i) The prices of securities traded **reflect** all the **relevant information**, which is **available** to the buyers and sellers. Share prices **change quickly** to reflect all new information about future prospects.

(ii) **No individual dominates** the market.

(iii) **Transaction costs** of buying and selling are **not so high** as to **discourage trading** significantly.

Strong form efficiency

The efficient markets hypothesis exists in a number of forms, which relate to the nature of the information available to investors. Strong form efficiency means that share prices **reflect all information** available from:

(i) Past price changes

(ii) Public knowledge or anticipation

(iii) Insider knowledge available to specialist or experts such as investment managers

If the stock market is believed to operate with strong level efficiency, this might affect the behaviour of the finance directors of publicly quoted companies in the following ways.

(i) Managers are likely to be aware that **share prices** will **change quickly** to reflect decisions that they take. This means that all financial decisions are likely to be evaluated in the light of their **potential impact** on the **share price**. A contrary view is that management should concentrate simply on **maximising** the **net present value** of its investments and need not worry about the **effect** on **share prices** of financial results in the published accounts. **Investors** will make **allowances** for low profits or dividends in the current year if higher profits or dividends are expected in the future.

(ii) Managers should be **discouraged** from attempting to **manipulate** their **accounting results**, since the truth will be realised quickly, and prices adjusted accordingly.

The company may concentrate on producing **constantly improving financial results** at the expense of the company's **responsibility** to **other stakeholders** in the business, such as its employees and the environment.

29   OBJECTIVE TEST QUESTIONS: SHORT-TERM FINANCE I

1   C   Since the compounding is to be done at six-monthly intervals, 5% (half of 10%) will be added to the value on each occasion. There will be six additions of interest during the three years, and the following expression can therefore be used:

$$S = x(1 + r)^6$$

where: S = Value of the investment at the end of the period

x = Initial sum invested

r = Interest rate

In this case:

$$S = 10,000(1 + 0.05)^6$$
$$S = £13,400$$

2   D   A property mortgage is generally for a term longer than five years, and this is therefore a long-term source of finance.

3   A   Interest is only paid on the amount borrowed, not on the full facility.

4   D   This is also known as a documentary credit.

5   D   The currency in which the loan is denominated will have little, if any, effect on the credit risk.

6   A   Short-term cash surpluses will not normally be invested in equities owing to the risks associated with achieving a return over a short period.

7   C   Sales order processing and invoicing will normally continue to be carried out by the company. The factor only steps in at the debt collection stage.

8   B   Although the level of return is a factor in the decision, it is more important to minimise the risk to the original capital invested.

9   B   The Miller-Orr model relates to cash management, not to interest rates.

10   A   The value can be found using the following expression:

$$PV = \frac{£1,000}{r} - \frac{£1,000}{r(1+r)^n}$$

where   PV   =   PV of annuity

          r   =   interest rate

          n   =   annuity term

In this case:

$$PV = \frac{£1,000}{0.08} - \frac{£1,000}{0.08(1.08)^5}$$

$$PV = 1,250 - 850 = 400$$

30   OBJECTIVE TEST QUESTIONS: SHORT-TERM FINANCE II

1   B   Treasury bills are issued by the Bank of England on behalf of the government, to raise short-term cash (mostly for 90 days). they are traded 'second hand' on the discount market, and carry a low rate of interest because they are risk free.

Other money market instruments carry slightly higher rates of interest. A sterling CD is issued by a bank, acknowledging that a certain sum of money that has been deposited with it will become available on a given date to the certificate holder. CDs are also traded, on the CD market. Local authority deposits and finance house deposits are time deposits with local authorities and finance houses respectively. Local authorities raise money for short-term cash needs and finance houses raise money for re-lending.

2   D $V = X(1 + r)^n = £14,000 (1 + 0.005)^{24} = £15,780$.

A includes 6% interest only.
B includes 12%, not compounded.
C includes 12%, compounded annually.

3   A   The company will be retaining the majority of its delivery vehicles, and it is safe to assume that reasonably priced contracted-out alternatives are available. This sale should not damage the long-term profitability of the company.

Option B is not correct. It can be assumed that the blending of pigments to go into the china products is a core activity of the business. This plant should not be sold in these circumstances.

Option C is not correct. Such a patent is likely to be a key to securing the long-term future profitability of the company. It should not be sold to meet short-term needs.

Option D is not the most appropriate option. A 60% stake constitutes a controlling interest in a company. It could therefore be unsafe to sell this shareholding.

4   B   Monthly rate = 0.5%

Annuity factor over 36 periods $= 1/0.005 \times (1 - 1/1.005^{36}) = 32.871$
Monthly investment required $= £10,000/32.871 = £304$

If you forgot about the interest, you may have got answer A. If you used the wrong annuity factor, you may have got answers C or D.

5   D   Convertible loan stock is a longer term investment, and transaction costs will be too high for a short-term investment.

The minimum term for a local authority deposit is normally overnight, and longer-term arrangements can also be made.

If the company is large enough to lend directly on the money markets, it will be able to negotiate overnight, daily or weekly terms.

Treasury bills have a term of 91 days to maturity. No interest as such is paid, but the bills can be sold at any time.

6   B   Present value of a perpetuity of £1 $= 1/r = 1/0.12 = 8.333$.
$8.333 \times £3,000 = £25,000$.

Errors of principle or miscalculations may have led you to other answers.

7   C   The interest yield is the gross yield divided by the market value of the stock expressed as a percentage, in this case $11,000 \times 10\% \div 10,000$.

Option A is not correct. The interest yield is the gross yield divided by the market value of the stock expressed as a percentage. You possibly arrived at Option A by multiplying the coupon rate by the market value and dividing by the nominal value. This is incorrect.

Option B is not correct. 10% is the coupon rate on this bond.

Option D is not correct. 12% is the average market rate of return which is irrelevant to the calculation of the yield of an individual bond.

8   B   As UK government securities, Treasury bills carry a low rate of interest because they are virtually risk-free.

A sterling CD is issued by a bank and will carry a slightly higher rate of interest than Treasury bills.

Finance house deposits are time deposits with a finance house, which can then re-lend the money. The higher interest rate reflects the risk that the finance house might default.

Time deposits with a local authority will be considered as slightly higher in risk than UK government securities, and so will carry a slightly higher interest rate.

9   C   Inflation does erode the capital value of amounts borrowed, but this favours borrowers and disfavours lenders. The value of the capital that borrowers have to repay is reduced.

Option A is not correct. The effect of inflation on the different costs and revenues of an enterprise cannot be known with certainty.

Option B is not correct. The fact that different elements of costs and earnings streams may have inflated at different rates makes comparison between business sectors and divisions of a business problematic.

Option D is not correct. There have, in fact, been negative interest rates in Japan at times. Effectively, people have had to pay their bank a percentage of the amount deposited to hold their money there.

10 A   With an inverted yield curve (short-term interest yields higher than long-term yields), bond prices will eventually fall as longer term interest yields are forced upwards. If bond yields rise and bond prices fall, shareholders will want higher yields too and so share prices will fall. Higher yields result in lower prices, for both bonds and shares.

31 INTEREST RATES

> **Pass marks**. Although the particular conditions which applied at the time of this question were soon out of date, parts (a) and (b) are standard questions in corporate finance and should be studied in detail.

(a) **Implications of a fall in interest rates for a typical company**

   (i)   The **cost of floating rate borrowing will fall,** making it more attractive than fixed rate borrowing. For most companies with borrowings, interest charges will be reduced, resulting in higher profitability and earnings per share.

   (ii)   The **value of the company's shares will rise,** both because of the higher level of company profitability and also because of the lower alternative returns that investors could earn from banks and deposits, if interest rates are expected to remain low in the longer term.

   (iii) The **higher share value results in a lower cost of equity capital,** and hence a lower overall cost of capital for the company. Investment opportunities that were previously rejected may now become viable.

   (iv)   As interest rates fall, consumers have **more disposable income.** This may increase demand for the company's products. Falling returns on deposits may, however, encourage many people to save more, rather than spend.

(b) As explained above, if interest rates are expected to remain low in the longer term, the company's overall cost of capital will fall. The discount rates used in investment appraisal will therefore be lower, making marginal projects more profitable, with a resulting increase in the company's investment opportunities.

The cash flows from all possible investments should be reviewed in the light of falling interest rates and the possible effects on consumer demand and the sterling exchange rate. These cash flows should then be appraised at the new lower discount rates and the project portfolio ranked and reviewed. The company's investment plans are likely to be expanded, unless constrained by other factors such as lack of skills or management time.

When interest rates are expected to fall in the future, an ungeared company may be tempted to introduce debt into its capital structure. If fixed interest rates are high at the moment, floating rate debt may be more attractive, because it allows the company to take advantage of falling interest rates.

New projects may be financed entirely by borrowings until an appropriate gearing level is reached. As gearing is increased, the company's cost of capital is usually reduced because of the tax relief on debt interest but, if gearing is increased to too high a level, increased risks of bankruptcy arise, causing the cost of capital to rise.

If the company is tempted to increase its debt financing substantially, this may affect which investment projects are undertaken, as some projects are more suitable for debt financing than others. Generally, a project with significant tangible assets and stable cash flows will be most suitable for financing by debt.

32   YIELD CURVE

(a)   A **yield curve** is a curve that can be drawn showing the relationship between the **yield on an asset** (usually long-term government stocks) and the **term to maturity** of that same asset. It shows how the rate of interest (yield) varies with different maturities. To construct a yield curve you need to gather information about the interest rates on short-term stocks, medium-term stocks and long-term stocks. These rates can then be **plotted on a diagram** against the maturity dates of those same stocks.

A normal yield curve looks like Figure 1.

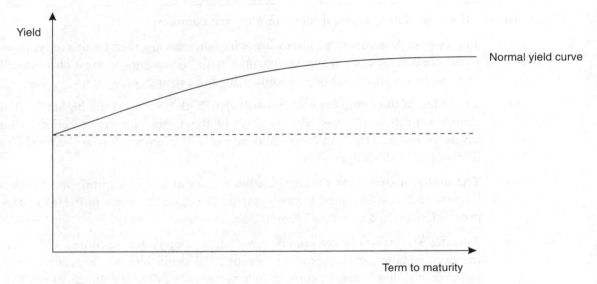

Figure 1

(b)   The **shape of the yield curve** depends very much on **expectations about the future.** Reward for loss of liquidity is likely to remain fairly constant. Reward for possible default is likely to remain constant also. Reward for the risk of having to cash in before maturity and suffering a loss are also likely to stay fairly constant. The only factor which will vary widely is expectations - in particular, expectations about future short-term interest rates.

Expectations about the future level of short-term interest rates are the most important factor in determining the shape of the yield curve. Although the normal yield curve is upward sloping, with higher yields being expected for longer maturity periods, expectations of rises in future interest rates can cause the yield curve to be steeper than the normal curve. Expectations of falls in interest rates can cause the yield to flatten, or, if substantial falls are expected, to become downward-sloping (Figure 2).

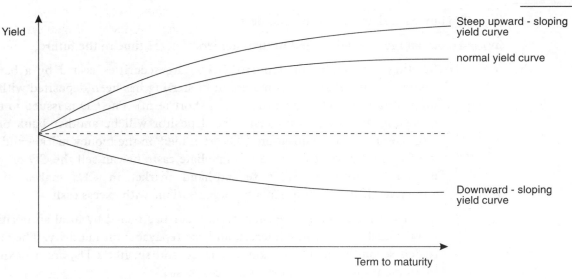

Figure 2

If interest rates are now **expected to rise**, investors will not wish to lock in to lower interest rates and will therefore sell short. Borrowers will wish to borrow at lower long-term rates to avoid exposure to the higher rates expected in the future. These demand and supply factors will result in a shortage of long-term funds, which will push up long-term money market rates, and to an excess supply of short-term funds, which will lead to a reduction in short-term rates. The resulting yield curve will be more steeply upward-sloping than the normal curve.

If there are **new expectations that interest rates will fall,** investors will prefer to lock in at higher long rates, while borrowers will not wish to be committed to higher long term rates and will prefer to borrow short. There will be an excess supply of funds at long maturities and a shortage of funds at short maturities. This will tend to lower the yield curve, possibly resulting in a flat curve or even in a downward-sloping curve.

Short-term interest rates are in turn determined partly by **expectations of inflation** rates in the near future. If high inflation is expected, investors will seek higher nominal rates of interest in order to achieve a real return. If people believe that inflation is falling, then they will not require such a high return.

33 EXCESS CASH AND MONEY MARKET INSTRUMENTS

(a) Surplus cash flows will be earned by a company that is trading profitably, and does not have high capital expenditures or other outlays to use up the cash inflows. Four possible reasons for a cash surplus are:

(i) Higher income from sales, due to an increase in sales turnover

(ii) Lower costs, due perhaps to a cost-cutting exercise or improved productivity

(iii) Lower capital expenditure, perhaps because of an absence of profitable new investment options

(iv) Income from selling off parts of the business

The board of directors might keep the surplus in liquid form:

(i) To benefit from high interest rates that might be available from bank deposits, when returns on re-investment in the company appear to be lower

(ii) To have cash available should a strategic opportunity arise, perhaps for the takeover of another company in which cash consideration might be needed

(iii) To buy back shares from shareholders

(iv) To pay an increased dividend to shareholders at some time in the future

(b) (i) (1) **Sterling certificates of deposits (CDs)** are securities issued by a bank, acknowledging that a certain amount of sterling has been deposited with it for a certain period of time (usually, a short term). The CD is issued to the depositor, and attracts interest. The depositor will be another bank or a large commercial organisation. CDs are traded on the money market and so if a CD holder wishes to obtain immediate cash, he can sell the CD on the market at any time. This second-hand market in CDs makes them attractive, flexible investments for organisations with excess cash.

(2) **Local authority bonds** are short-term securities issued by local authorities to raise cash. They carry interest, and are repayable on maturity. They are traded secondhand in the money market, and so, like CDs, are a flexible investment for organisations with excess cash.

(3) **Finance house deposits** are non-negotiable time deposits with finance houses (usually subsidiaries of banks). Finance houses specialise in lending money, and have to raise the funds (much of them from the money market) for re-lending.

(4) **Treasury bills** are short-term debt instruments issued by the Bank of England, to raise cash for the government's spending needs. The bills are sold by tender, each week, at a price which is at a discount to their nominal value. They are redeemable at their nominal value, and so there is an implied rate of interest on the bill.

Treasury bills are bought initially by money market organisations with which the Bank of England has a special relationship, mainly the discount houses. The discount houses then carry out secondhand trading in Treasury bills (and other bills) on the discount market. Treasury bills are therefore negotiable.

(ii) **Differences in interest rates between instruments**

Some money market instruments carry a higher interest rate than others. The main reasons for this are differences in their relative marketability and risk.

(1) **Treasury bills** are government debt, and therefore the most secure form of short-term debt available. Interest rates on Treasury bills should therefore be lower than on other money market instruments. Interest rates at which the Bank of England deals in bills in the money market usually set the level of interest rates for all other money market instruments.

(2) **Finance house deposits** are not negotiable, and so are less marketable than the other money market instruments in the list. For this reason, interest rates on them are slightly higher. Similarly, CDs are more marketable than ordinary money market bank deposits, which are for a given (short) term; thus CD interest rates will be slightly lower than LIBID (the London inter-bank bid rate).

Differences in interest rates over time

Interest rates over time are affected by the supply and demand of funds, and by expectations of future changes in interest rates. Broadly speaking, interest rates on longer-term investments will be higher, and the 'yield curve' (a graph of interest rates against term to maturity) will normally be upward-sloping. In the data given, we see that interest rates are increased with the term of the deposit/bond/bill.

However, when there are expectations of a future fall in interest rates, because current rates are high, the yield curve may slope downwards, with yields on long term debt being lower than yields on shorter term debt.

34 4D PLC

> **Pass marks**. In part (a) it is necessary to define the likely investment criteria before going on to consider the individual factors to be taken into account. In part (b)(ii) you should consider both the systematic and unsystematic risk components of the proposed portfolio, and seek to relate these to the objectives of the company and to its existing risk position.

(a) When selecting marketable securities in which to invest, the treasurer will normally be doing so with the aim of **maximising the return on short-term cash surpluses**. In this situation, the criteria are likely to include the following.

  (i) The amount of funds available for investment will influence the type of security that will be appropriate.

  (ii) Since the company is not seeking a speculative gain, the level of risk should be as low as possible. However, he must ensure that funds which are intended for specific future purposes do not lie idle.

  (iii) The level of return should be as high as possible within the class of risk which the company is prepared to accept.

  (iv) The level of transaction costs and the complexity of administration should be kept to a minimum.

  (v) The securities should be easily marketable so that if the funds are required at an earlier date than anticipated this can be achieved without a significant loss of revenue.

(b) (i) The **risk of the portfolio** can be calculated using a weighted average of the beta values of the different securities. It is assumed that in the case of security 3, the required rate of return is a sterling figure. If this is the case, then this corresponds with the market average which means that the beta can be assumed to be 1.0.

	Proportion	*Beta*	*Weighted*
Security 1	30%	1.2	0.36
Security 2	30%	1.6	0.48
Security 3	20%	1.0	0.20
Security 4 (risk free)	20%	0.0	0.00
			1.04

Assuming that the historical performance of these securities will continue into the future, this beta value can be used in the CAPM to calculate the expected return for the portfolio:

$$k_e = R_f + (R_m - R_f)\,\beta$$

where
$$k_e = \text{expected return}$$
$$\beta = \text{beta value (1.04)}$$
$$R_f = \text{risk free rate of return (5\%)}$$
$$R_m = \text{market rate of return (12\%)}$$

$$k_e = 5\% + (12\% - 5\%) \times 1.04$$
$$= 12.28\%$$

(ii)

REPORT

To: Board of Directors
From: Management Accountant   Date: 15 May 20X6
Subject: Investment portfolio of marketable securities

Introduction

The purpose of this report is to consider the choice of marketable securities for 4D for the coming twelve months. The securities already proposed will be considered, together with other available alternatives.

Proposed portfolio

The securities selected must meet the Board's criteria in terms of **risk profile, liquidity, return** and **transaction and administration costs**. The proposed portfolio would offer a level of risk slightly in excess of the market level of risk, with a return similarly slightly above the market rate of return. In the context of the purpose for which the investment is being made, and assuming that the funds will be required in full at the end of the twelve month period, one might consider that this is too high a level of risk to accept for such a portfolio. In fact, the beta of the portfolio is significantly in excess of our own beta which suggests that the portfolio may not conform to our financial objectives.

When the individual securities are considered, it is apparent that the portfolio beta is only brought down to its existing level by the inclusion of 20% short-dated government bonds; the remainder of the portfolio carries a level of risk significantly above that of the market. Although the US shares carry an apparently lower beta, their inclusion in the portfolio would introduce a level of exchange rate exposure, thus increasing their real level of risk. The UK equity investments are also relatively risky, particularly the small high technology company.

A further factor to be considered is the **spread of the portfolio.** It is generally considered that a portfolio of at least twenty securities is required in order to eliminate unsystematic risk, but in this case, only four securities are being considered. It is not as yet clear what the exact amount of the funds available for investment will be, and it may be that if the amount is relatively low, the benefits of diversification could be outweighed by the higher level of transaction costs.

Alternative options

A number of other options are available. These include:

(1) Other UK equities
(2) Loan stock or debentures
(3) Commercial paper
(4) Bank deposits
(5) Local authority bonds
(6) Bills of exchange
(7) Investments that offer a spread themselves, such as unit trusts

Conclusions

The Board should give consideration to the investment criteria in terms of risk, return and transaction costs that it wishes the portfolio to meet. The proposed portfolio carries a relatively high level of systematic risk and is unlikely to succeed in eliminating unsystematic risk. A number of other alternatives are available, and it is suggested that further consideration should be given to these before the final decisions are made.

Signed: Management Accountant

35 RT PLC

(a) (i)   Since interest rates are forecast to rise, the best solution is likely to be one in which only **short-term deposits** are made, thus allowing advantage to be taken of the rise in rates. Options structured in this way include the following.

	Amount £'000	Month invested	Period Months	Rate	Income £
1	2,000	0	2	7.3%	24,333
	6,000	2	2	8.0%	80,000
	4,000	4	2	8.3%	55,333
	Transaction costs				(300)
					159,366
2	2,000	0	4	7.4%	49,333
	4,000	2	4	8.1%	108,000
	Transaction costs				(200)
					157,133
3	2,000	0	4	7.4%	49,333
	4,000	2	2	8.0%	53,333
	4,000	4	2	8.3%	55,333
	Transaction costs				(300)
					157,699
4	2,000	0	2	7.3%	24,333
	2,000	2	2	8.0%	26,667
	4,000	2	4	8.1%	108,000
	Transaction costs				(300)
					158,700
5	2,000	0	6	7.5%	75,000
	2,000	2	4	8.1%	54,000
	2,000	2	2	8.0%	26,667
	Transaction costs				(300)
					155,367

	Amount £'000	Month invested	Period Months	Rate	Income £
6	2,000	0	6	7.5%	75,000
	4,000	2	2	8.0%	53,333
	2,000	4	2	8.3%	27,667
	Transaction costs				(300)
					155,700

It can be seen that Option 1 yields the best return.

(ii)   When selecting marketable securities, the company is normally doing so with the aim of **maximising the return on short-term cash surpluses**. With this aim in mind, the criteria are likely to include the following.

(1)   The level of risk should be as low as possible since the company is not seeking a speculative gain, but to ensure that funds which are intended for specific purposes in the future do not lie idle.

(2) The level of return should be as high as possible within the class of risk which the company is prepared to accept.

(3) The level of transaction costs and the degree of complexity of administration should be as low as possible.

(4) Ideally the securities will be easily marketable so that if the funds are required at an earlier date than anticipated this can be achieved without significant loss of revenue.

(5) The amount of funds to be invested will influence the types of security that will be appropriate.

(b) (i) Long-term business investment tends not to be driven by the **availability of funds** but rather by the **opportunities in which to invest**. In practice, if a company perceives an investment opportunity, it will firstly evaluate it against its cost of capital to determine whether or not the project will enhance the net worth of the company. Thus the interest rate is only important at this stage in so far as it forms a component of the hurdle rate used by the company.

When interest rates are relatively very high this may mean that the availability of funds to invest is limited and this may mean that the company is unable to finance projects which it would like to undertake. Thus high interest rates can act as a constraint on investment, but relatively low rates are unlikely to act directly and proportionately to increase the rate in investment.

In terms of **liquidity,** when interest rates are high companies will try to keep short-term borrowings at as low a level as possible by putting pressure on to speed up the transmission of cash through the cycle. When rates are low, there will be less pressure to do this, and thus it is likely that the liquidity position of companies does relate more closely to the level of interest rates.

(ii) The type and use of **cash management models** differs with the size and complexity of the organisation. In small companies, the weekly or monthly cash forecast can be very helpful in order to ensure the best timing of payments, and can also act as a spur to debt collection.

In large organisations, models are much more sophisticated and allow all free funds to be placed on deposit whenever possible, minimising the costs of holding cash.

Models such as that of **Miller and Orr,** which triggers the buying or selling of securities when cash balances reach an upper or lower limit, can help to free up management time which might otherwise be spent responding to day-to-day fluctuations in cash balances.

Cash management models can also be used to evaluate the relative costs and benefits of switching between alternative short-term investments.

Thus cash management models can be useful to companies at a variety of levels although it is unlikely that in practice they will be used to their fullest extent: in many cases, large cash movements which are predictable, as with tax and dividend payments, can be best managed without using a formal model.

36   **EXPANDALOT LTD**

> **Pass marks**. In part (a) when discussing the causes of overtrading, do not forget to include the effects of inflation and a reduction in the level of long-term capital as well as the more obvious increase in the level of activity. In part (b) the return on the investments can be evaluated at the cost of capital at the end of the year.

(a)   **Overtrading** occurs when a business tries to do too much too quickly with too little long term capital, so that it is trying to support too large a volume of trade with the capital resources at its disposal.

Overtrading arises as the company seeks to increase the level of sales but fails to provide enough resources to finance the required increase in working capital. If stock turnover, and debtor and creditor days, remain constant, an increase in sales will result in an increase in the required level of working capital. This is because the absolute level of stocks and debtors will increase, and except in unusual circumstances, this increase will be larger than the similar rise in the absolute level of creditors.

Other causes of overtrading include the repayment of loans without their replacement by alternative sources of finance ie the level of activity remains the same but the level of finance to support it falls. Inflation may also cause an erosion of the real capital base making it difficult to replace assets and causing an increasing reliance upon credit.

Symptoms of overtrading include the following.

(i)   There is a rapid increase in sales.

(ii)   There is a rapid increase in the volume of current assets and possibly also fixed assets.

(iii)   The increase in assets is financed primarily from short-term credit as evidenced by a rising level of overdraft and trade creditors. The payment period for creditors is likely to extend. The relative level of equity falls.

(iv)   Liquidity (ie current and quick) ratios fall.

Overtrading may be improved by tightening the control of working capital, in particular ensuring that debtors pay to terms and that the levels of stock carried are not excessive. Beyond this, the company will need to secure additional sources of long term capital either in the form of long-term debt such as a bank loan or further equity.

(b)   During the year in question sales have doubled to £1m, but this has been at the expense of gross margin which has fallen from 20% to 15%. It is apparent that the assumed inflation of 5% in the cost of sales has not been passed on to the customers and that in fact prices have fallen (if selling prices had remained static and the cost of sales had increased in line with inflation, the gross profit would have been £160,000). At the same time overheads have risen from an inflation adjusted £78,750 to £120,000, a real increase of 52.4%. The combined effect of these factors is that net profit has risen by only £5,000, and the ratio of net profit to sales has fallen from 5% to 3%. This is very low and means that the growth in sales is not providing any significant increase in retained earnings with which to finance the expansion.

The small increase in retained profits has apparently been used to finance the 20% increase in fixed assets which is low in relation to the doubling of sales. However, the level of current assets has risen dramatically, stock having gone up 2.5 times and debtors 2.65 times. These increases exceed the relative increase in sales and suggest that control of working capital has deteriorated. The absolute size of the increase in stock and debtors is £116,000. At the same time there has been no injection of further

123

long-term capital to support this rise in current assets. This has been financed by a significant increase in the level of overdraft to £50,000, with which it appears that the bank is less than happy. Most significantly, trade creditors have increased fourfold and other creditors have doubled. Since Expandalot is a manufacturing company, there is insufficient information to extract the actual level of purchases and hence the creditor payment period, but it is most unlikely that the company can sustain this position for long.

It thus appears that **Expandalot is exhibiting all the symptoms of overtrading.** Unless it secures additional long term finance quickly and improves its control of working capital and overheads it may not be able to survive at its existing level of operations, let alone continue its expansion programme.

37 OVERDRAFT USAGE

> **Pass marks.** Ensure that your answer does more than simply listing the alternatives.

(a) An **overdraft** is a negative balance on a current account at a bank. This constitutes borrowing and, because the balance will vary daily, the interest on the borrowing is normally computed on a daily basis at an agreed rate. A maximum limit to the overdraft is agreed with the bank and above this limit penalty charges will apply. In theory, the overdraft can be cancelled immediately if the bank is not happy with the company's **credit worthiness**. An overdraft can be **unsecured**, or **secured** on company assets or the personal assets of the proprietors.

The overdraft is a key source of finance for working capital because of its flexibility: the finance varies automatically up to the agreed limit, enabling the company to handle peaks and troughs in cash flows without incurring excess interest charges with the company's cash flow. The potential disadvantage for an expanding company is that the overdraft limit may have to be frequently renegotiated. There is also a tendency for expanding companies to ignore the need to underpin their growth with longer term finance.

When considering alternatives to the bank overdraft, it is essential to consider the need for longer term funds (loans or equity funds) to finance the permanent element of working capital. Although such funds may be more expensive than short term finance, they provide a longer term stability for planning.

(b) Alternative short-term sources of finance include the following.

Short-term bank loans. A short-term bank loan (eg six months) can be arranged to cover a forecast cash deficit. The disadvantage compared with the overdraft is that the interest is chargeable on the full amount of the loan even if the finance is not required for part of the period.

Commercial paper. Large companies can issue certificates promising to pay the bearer a given amount on the maturity date in, say, one year's time. These certificates can be sold at a discount to provide immediate cash.

Debt factoring. A specialist organisation will collect the company's debts and advance cash, effectively on the security of the company's debtors. The effective cost of the finance is sometimes difficult to compute but, for an expanding company, an advantage over overdrafts is that the source of finance effectively grows with the sales ledger.

Discounting of invoices and bills of exchange. The company presents invoices or bills of exchange to the bank in return for immediate cash, slightly less than the face value (ie discounted). When the debtors pay, the cash goes direct to the bank. The discount represents the effective interest on the funds advanced. An extension of this process is the **acceptance credit**, whereby the company draws a bill of exchange on a bank, on the security of debts owed by customers. This banker's bill can then be discounted for immediate cash.

Supplier finance. Some suppliers will provide extended credit periods on stock, or alternatively finance can be raised from finance houses on the security of stock.

The key to evaluating these different sources of finance is to compute the true annual percentage interest rate implicit in each arrangement and to quantify other relevant cash flows, such as administration costs, variations to selling prices and the likely effect on bad debts. Other issues which are less easy to quantify include the effect on customer, supplier and lender loyalty.

38   OBJECTIVE TEST QUESTIONS: WORKING CAPITAL MANAGEMENT I

1   A   Short-term finance is matched to fluctuating current assets. B is a conservative policy, while C and D are aggressive policies.

2   B   This is the ratio of current assets to current liabilities. The five year bank loan would not normally be included with current liabilities.

3   C   This is the ratio of current assets excluding stock to current liabilities. The debenture would normally be included with long-term liabilities.

4   B

5   A   The credit cycle begins with the receipt of the customer's order. Price negotiations take place prior to this point.

6   D $365 \times$ year end debtors $\div$ total sales

7   D   Total sales $\times$ 2% + £5,000. 'Without recourse' means that the factor carries the risk of the bad debts.

8   A   Answer C ignored the effect of the changes on the level of stocks and creditors. B and D are wrong because they assume that the financing cost will increase rather than decrease. Workings are as follows:

Current level of debtors $= £2m \times 90/365 = £493,150$
New level of debtors $= £2m \times 80\% \times 30/365 = £131,507$

Current financing requirement $= £500,000 + £493,150 - £30,000 = £963,150$
New financing requirement $= £400,000 + £131,507 - £24,000 = £507,507$

Reduction in financing requirement $= £963,150 - £507,507 = £455,643$
Reduction in financing cost $= £455,643 \times 10\% = £45,564$ (round to £46,000)

9   C   Dividend payments are sums owed by the company to its shareholders. They are therefore current liabilities and not assets.

10 D   Interest due on marketable securities is money owed to the company, and is therefore an asset, not a liability.

39   OBJECTIVE TEST QUESTIONS: WORKING CAPITAL MANAGEMENT II

1   D   Depreciation is a non-cash item and should therefore be excluded.

2   B   Since monthly sales are stable, receipts will equal monthly sales, less bad debts.

3   C   An increase in the stock level would increase the cash requirements, and therefore the size of the cash deficit.

4   B

			£
Direct materials	$= 800 \times £100 \times 30\%$	=	24,000
Direct labour	$= 800 \times £100 \times 20\%$	=	16,000
Variable overhead	$= 600 \times £10$	=	6,000
Total cash outflow			46,000

5   D   Wages are paid in the month in which they are incurred, and therefore the cash outflow will be the same as the charge in the profit and loss account.

A: the sales forecast will need adjustment to arrive at the receipts figure.
B: corporation tax will not be paid until the following year.
C: depreciation is a non cash item.

6   A   Cheque payments will take the longest to clear through the banking system. Time will also be taken in the postal system and administration. The other methods can be cleared through the system much more quickly.

7   B   CHAPS stands for Clearing House Automated Payment System. It provides same day settlements for amounts of £10,000 or more between banks that are members of the clearing system.

8   A   The Baumol model identifies the optimum amount of Treasury bills to sell, by value, each time that the cash balance needs topping up.

9   C   The model assumes that cash flows are entirely unpredictable.

10 B   Transmission delay refers to delays in delivering the cheque to the company.

Clearance delay is the time needed for a bank to clear a cheque.

Float is the amount of money tied up between the time when a payment is initiated and the time when the funds are available for use in the recipient's bank account.

40   OBJECTIVE TEST QUESTIONS: WOKING CAPITAL MANAGEMENT III

1   C   The annual cost can be found using the following expression:

$$i = \frac{d}{100-d} \times \frac{365}{t}$$

where
- i = implied annual cost in interest per annum
- d = the size of the discount
- t = reduction in payment period in days which would be necessary to obtain the discount

In this case:

$$i = \frac{2.5}{100-2.5} \times \frac{365}{60-10}$$

$$i = 18.7\%$$

2   D   Standing orders are used to make regular payments of a fixed amount. Payments to trade creditors will vary in amount, and therefore a different method would be more appropriate.

3   B   The other main difference is that the payment can be for a variable amount each time, rather than for a fixed amount.

4   B C_o is the cost of making one order. It could not be the cost of placing orders for one year, since until Q is determined it is not known how many orders will be placed in a year.

5   D   The EOQ model can be used:

$$Q = \sqrt{(2C_oD)/C_h}$$

where   Q   =   the reorder quantity
        C_o =   cost of making one order
        C_h =   holding cost per unit of stock per year
        D   =   usage in units per year

In this case:

$$Q = \sqrt{(2 \times £25 \times 10,000)/£0.50}$$
$$Q = 1,000$$

6   B   The EOQ model can be used:

$$Q = \sqrt{(2C_oD)/C_h}$$

where   Q   =   the reorder quantity
        C_o =   cost of making one order
        C_h =   holding cost per unit of stock per year
        D   =   usage in units per year

In this case:

$$Q = \sqrt{(2 \times £25 \times 10,000)/£0.50}$$
$$Q = 1,000$$

Since 10,000 wheels are required each year, 10 orders will be placed.

7   C   The EOQ model can be used:

$$Q = \sqrt{(2C_oD)/C_h}$$

where   Q   =   the reorder quantity
        C_o =   cost of making one order
        C_h =   holding cost per unit of stock per year
        D   =   usage in units per year

In this case:

$$Q = \sqrt{(2 \times £25 \times 10,000)/£0.50}$$
$$Q = 1,000$$

Since 10,000 wheels are required each year, 10 orders will be placed.
The length of the stock cycle is therefore 52 ÷ 10 = 5.2 weeks.

8   D   Although the purchasing manager may sanction payments to suppliers, the payment will normally be raised by the finance department.

9   B   A standing order is the simplest method to use for regular fixed payments. It is preferred to a direct debit because the person making the payment retains control over the amount paid.

10 D   A banker's draft cannot be stopped or cancelled once it is issued, and is effectively a cheque drawn on the bank. It is accepted by most people as being as good as cash, but has none of the inconvenience that cash would involve in a payment of this size.

41 OBJECTIVE TEST QUESTIONS: WORKING CAPITAL MANAGEMENT IV

1   B   An increase in the time from the outlay on wages and raw materials to the inflow of cash from customers will increase the level of working capital required.

The trading cycle is another name for the operating cycle. Therefore a reduction in one is synonymous with a reduction in the other.

An increase in the payment period (C) to suppliers will decrease the net length of the cycle since this factor is subtracted from the stockholding time, production time and debt collection period to arrive at the length of the cycle.

Option D is not correct. This will shorten rather than lengthen the overall length of the cycle.

2   B   An excess of current liabilities over current assets indicates an insufficiency of capital to support the level of sales.

Option A is not correct. When a company overtrades, the level of sales exceeds the capacity of the capital base to support it. It is therefore characterised by an increase in turnover.

Option C is not correct. A shortening period of credit taken from suppliers suggests a lessening pressure on capital resources.

Option D is not correct. A rise in the quick ratio indicates an improvement in the cash base of the business. This is the opposite to what might be expected in a period of overtrading.

3   A   If transactions costs rise, then the firm will want to buy or sell securities on fewer occasions, and so control limits should be widened.

4   B   Optimal sale $= \sqrt{\dfrac{2FS}{i}} = \sqrt{\dfrac{2 \times 2,450,000 \times 25}{0.07}}$

$= £41,833$

Errors of principle may have led you to answers A, C or D.

5   D   The capital base has been reduced while the activity level remains constant. This could lead to overtrading.

Option A is not correct. Since the loan is replaced, the capital base is essentially unchanged and, provided that sales are stable, overtrading should not occur.

Option B is not correct. If the capital base is not increasing to support a *rise* in sales, this is likely to result in overtrading.

Option C is not correct. High inflation can increase stock and asset replacement costs at a rate that is greater than the rate of increase in profits to pay for it, thus causing overtrading. However, there should be no such problems in a time of low inflation.

6   C   The policy of suppliers is irrelevant to the company's relationship with its customers.

Option A is not correct. This is an important consideration, since if customers are generally indifferent to the length of credit period offered, there is unlikely to be a positive effect on sales. In this situation, the company's profitability will reduce since it will have to carry the cost of the additional debtors.

Option B is not correct. The rate of return achieved on the investment in additional debtors should exceed the rate of return that could be obtained by investing the money elsewhere.

Option D is not correct. The company must be broadly competitive in this area with other firms in the market unless it can offer further unique services that would compensate for a poorer than average credit policy.

7   D $$\text{Spread} = 3 \times \left(\frac{\frac{3}{4} \times 25 \times 200,000}{0.00020} \right)^{\frac{1}{3}} = £7,970$$

Upper limit = £7,970 + £2,500 = £10,470

The incorrect answers are reached by missing out the fraction of 3 and/or not adding the lower limit to the spread.

8   D

9   B   A slowdown in trading is likely to be associated with a lengthening stock turnover period since it usually takes time for production to be reduced in response to the downturn in sales.

Option A is not correct. If sales are increasing, it is more likely that the stock turnover period will decrease as stocks are held for a shorter period before sale.

Option C is not correct. A decrease in any type of stock, be it finished goods, raw materials or work in progress is likely to be reflected in a shortening of the stock turnover period.

Option D is not correct. A reduction in the operating cycle means that the length of time from the purchase of raw materials to the collection of debt from the customers becomes shorter. This is likely to be reflected in a shortening of the stock turnover period.

10   C   If the workers have only just been made redundant, the company will have had to pay redundancy pay, but there will not yet have been time for the cost savings to work through. This is therefore likely to have a negative effect on the cash position in the short term.

Option A is not correct. Labour costs will be significant in this type of business. Low sales, combined with a piecework system, means that cash outflows for the month will have been reduced. However, customers will still have been paying the larger debts incurred in earlier months, keeping receipts at a good level. This is therefore a timing effect.

Option B is not correct. The price increase implemented two months ago will now be working through into the cash receipts from debtors, and this will boost the cash balance.

Option D is not correct. If capital expenditure has fallen behind schedule, the cash position will be better than budgeted.

42   OBJECTIVE TEST QUESTIONS: WORKING CAPITAL MANAGEMENT V

1   B   This suggests that stock levels are falling. This would be unlikely if the company is over-capitalised with respect to working capital.

Option A is not correct. A current ratio at this level suggests that a large amount of money is tied up in current assets and working capital.

Option C suggests that the emphasis is on speedy settlement of accounts rather than on the proper use of credit facilities to minimise working capital requirements.

BPP PUBLISHING

Option D is not correct. A relatively low level of the sales:working capital ratio suggests that the overall level of working capital may be too high.

2   C   A risk of deterioration in the company's credit rating brings the prospect that the company may be unable to renew its borrowing facilities, and so long-term loans arranged now may be preferred.

Option A is not correct. Exposure to interest rate movements will make treasury managers seek a balance between long-term and short-term borrowings in their debt portfolios.

Option B is not correct. Inaccurate cash flow forecasts, possibly leading to excessive cash holdings but 'locked-in' long-term debt, or a short-term cash deficit, are likely to increase reliance on short-term borrowings.

Option D is not correct. Exposure to exchange rate risk will not, in itself, affect the preference for long-term debt over short-term debt.

3   B   There may be delays between recording a payment in the cash book and the cash leaving the bank account, and between recording a receipt in the cash book and the cash becoming available.

Option A is not correct. With this knowledge, the treasurer can increase profits by investing cash overnight or for longer durations.

Option C is not correct. The Miller-Orr model assumes that cash flows are unpredictable. In practice, many flows - such as dividend and tax payments - will be known in advance.

Option D is not correct. A typical example is the time between the time when a debtor posts a cheque and the time when the money paid is available as cleared funds.

4   A   The current ratio is likely to be low for an overtrading company.

Option B is not correct. Overtrading means trying to carry out an excessive volume of business for the size of the company's capital base.

Option D is not correct. The overtrading company is likely to seek longer credit from suppliers.

5   B   This is concerned with the method of financing new assets, and is therefore a financing decision.

Options A and C are investment decisions rather than financing decisions.

Option D is a disinvestment decision rather than a financing decision. It may in some instances be undertaken to solve a funding crisis.

6   D   Interest cover $= \dfrac{\text{PBIT}}{\text{Interest}} = \dfrac{200}{80} = 2.5$

This is very low and potentially a very serious problem.

7   B

	£
Capital employed	480,000
Fixed assets ($^2/_3$)	320,000
Working capital ($^1/_3$)	160,000

If current assets = CA and current liabilities = CL

CA – CL = £160,000

CA = 3CL

CA = £240,000

CL = £80,000

8   D

		£
Net profit = 25% of £960,000 =		240,000
ROCE = 10%		
Capital employed (× 100% + 10%)		2,400,000
Fixed assets (50%)		1,200,000
Working capital (50%)		1,200,000

If current assets – CA and current liabilities = CL

CA – CL = £1,200,000 and CA = 1.5CL

CL = £2,400,000

9   D   Credit cards are widely used and if retailers did not accept them, sales volume would almost certainly be much lower. The problem of bad debts is less with credit cards than with cheques. If the retailer uses the Cardnet service, cleared funds are available one day later – faster than with cheques. The cost of credit cards to retailers is higher than cheques – with retailers paying a commission of perhaps 2-3% (or even more) to the credit card company.

10   C $EOQ = \sqrt{\dfrac{2 \times 259 \times 3,000}{27}}$

= 240 units

Frequency of ordering $= \dfrac{240}{3,000} \times$ weeks = 4 weeks

43   MORIBUND

(a)   The operating cycle of a company is the length of time between the outlay on raw materials, wages and other costs and the inflow of cash arising from the sale of the product. In a manufacturing company this can be determined as follows.

Average raw material stockholding period
        plus
Time taken to produce goods
        less
Period of credit taken from suppliers
        plus
Average finished goods stockholding period
        plus
Average debt collection period

Thus as stock and debtor turnover periods improve and the creditor payment period lengthens, the operating cycle shortens and the investment required in working capital falls. The operating cycle therefore represents the relative investment in working capital; however it does not by itself indicate the absolute amount of working capital that will be required at different points in the cycle.

(b)   There is sufficient information for 20X2 to calculate average stockholding periods. However, since this is not available for 20X1, closing figures will be used to allow direct comparison of performance in the two years.

The operating cycle can be found as follows.

Average stockholding period: $\dfrac{\text{Total closing stock} \times 365}{\text{Cost of goods sold}}$

        plus

Debt collection period: $\dfrac{\text{Closing debtors} \times 365}{\text{Sales}}$

less

Length of trade credit taken: $\dfrac{\text{Closing creditors} \times 365}{\text{Purchases}}$

	20X2	20X1
Total closing stock (£)	410,000	330,000
Cost of goods sold (£)	750,000	650,000
Stockholding period	199.5 days	185.3 days
Closing debtors (£)	230,000	180,000
Sales (£)	900,000	800,000
Debt collection period	93.3 days	82.1 days
Closing creditors (£)	(120,000)	(90,000)
Purchases (£)	500,000	450,000
Trade credit period	87.6 days	73 days
Length of operating cycle	205.2 days	194.4 days

(c) The steps that could be taken to reduce the operating cycle include the following.

(i) **Reducing the average raw material stockholding period.** Some of the practical steps that could be taken to achieve this include the following.

(1) **Ordering in small quantities** to meet immediate production requirements. This could mean that the company loses the benefit of quantity discounts from suppliers.

(2) **Reducing the level of buffer stocks** if these are held. This will increase the risk of production being halted due to a stock-out.

(3) **Reducing the lead time allowed to suppliers**. This could also increase the risk of a stock-out

(4) **Reducing the range of products made.** This means that a smaller number of raw materials will need to be stocked. However sales may be lost if customers cannot be persuaded to switch to different products.

(ii) **Increasing the period of credit taken from suppliers**. If the credit period is extended then the company may lose discounts for prompt payment. The financial effect of this should be calculated and compared with the cost of funds from other sources. If the credit period is extended beyond the terms allowed by suppliers then not only may goodwill be lost which is important in the event of goods being required urgently, but regular supplies may also be put into jeopardy. The credit period has increased significantly over the last year and already seems very long unless the company is allowed three months credit by its suppliers.

(iii) **Reducing the time taken to produce goods.** Provided that goods continue to be made in economic batch quantities, this should only lead to improvements in efficiency. However, the company must ensure that quality is not sacrificed as a result of speeding up the production process.

(iv) **Reducing the average finished goods stockholding period.** The savings arising from this must be evaluated against the cost of a stock-out, together with the effect on customer service.

(v) **Reducing the average debt collection period.** The administrative costs of speeding up debt collection and the effect on sales of reducing the credit period allowed must be evaluated. However, the credit period has increased significantly over the last year and does seem very long by the standards of most industries. It may be that generous terms have been allowed to secure large contracts and little will be able to be done about this in the short term.

44   RATIOS

> **Pass marks**. Part (a) of this question is divided into three sections. You may have chosen to keep to this division, or to answer all three sections together for each ratio in turn. If you chose the latter course, you should have concluded with a general review of X plc, as a combination of trends in several ratios may be more informative than the separate trends.
>
> In part (b), the years to compare are specified in the question, so you should limit your analysis accordingly.

(a) (i) The **working capital: total assets ratio** shows the investment in working capital (current assets less current liabilities) as a proportion of a business's total assets. A high ratio would suggest an excessive investment in working capital, perhaps because of poor credit control, whereas a very low ratio would suggest overtrading, which can lead to insolvency.

The **retained earnings: total assets** ratio shows the retained earnings as a proportion of total assets. One would not expect this ratio to be very low. A company with substantial fixed assets will need substantial new finance to ensure their continued maintenance, effective use and eventual replacement. Retained earnings are a major source of new finance for most businesses.

The **earnings before interest and tax: interest charges plus annual repayment of loans** ratio indicates a company's ability to meet its obligations to the providers of debt finance. Earnings should be significantly higher than those obligations, perhaps two or three times higher, so as to ensure that the company can survive a temporary fall in earnings and that in most years there will be surplus earnings for re-investment in the business. In interpreting this ratio, one should bear in mind that although it is appropriate to compare interest with earnings before tax, as interest is an allowable expense for tax purposes, loan repayments are not allowable and must be made out of earnings after tax or covered by new loan or share capital.

(ii) Relevant data on **X plc** are as follows.

	Year 1 £'000	Year 2 £'000	Year 3 £'000	Year 4 £'000
Working capital (net current assets)	1,130.7	962.3	867.5	645.5
Total assets (fixed and current)	2,936.7	2,911	3,205	3,571
Retained earnings (brought forward plus current year)	1,389.7	1,395.3	1,450.5	1,501
Earnings before interest and tax	274.5	284	285.5	205.5
Interest charges plus annual repayment of loans	273	384	310	235

It has been assumed that loan repayments in year 1 were the same as in years 2 to 4, £124,000 a year.

Ratios, expressed as percentages, are therefore as follows.

	Year 1	Year 2	Year 3	Year 4
	%	%	%	%
Working capital: total assets	38.5	33.1	27.1	18.1
Retained earnings:				
total assets	47.3	47.9	45.3	42.0
EBIT: interest charges				
plus annual loan repayments	100.5	74.0	92.1	87.4

(iii) **Trends in ratios**. Working capital has fallen steadily, both in pounds and as a percentage of total assets. This is mainly due to a growth in current liabilities, most noticeably the bank overdraft.

The fall in retained earnings as a proportion of total assets over the last two years, despite the rise in the amount of retained earnings, suggests that the dividend policy is too generous for a company with rapidly growing assets.

Earnings have not covered interest charges and loan repayments in any of the last three years. This may explain the company's increasing reliance on short-term credit.

(b) Between year 1 and year 4, both **fixed and current assets** grew significantly. This growth has had to be financed. The company has clearly been committed to regular repayments of its long-term borrowings, and has not obtained replacement long-term loans, so the burden has fallen on current liabilities and on shareholders' equity. There has been no new share capital, and while total retained earnings have increased the company has had to rely on current liabilities for most of the new finance. There was no bank overdraft in year 1, and an overdraft of £504,000 in year 4. In addition, trade credit has increased from 12.4% of turnover in year 1 to 14.4% of turnover in year 4, and other current liabilities (possibly including taxation and proposed dividends) have more than doubled over the same period.

This policy of **funding increases in total assets**, particularly fixed assets, almost entirely by increases in **current liabilities**, is most unwise. Bank overdrafts are often in practice renewed indefinitely, but they are still repayable on demand, and the bank could require repayment if ever it thought that the company was getting into difficulties. Similarly, further trade credit could be denied at any time. If all debtors realised their book values, the current liabilities could be met, avoiding immediate insolvency, but the company might then find it very hard to continue trading. A fresh injection of equity or long-term debt is clearly called for.

45 YZPK PACKING CO LTD

Pass marks. The question is concerned with the pressures of growth on working capital. You may find it helpful to consider the typical reactions of a fast growing company to these demands and compare them with the actual performance of YZPK.

(a) Growth over the last four years has been extremely rapid, sales having increased 6.36 times, profit having increased 18.55 times and profitability (net profit/ turnover) having increased from 2.48% to 7.25%.

Some of the problems associated with rapid growth include the following.

(i)   **Cash flow shortages** may occur as companies have to finance a larger amount of working capital and fixed assets.

(ii)   The **management style** and the skills demanded from management are likely to change, particularly if the process is labour intensive resulting in a large increase in the number employed. This may put pressure on the existing management, some of whom may not be up to working at a senior level in a much larger firm, with probably a much more specialised brief than previously. In the short to medium term this may lead to some loss of control.

(iii)   Although in this case growth in sales has not been at the expense of margin, if the additional sales are achieved by offering **low prices** there may be a decline in the productivity of labour and/or assets.

(b)   Possible reasons for the low stockholding periods may include the following.

(i)   The company may have put **tight stock control policies** into force, either through choice or necessity in order to minimise the working capital requirement during a period of growth.

(ii)   The company may use superior manufacturing process controls compared to the other firms in the industry, eg **just in time (JIT)** or **material requirement planning (MRP)** systems. This will minimise the levels of raw material stocks and work in progress.

(iii)   The company may occupy a particular **niche in the market** which means that its product range is small by comparison with other firms in the industry. This would mean that it would have to hold a lower level of stock than other firms in the industry.

It would be equally interesting to know why the stock turnover has been increasing steadily over the period in question.

(c)   MEMO

To: Board of Directors
From: Chief Accountant
Date: 15 December 20X5
Subject: Debtor and creditor management

The purpose of this memorandum is to propose potential areas of improvement to our control of debtors, and to discuss the risks of taking extended credit from our suppliers.

Potential credit control improvements

Throughout the last four years the average debtor collection period has been consistently above the industry average, increasing from 63 days in 20X3 to 76 days in 20X5, although it has fallen back to 64 days in 20X6. This is somewhat surprising given the pressure on cash resources during the period. Possible reasons for this include poor control of debtors during a time of rapid growth when other areas of the business were seen as more important, and the conscious decision to gain additional business through a generous credit policy.

Although the collection period has fallen a little in 20X6, it is recommended that a **thorough review** should be undertaken of the credit control and debt collection policies, including an assessment of the effects of any change in policy on the trading performance of the company.

Specific measures to be considered

(i) Tightening up the procedures for chasing up slow payers, including the system for telephoning to request payment and placing consistently late payers 'on stop'

(ii) Evaluating the relative costs and benefits of introducing a settlement discount scheme

(iii) Assessing the feasibility of levying a credit charge on accounts that remain unpaid after the due date

(iv) Reviewing the procedures by which customers are granted credit, the terms negotiated and the setting of credit limits

Policy with respect to creditors

Although creditors are now being paid faster than during the last two years, the average payment period is still 118 days which is well in excess of the industry average (72 days). The extent to which this is a cause for concern depends of course on the details of the payment terms negotiated with the suppliers. However it is most unusual for suppliers to offer a credit period in excess of three months, and the most likely inference is that the terms are regularly being exceeded. This is a dangerous situation to allow to continue since, taken with the low level of the acid test ratio, the company is vulnerable to liquidation in the event of pressure from the creditors.

46   **IMPROVING CASH FLOW**

It would seem that B Ltd relies entirely on A plc for finance, and so cannot raise money from a bank loan or overdraft. The maximum loan from A plc is £50,000, but the cash budget projects an 'overdraft' of up to £262,000 (month 10).

B Ltd would appear to be profitable and growing. A very rough estimate of profits in the year could be made by preparing a funds flow statement in reverse.

	£'000
Increase in bank balance (35 – 30)	5
Increase in finished goods stock	114
Net increase in debtors and raw materials stocks less creditors	x
Purchases of fixed assets (70 + 10 + 15 + 5)	100
Dividend paid	80
Tax paid	120
	419 + x
Less depreciation	– y
Profit before tax	419 + x – y

A combination of seasonal business, growth in trading and fixed asset purchases would appear to be the reason why B Ltd is only expected to increase its cash balance by £5,000 over the whole year, in spite of these profits.

Possible measures to reduce the requirement for cash include the following.

(a) **Do not pay the dividend to A plc in month 3**. However, A plc is short of cash, and is probably relying on the dividend income. It would therefore seem unlikely that A plc would agree either to cancel the dividend or to lend more than £50,000.

(b) **Delay the payment of corporation tax** from month 9 (presumably, this is the statutory payment date, 9 months after the year end). The Inland Revenue might allow B Ltd to do this, although there would be an interest charge for the delay.

(c) **Improve stock control**. We do not know the total of finished goods, but stock levels will rise by £114,000 in the year. Clearly, the increase in stock is expected because of the company's sales growth. However, some reductions in the investment in stocks might be possible without prejudice to sales, in which case the cash flow position would be eased by the value of the stocks reduction.

(d) **Improve creditors control**. Three months credit is taken from suppliers, but raw material purchases are every 2 months. The credit period already seems generous, and some suppliers are probably making a second delivery of materials before they are paid for the first. Taking longer credit would be difficult to negotiate. However, if B Ltd is on very good terms with its suppliers, and is a valued customer of those suppliers, it might be possible to defer by a further month payments due in months 6, 8 and 10, which cover the cash crisis period.

(e) **Improve debtors control**. Two months' credit is allowed to customers. If all sales are on credit, customers are likely to be commercial or industrial buyers, who would expect reasonable credit terms. A shortening of the credit period is probably not possible, without damaging goodwill and sales prospects, unless an incentive is offered for early payments, in the form of a discount. The discount would have to be sufficiently large to persuade customers to take it. Suppose, for example, that from month 5 sales onwards, a 10% discount were offered for payments inside a month. (10% would be very generous and unrealistic perhaps, but is used here for illustration). If all customers accepted the offer, this would affect cash flows from month 6 on, as follows.

Month	Original budget £'000		Revised budget £'000	Net change £'000
6	75	+ (90% of 80)	147	+72
7	80	−80 + (90% of 90)	81	+1
8	90	−90 + (90% of 110)	99	+9
9	110	−110 + (90% of 150)	135	+25
10	150	−150 + (90% of 220)	198	+48
11	220	−220 + (90% of 320)	288	+68
12	320	?	?	?

The effects on cash flow would then be substantial, although the cost of the discounts would reduce profits by a substantial amount too.

(f) **Postpone capital expenditure**. Since the company is growing, the option to postpone capital expenditure on new equipment, building extensions and office furniture is probably unrealistic. The routine replacement of motor vehicles should be deferred, but this would only ease the cash situation by £10,000.

(g) B Ltd has an investment which will pay a dividend of £45,000 in month 7. This is obviously a fairly large investment. If B Ltd's cash flow problems cannot be solved in any other way, the company's directors might have to consider whether this investment could be **sold** to raise funds.

Summary

B Ltd is a profitable company, but is faced with serious cash flow problems which would seem to be hard to overcome without drastic measures being taken. Because B Ltd is profitable, closure of the company is unthinkable, and it would be against the company's long-term interests to abandon its plans for growth. A plc is acting as a serious constraining influence on B Ltd.

However, the sort of radical action and response outlined above for debtors, coupled with a postponement of the tax payment by 3 months or so and a deferral of £10,000 in motor vehicle purchases until next year, would be virtually sufficient to overcome the firm's cash flow problems in the year, with a slight problem still in month 8: see workings below.

					Month (£'000s)			
	5	*6*	*7*	*8*	*9*	*10*	*11*	*12*
Postpone purchase of vehicles	10							
Defer tax payment					120			(120)
Discounts for early payment by debtors - possible effect		72	1	9	25	48	68	?
Change	10	72	1	9	145	48	68	?
Cumulative change	10	82	83	92	237	285	353	?
Original cash budget	1	(71)	(66)	(144)	(216)	(262)	(130)	35
Revised cash budget balances	11	11	17	(52)	21	23	223	?

If B Ltd is to overcome its problems within the constraints set by A plc's financial policy, it is likely that **action on debtors** is the key to a practical solution.

47   PHOENIX PLC

> **Pass marks**. This question is mainly a narrative discussion comparing two possible uses of surplus funds: increasing the dividend or repaying loans. Because there are many other potential uses for the money, no final recommendation can be made, but the marks will go for discussing the very important principles which are involved.
>
> Part (a) of the question is easy but is slightly marred by the use of incorrect terminology in the question (see tutorial note below).

(a)   *Dividend payout ratios and dividend covers*

	20X5-6	20X6-7	
	£m	£m	
Profit before interest and tax	25.00	40.00	
Less: interest: £10m × 7%	0.70	0.70	
Profit before tax	24.30	39.30	
Tax	8.02	12.97	
After tax profit	16.28	26.33	
Total dividend: 280m shares × 1.5p	4.20		
£4.2m + £10m		14.20	
Pay-out ratio (dividend / after-tax profit)	25.8%	53.9%	
Dividend cover (after-tax profit / dividend)	3.88	1.85	times

(b)

To: Finance Director
From: Financial Strategist
Date: 15 December 20X7

Report on proposals for using cash surpluses

Under the terms of reference for this report I am required to evaluate two proposals for the use of the company's £10 million cash surplus:

(i)   Redeeming the £10 million secured 7% loan
(ii)   Increasing the dividend payout by £10 million

Before making a final decision, however, other possible uses for the cash should be considered, including:

- Placing the money on deposit or in liquid investments
- Capital investment for organic growth
- Acquisition of other businesses
- Share buyback

These other alternatives are not specifically discussed in this report.

(i)   **Background**

The cash surplus has arisen because of a marked expansion in the volume of our business as the economy emerged from the recession. We should, however, bear in mind that ours is an industry which suffers from volatile fluctuations in demand and in future years we might suffer cash shortages.

(ii) **Proposal to redeem the £10 million secured 7% loan**

If the loan is redeemed, eliminating future interest payments, then future dividends can be increased. Because share prices of quoted companies reflect expectations of future dividend payouts, the company's share price should increase.

Thus, from the shareholders' point of view, the effect of the loan redemption can be seen as a sacrifice of a potentially large dividend now in return for an increased 'ex div' share price. Shareholders seeking capital gains as opposed to cash dividends (usually for tax reasons) will prefer this option.

Eliminating debt also means that the shareholders will suffer less risk: the volatility of their earnings ('**financial risk**') will decrease and the chances of bankruptcy or financial distress are lessened.

Arguments against redemption of the loan

- The company's gearing is very low compared with the sector average. This implies that the bankruptcy risk mentioned above is not significant. Gearing (debt/shareholders funds) at present is £10m/£200m = 5% compared with the sector average of 45%, and interest cover is £25m/£0.7m = 35.7 times at the moment compared with the sector average of 6.5 times.

- Loan interest is an allowable expense against corporation tax. The return on shareholders' investment is increased by this tax saving if loan finance is used. The benefits of this tax reduction (known as the '**tax shield**') will be lost if the loan is redeemed.

- If not properly explained to the market, the loan repayment may be interpreted by shareholders as a sign that there are difficult times ahead. This may cause the share price to fall, rather than rise.

An important point when deciding whether to redeem a fixed interest loan is its interest rate compared with expected future market interest rates. For example, if the loan is redeemable now *at par* but to borrow in future would cost more than 7% then redemption would probably be unwise. However, if the loan stock is quoted with a market value, the price at which it can be purchased and cancelled will adjust to take account of this effect.

(iii) **Proposal to increase the equity dividend by £10 million**

This proposal is the extreme alternative to the previous one: a large dividend is paid immediately but future dividends cannot be as large as if the loan were repaid; hence there will be no increase in 'ex div' share price.

This proposal will be preferred by those shareholders who want a large immediate cash distribution and will not suffer any adverse tax consequences if it is received as a dividend. Such shareholders are often tax-exempt institutions. However, higher rate tax payers may regard the increased dividend as very unwelcome if they were looking for share price growth rather than a taxed dividend. These shareholders may sell their shares, assuming that the company had changed its dividend policy to one of high taxable dividend payouts.

If the loan not repaid, the advantage of the **tax shield** from loan interest is retained.

The main problem with the proposed increase in dividend is that it is very large in percentage terms (a 238% increase). Unless the reasons for the increase are carefully explained to the market, the wrong signals can be picked up. Some shareholders may assume that dividends in future years will continue to increase at the same rate, whereas others may assume the company has run out of investment ideas and is signalling an end to growth. It is best to avoid confusion of this sort, as it can have an adverse effect on the share price. Companies wishing to pay large increases in cash to shareholders have avoided this confusion either by announcing 'one-off' **special dividends** or by making **share buy-backs**.

Most finance directors tend to believe that dividend policy should be managed in such a way that dividends show a steady rate of increase over time, rather than just being a residual balancing figure after investment and financing decisions have been made. This positive management of dividend policy is said to increase investor confidence, though the matter is far from proved.

(iv) **Making the choice**

As stated at the outset, the choice is not a simple alternative between paying a £10 million dividend and repaying the £10 million loan. There are several alternatives which must be discussed carefully, each of which could merit a report longer than this one. The end result is likely to be a combination of several applications for the money. We cannot at this stage, therefore, make any recommendations.

48 RIPLEY PLC

> **Pass marks**. In part (a) it is helpful to structure your answer so as to discuss the rationale, benefits and disadvantages of the two policies. This should then allow you to identify the key issues to be addressed in making the decision. Alternative approaches are possible in part (b) regarding the treatment of the interest forgone on the short-term securities. The answer includes the amount forgone as part of the cost of the first option. It would be equally correct to calculate the amount of interest received from the securities under each of the two options and to make the evaluation on this basis.

(a)   MEMORANDUM

To: Board of Directors
From: Assistant Treasurer
Date: 15 December 20X6
Subject: Alternative financial policies

The purpose of this memorandum is to explain the rationale behind our current financing policy and the proposed policy currently under discussion. The final section will deal with the key issues that need to be considered in making a decision between the two alternatives.

Current policy

Our current policy is based on the principle of **matching**, whereby we attempt to match the timespan of our financial liabilities to the lifetime of the assets with which they are associated. Thus our fixed assets are of approximately equal magnitude to our long-term debt and equity financing. Short-term assets such as stock and debtors are funded out of shorter term finance such as creditors and bank overdraft.

The benefits of this policy are as follows.

(i)   Expensive longer term finance is only used to support those assets which have a longer life - it is not used to finance more ephemeral assets which can be supported with cheaper shorter term finance.

(ii)   It reduces the risks associated with under-capitalisation whereby the company runs the risk of short-term financing being withdrawn at short notice when it cannot easily liquidate the associated assets. Such a situation carries significant levels of financial risk.

Proposed policy

The proposal under consideration is an **'aggressive' policy** involving a **greater use of cheaper short-term finance**. It implies the need for very careful management of the current assets, particularly debtors and creditors. The use of short-term finance to support long-term assets does carry financial risks as outlined above. However, the adoption of such a policy could result in a significant reduction in our financing costs. The implementation of this policy also assumes that the term structure of interest rates will continue in its present form with shorter term finance being significantly cheaper than longer term finance. Obviously if this relationship changes the benefits of the policy could be diminished.

Key issues

The key issues that the Board must consider before reaching the decision to change policy include the following.

(i)   Is there likely to be any significant change in the **term structure of interest rates**?

(ii)   How practical is it to increase the **payment period** to creditors - will this have an adverse affect on the operations of the business in terms of quality and continuity of supply?

(iii) What is the **nature of our fixed asset base** - would it be possible to liquidate any of the assets quickly without damaging the operations of the business? Alternatively could we consider refinancing some of the assets differently, for example using finance or operating leases.

(iv)   What is the degree of **volatility in our cash flows** and are there significant seasonal fluctuations that must be taken into account?

(v)   Do we have any **financial 'safety nets'** to back up this policy, for example any holdings of easily marketable securities or currently unused lines of credit?

(b)   The two alternative policies will be evaluated separately to determine the most beneficial in financial terms.

(i)   **Selling securities**

The first step is to determine the optimal amount of cash that will be raised in each transaction, and hence the number of transactions and the level of transaction costs.

$$Q = \sqrt{\frac{2FS}{i}}$$

where: i   = average % rate of return   12%

   F   = cash payments   £1.5m

   S   = transaction fee   £25

$$Q = \sqrt{\frac{2 \times £1.5m \times £25}{12\%}}$$

   = £25,000

In order to raise £1.5m, Bramham must make 60 sales (£1.5m/£25,000) thereby incurring transaction costs of £1,500 (60 × £25).

Since the cash payments will become due at a steady rate it is possible to calculate the average level of cash balances held ie £25,000/2 = £12,500. This cash will be placed on short-term deposit earning interest at 5%, thus generating income during the year of £625 (£12,500 × 5%).

The net cost of this policy is therefore the transaction costs of £1,500 less the interest received of £625, giving a total of £875.

In addition, the company will lose income from the portfolio of securities. This will amount to 12% of the average balance held (£1.5m/2) ie £90,000, and this income forgone must be added to the net cost of the policy, giving a total cost of £90,875.

(ii) **Secured loan**

Since the cash payments will become due at a steady rate it can be assumed that the average value of the cash remaining will be £750,000 (£1.5m/2), and that this will earn interest at 9% amounting to £67,500 (£750,000 × 9%).

Interest will be paid at 14% on the full amount of the loan for the year, amounting to £210,000 (£1.5m × 14%).

The cost of this policy is therefore:

	£
Interest paid	210,000
Interest received	(67,500)
Arrangement fee	5,000
	147,500

The figures suggest that the policy of selling securities is to be preferred since this has a net cost of £90,875 which is £56,625 less than the cost of taking out a secured loan for the period.

The company should also take into account the following **other factors** associated with the policies.

- The value of the short-term securities is likely to fluctuate and Bramham must consider the possibility that the value could fall to below that required to meet the cash payments.

- Use of the securities will eliminate them as a future source of finance.

- If Bramham takes out the loan, it must have funds available with which to repay it at the end of the period.

(c) **Limitations of the model**

(i) It assumes a steady rate of return from the securities although this may be very uncertain. Bramham should consider the effect of fluctuations in this rate on the model.

(ii) It does not allow for a buffer stock of cash but assumes that further securities will only be sold when the cash balance reduces to zero. This is unlikely to be realistic in practice.

(iii) It assumes that the level of transaction costs is independent of the size of the transaction - again this is unlikely to be true in practice.

(iv) In reality, payments will not be made continuously but at regular intervals. The effect of this 'stepped' effect on the operation of the model should be considered.

49   RECENT RESEARCH

> **Pass marks**. With the exception of a very small computation, this question is entirely narrative. It really covers most of the syllabus for credit control and management of debtors and shows that, in this paper, a broad grasp of the problems and principles is as valuable as detailed knowledge, provided that you can explain the concepts in words under exam conditions.

(a)   Small companies face a number of **problems in respect of credit management,** as follows.

   (i)   Small companies are often under pressure from large customers to give over-generous credit facilities. Sometimes these customers negotiate long payment periods and sometimes they just take them. The average small company has little bargaining power to resist such pressures.

   (ii)   The business is too small to justify the appointment of a skilled credit controller. If the job is only part of someone's overall responsibilities, it may be shelved behind other more pressing tasks. It is not always obvious to employees that prompt collection of cash has an impact on profitability and the situation may be allowed to drift until the company reaches its overdraft limit.

   (iii)   Small companies do not usually have documented systems on their credit control policies. Neither do they invest much in training their staff in financial skills and awareness of credit problems. This may result in the granting of credit to high-risk customers.

   (iv)   Many small companies are undercapitalised and operate with a bank overdraft as the main source of external finance. Consequently poor cash collection will quickly result in the overdraft limit being reached and recurrent problems with the bank.

The following actions could be taken to minimise the effects of these problems.

   (i)   Ensure that all top management are adequately trained in the importance of cash and credit management to the profitability, liquidity and survival of the company.

   (ii)   Obtain benchmark figures for payment periods and bad debts to determine how efficient the company is compared with others in the same industry.

   (iii)   Analyse the company's strengths and weaknesses to see whether it is able to exercise more bargaining power with large customers. A company with above-average products and services will be able to operate a stricter credit control policy than one which is only average.

   (iv)   Decide whether credit control should be managed in-house or whether it should be passed to an external expert, such as a factoring company or even a freelance credit consultant.

   (v)   If credit is to be managed internally, invest in designing and documenting a proper system, assigning clear responsibilities and training the appropriate staff. Ensure that customers are informed of the new rules.

   (vi)   Consider discount schemes for prompt payment.

   (vii)   Consider a strategic alliance with a larger company in order to gain more bargaining power with large customers.

(b) To: Credit Manager
    From: Management Accountant   Date: 11 November 20X7
    Subject: Credit control policy and discounts for prompt payment

(i)   Credit control has an impact on many aspects of business strategy, including **marketing, production** and **financial strategy**.

In formulating marketing strategy, emphasis is rightly given to achieving **growth** through **customer satisfaction**. Credit control may be seen as a boring operational job which has little to do with the company's strategic plans. It is important for you to refute these assumptions. Cash, after all, is the life-blood of the company and in these volatile times no sale can be regarded as safe until the cash is collected.

When deciding which customers to target, their **ability to pay** is of major concern. A review of the creditworthiness of the existing customer base may result in a revised target clientele.

On the other hand, the extension of credit periods or the granting of prompt payment discounts as special offers can act as a positive marketing tool (see (ii) below).

The **costs of collecting late debts and writing off bad debts** can be viewed as one of the costs of the product itself. In order to achieve cost efficiency and effective pricing, the company must have strategic plans for credit control.

The need to ensure **prompt payment of debts** will also motivate the organisation to produce products of above-average quality so that late payment can be more easily countered by the threat of cutting off the supply. In this way, credit control has an impact on product design and manufacture and can be seen to form part of a total quality management programme.

Credit control has an obvious impact on **financial strategy**. The company needs to be able to forecast its debtor levels as accurately as possible in order to determine its financing requirements.

Since credit policy impacts on marketing, production and finance, it is important to elevate it to the level of strategic planning so that the company's resources are properly co-ordinated.

(ii)   **Advantages of introducing prompt payment discounts**

(i)   If customers are attracted by the discount, there will be an immediate cash inflow which will lower the company's interest costs by, for example, lowering the overdraft requirement.

(ii)   Total sales will increase if customers view the discount as a price reduction.

(iii)   Bad debts are likely to be reduced, because default risk increases with the time a debt is outstanding.

Disadvantages

(i)   The cost of the discount itself often has to be substantial to induce prompt payment.

(ii)   The effect on customers who miss the prompt payment period is that sometimes they will delay payment more than they otherwise would.

To illustrate the cost of the cash discount, imagine that our company offers a 1% discount for payment within 10 days when the normal credit period is 30 days. In other words, cash is received 20 days earlier in return for a cost of 1%. A rough estimate of the effective annual cost is $1\% \times 365/20 = 18.25\%$. The true annual compound rate of interest will be higher than this. This is an expensive discount, but it is likely to increase demand for our products if customers regard it as a price reduction.

Signed: Management Accountant

50   WHICHFORD PLC

(a)   At present, the expected delay in invoicing is as follows.

Days of delay	Probability	Expected delay in days
3	20%	0.60
4	6%	0.24
5	40%	2.00
6	22%	1.32
7	12%	0.84
		5.00

The cost of five days delay in invoicing sales of £25,000,000 is £25,000,000 $\times$ 15% $\times$ 5/365 = £51,370 a year.

Under the proposed new system, the expected delay in invoicing would be as follows.

Days of delay	Probability	Expected delay in days
0	50%	0
1	40%	0.4
3	10%	0.3
		0.7

The cost of 0.7 days delay in invoicing sales of £25,000,000 is £25,000,000 $\times$ 15% $\times$ 0.7/365 = £7,192 a year.

The annual saving under the new scheme is therefore:

	£
Reduction in cost of financing debtors £(51,370 – 7,192)	44,178
Reduction in other costs	48,000
	92,178

The company is therefore justified in paying for the system a monthly rental of £92,178 ÷ 12 = £7,681.

(b)   If the **debtors collection period** is reduced to 30 days, a saving of five days will have been achieved. As calculated in (a) above, this is worth £51,370 a year to the company. The total annual savings are as follows.

	£
As in (a) above	92,178
Add	51,370
	143,548

The company is therefore justified in paying for the system a monthly rental of £143,548 ÷ 12 = £11,962.

(c)   When a **policy for credit control** is being formulated, management should consider the following issues.

(i)   The average period of credit to be given. Whether this should be longer than average to encourage sales or less than average, to speed up sales.

(ii)   Policy for making decisions on granting credit to individual customers:

(1)   How customers are to be investigated for creditworthiness (eg by direct assessment by the company, or indirect assessment using credit references from banks, or other assessment agencies)

(2) How the amount and timing of credit is to be decided (eg whether credit is to increased progressively)

(iii) Debt collection policies. Whether to employ specific staff on this task. Issue of debtors' statements, reminder letters, whether and when to make use of professional debt collectors. When to consider legal action.

(iv) Accounting reports required: aged debtors lists etc.

(v) Policies on persuading debtors to pay promptly eg discount schemes.

(vi) Whether to make use of factoring services.

For all the above, it will be necessary to consider the costs and benefits of the alternative courses of action. This will include considerations on how credit is to be financed.

51   DISCOUNT

> **Pass marks**. Part (a)(i) requires an understanding of the relative costs of offering a trade discount as against accepting a longer payment period. Do not forget to mention the less easily quantifiable aspects such as the effect of a longer credit period on the risk of default.
>
> Part (b) is looking for a broader discussion of the conflicting objectives that must be held in balance when determining working capital policy. Define how you are interpreting the terms 'aggressive' and 'conservative' since these can be used in different ways.

(a) (i) The company is offering its customers a 2% discount in return for the loss of 20 days credit. This represents an annualised rate of interest of $1.02^{365/20} - 1 = 0.435$, ie 43.5%. The cost of offering the discount must be compared with the opportunity cost of capital in deciding whether the policy is appropriate.

Other factors must also be taken into account such as any potential improvements in bad debts which might result from speeding up payments.

(ii) **A debt factoring organisation** manages the debts owed to a client on the client's behalf. Services offered by a factor may include:

(1) Administration of invoicing, sales accounting and debt collection

(2) Credit protection, whereby the factor undertakes to take over the risk of bad debts

(3) Provision of finance to the client secured on the outstanding debts

Factoring can therefore provide a significant source of credit to a business and can reduce the overheads associated with debt collection. However there is a cost for the service and it may well be more economic to continue to operate the sales ledger directly.

A company may be unable to avoid offering some form of settlement discount if this is common practice in the industry. An efficient sales administration system is essential to ensure that discounting does produce its full potential cash flow benefits. It should also be borne in mind that the sales administration department can be an important point of contact with the customer and can glean information essential to maintaining the smooth running of the account, as well as fostering a good long-term relationship.

(b) It is assumed that the degree of **aggression** or **conservatism** in the management and financing of current assets relates to the degree of risk which the company is prepared to accept. This can be assessed by taking each element of the current asset base in turn.

(i) **Cash and marketable securities.** All companies will require a certain amount of cash to be available for their day to day operations - to pay suppliers, wages, expenses and so on. The precise amounts required will be determined by means of a regularly updated short-term cash flow forecast which will highlight peaks and troughs in cash demands. A company with a conservative cash policy will probably maintain a bank balance which is sufficient to cover the normal peaks in demand. The cash forecast will be updated less often, perhaps twice a month, and the company will accept that there is likely to be some idle cash in the account.

A company with an aggressive policy will monitor the cash position throughout the day and will seek to minimise the amount held in the bank account. Wherever possible surplus funds will be transferred to other accounts and investments, or alternatively placed on overnight deposit to ensure that interest is maximised.

The **downside** of such a policy is that there will be an overhead incurred in monitoring the situation and moving the funds around. There is also the risk that if forecasts are inaccurate the company may need to call on other reserves at short notice and so incur a loss of interest. It may even face the embarrassment and loss of confidence of its suppliers if mistakes result in some of its cheques being bounced.

(ii) **Stock and work in progress.** The first decision to be faced by a company is whether to manufacture to order or to supply from stock. If it chooses the latter option it must then decide on the level of stock it should carry, and to do this it will need to make demand forecasts. The key problem is that all such forecasts are subject to some degree of error and the company must decide what level of buffer stock is appropriate to minimise the risk of a stock out occurring.

Although models are available which attempt to quantify the relative costs of carrying excess stocks as against a stock out, it is very difficult to estimate what the effect of a stock out will be on future business. A company which chooses an aggressive policy in the sense of being prepared to accept a higher level of risk will probably choose to stock at a lower level than one which adopts a more conservative policy.

(iii) **Debtors.** An **aggressive** policy in respect of debtors could be one of two things. If aggression is to be defined in terms of attitude to risk, then a company with an aggressive policy is likely to have a high level of debtors, being generous in allowing credit in order to achieve the maximum level of sales. A more **conservative** company would be more cautious in both granting credit to a customer and in the size of the credit limit applied and this may mean that some sales are sacrificed as a result.

Alternatively, an aggressive approach to the level of debtors might mean that the company seeks to minimise the amount of capital tied up by debtors. In this situation the aggressive policy would be to allow the minimum amount of credit to customers, to chase up payments as soon as they become due and to place 'on stop' customers who exceed their credit limit or who are late with their payment.

The **traditional view** is that short-term assets should be financed from short-term sources of capital such as the bank overdraft. However it is commonly accepted that in practice working capital is unlikely to fall below a certain amount and that this level can be regarded as semi-permanent requiring a longer term more secure source of finance.

The more aggressive company is likely to try to minimise interest costs by using a source of finance which can be varied in amount to match the fluctuations in requirements, rather than committing itself to a longer term loan. It is also likely to try maintain a high level of trade creditors and to use this as a source of finance, although such a policy obviously carries a risk of interruption of supply or litigation if creditors' terms are not complied with.

52   MP LIMITED

Pass marks. This is a slightly unusual question in that it relates to a company that is taking a surprisingly long credit period on a regular basis. You should think through the practical implications of implementing such a policy as well as the financial costs involved when drafting your answer

---

To: Financial Manager
From: Assistant Financial Manager
Date: 15 November 20X8
Subject: **Review of the policy concerning trade credit terms**

The purpose of this report is to evaluate the costs of our existing trade credit policy, and to discuss the arguments for and against using trade credit as a source of funds. The final section of the report will deal with the advantages and disadvantages of introducing standard terms of trade for all suppliers.

Evaluation of the existing policy

MP's current policy is to take 90 days credit on all supplier invoices. The result of this is that we routinely incur a variety of penalties and charges from a number of our suppliers for exceeding their terms of trade. An **analysis of the costs** in relation to three randomly chosen suppliers is outlined below. For the purposes of calculation it is assumed that we purchase £1,000 worth of goods from each supplier every month.

Supplier A charges a fixed penalty of 2% of invoice value for late payment. This penalty does not increase with the length of the credit period taken. Since under our existing policy, all invoices are paid late, the cost per invoice is £20, and the cost per year is £240. The average amount by which we exceed the supplier's terms at any one time is £2,000 (two months invoices), and therefore the annualised cost in percentage terms is 12% (240/2,000).

Supplier B charges compound interest at 2% per 30-day period after the due date of payment. Each invoice is paid two months late, and therefore the cost per invoice is as follows:

			£
Month 2	£1,000 × 2%	=	20.00
Month 3	£1,020 × 2%	=	20.40
			40.40

The cost per year is therefore £484.80, and the annualised percentage cost on an average credit level of £2,000 is 24.2%.

Supplier C charges simple interest at 10% per annum on the invoice value if payment is late. We always forego the opportunity to receive settlement discount. Each invoice is outstanding for two months, and therefore the cost per invoice is £1,000 × 10% × 2/12 = £16.60. The cost per year is £200.00 compared with paying on the due date, and the annualised percentage cost is 10% (200/2,000).

There is a further opportunity cost of not paying supplier C within 10 days of the invoice date, amounting to the discount of 2%. £1,000 × 2% = £20. The annual cost is then £16.60 + £20 = £36.60 per invoice.

Payment would need to be advanced by 2.67 months to get the discount.

Annualised percentage rate = £36.60/2,670 = 13.7%

The use of trade credit as a source of funds

Taking credit from suppliers is a normal feature of business. It is a source of short-term finance because it helps to keep working capital down. If the purchaser keeps to the terms of trade, it will be a cheap source of finance because in this situation suppliers rarely charge interest. However even in this situation there is some cost where settlement discounts are foregone, as in the case of Supplier C above. In this case the cost can be estimated using the formula:

$$\frac{d}{100-d} \times \frac{365}{t}$$

where   d   is the size of the % discount (in this case, 2)

   t   is the reduction in the payment period in days which would be necessary to obtain the early payment discount (in this case, 30 − 10 = 20)

The cost of forgoing the discount is therefore 37.2%.

The situation is different when credit periods taken regularly **exceed the terms of trade**. Many suppliers now impose a cost for the additional credit taken, as demonstrated above, and this should be compared with the cost of alternative short-term sources of funds to ensure that the cost of trade credit is not in fact greater than that of other funds. There are also further disadvantages to taking long credit periods, including the following.

- The company's credit rating will be reduced.

- It may be difficult to obtain additional credit from suppliers.

- The company may rank behind other customers due to its payment record if shortages of materials arise.

- The goodwill between the company and its suppliers will be eroded. This may damage the business in other ways, for example, it may be difficult to get extra goods at short notice.

- Extra administrative costs will arise from the fact that suppliers will be continually chasing for payment.

- Staff morale may be eroded if those who are regularly deal with suppliers feel that they are unable to do an efficient job due to the payment policy in place.

In general therefore, it is recommended that trade credit should be used judiciously as a source of finance, but it is inadvisable for a variety of reasons greatly to exceed suppliers' terms on a regular basis.

The merits of standard terms of trade

The introduction of standard terms of trade for suppliers has a number of merits.

- It greatly simplifies the administrative processes for dealing with supplier invoices

- It makes cash flow forecasting more straightforward.

- If the terms are communicated clearly to suppliers and formally agreed, the relationship between customer and supplier will be smoother, and the number of payment queries reduced.

However, it is important that the terms are both reasonable and flexible and not imposed unilaterally. Possible problems that could arise include the following.

- There will always be some suppliers for whom different terms will be required, for example, telephone accounts normally have to be settled within ten days, and there must be procedures for dealing with these situations.

- The company must ensure that it does not forego valuable settlement discount opportunities in the process. Where such opportunities exist, they must be evaluated in financial terms, and the system must be able to deal with earlier payments if necessary.

- There must be procedures in place to ensure that even within the policy, credit opportunities are maximised, for example, credit notes should be taken immediately where they relate to earlier invoices, and not also held for the standard credit period.

53   OVERDRAFT

Pass marks. Be careful to make the calculations in relation to credit customers only and not to total sales. Show clearly how the ratios have been calculated. When making recommendations, take into account the objectives of the firm. You may wish to comment on the practicalities of your recommendation.

The three options are evaluated below as (a) and (b) respectively.

(a)   (i)   The first step is to calculate the forecast level of credit sales for 20X5:

£4,850,000 × 70% = £3,395,000

If it is assumed that the closing debtors figure is representative of the 'normal' level of debtors, then the average collection period can be found.

£850,000 ÷ (£3,395,000/365) = 91.4 days

If 50% of the customers take advantage of the discount scheme, the average debtor days will fall to:

(91.38 ÷ 2) + (10 ÷ 2) = 50.7 days.

Thus the average level of debtors will fall to:

(£3,395,000/365) × 50.7 = £471,580.

This represents a reduction of £378,420.

The **financial effect of the proposal** can now be evaluated.

	£
Reduction in interest costs on overdraft	
£378,420 × (11% − 5% + 4%)	37,842
Reduction in level of bad debts	24,000
Cost of discount	
£3,395,000 × 50% × 1.5%	(25,462)
Total annual savings	36,380

By the end of the first year, the overdraft should have fallen to £565,000 − £378,420 − £36,380 = £150,200.

(ii)   The **current ratio**, if no action is taken, is projected as:

$$\frac{£455,000 + £850,000}{£550,000 \ + \ £565,000} = 1.17$$

Under these proposals it would improve to:

$$\frac{£455,000 + £471,580}{£550,000 \ + \ £150,200} = 1.32$$

As calculated above, the debtor days would fall from 91.4 to 50.7 days.

(b) (i)   The factor would enable 90% of the debtors to be converted into cash, thus releasing capital amounting to:

£850,000 × 90% = £765,000

This would give rise to a cash surplus of £765,000 – £565,000 = £200,000. If it is assumed that these funds can be invested at, say base + 3% ie 9%, the financial effect of this proposal can be estimated as follows.

	£
Saving in overdraft interest	
£565,000 × 10%	56,500
Interest on cash surplus	
£200,000 × 9%	18,000
Saving in administration costs	65,000
Factor's commission	
£3,395,000 × 90% × 2%	(61,110)
Finance charge	
£765,000 × 11%	(84,150)
Net cost of proposals	(5,760)

By the end of the first year, the cash surplus should therefore amount to £200,000 – £5,760 = £194,240.

(ii)   Assuming the cash surplus is treated as a current asset, the current ratio can be calculated as follows.

$$\frac{£455,000 + £194,240 \ + \ £85,000}{£550,000} = 1.33$$

The appropriate average debtor days would become:

£85,000 ÷ (£3,395,000/365) = 9.1

However, it could be argued that this ratio should be calculated in relation to the actual sales to which the remaining debtors relate, in which case the ratio would be unchanged at 91.4 days.

The preferred course of action to be taken by XYZ will depend on its detailed **financial circumstances** and the importance of the **ratios**. Assuming that the level of the ratios will not materially affect its cost of borrowing, the choice can be made on the basis of the impact of the various options on the total value of the firm. The first option is the one which maximises the total value, giving annual savings of £36,380, and it is therefore recommended that the discount scheme should be implemented.

However, this does assume that the projected effects on customer behaviour are realistic - that at least 50% of the customers will pay within 10 days and that the average collection period for those who do not opt for the discount is not longer than the existing average. It is also suggested that XYZ should encourage its customers to adhere more closely to their credit terms in the future.

54   **KESWICK PLC**

(a)   (i)   The net working capital of a business can be defined as its current assets less its current liabilities. The management of working capital is concerned with ensuring that sufficient liquid resources are maintained within the business. For the majority of businesses, particularly manufacturing businesses, trade creditors will form the major part of the current liabilities figure, and will be a significant element in the make-up of the working capital balance.

It follows that the **trade credit period** taken will be a major determinant of the working capital requirement of the company. This is calculated (in days) as the total value of trade creditors divided by the level of credit purchases times 365. The actual length of the period will depend partly on the credit terms offered by suppliers and partly on the decisions made by the company. For example, the company may choose to negotiate longer terms with its suppliers although this may be at the expense of any available settlement discounts.

A link can be made between working capital and liquidity by means of the **cash conversion cycle**. This measures the length of time that elapses between a firm paying for its various purchases and receiving payment for its sales. It can be calculated as the debtor days plus the stock period less the trade credit period, and it measures the length of time for which net current assets must be financed. This emphasises the important role of the trade credit period in the overall liquidity of the company.

(ii)   For many firms, trade creditors provide a very important source of short-term credit. Since very few companies currently impose interest charges on overdue accounts, taking extended credit can appear to be a very cheap form of short-term finance. However, such a policy entails some risks and costs that are not immediately apparent, as follows.

(1)   If discounts are being forgone, the **effective cost** of this should be evaluated - it may be more beneficial to shorten the credit period and take the discounts.

(2)   If the company gains a reputation for slow payment this will **damage its credit references** and it may find it difficult to obtain credit from new suppliers in the future.

(3)   Suppliers who are having to wait for their money may seek recompense in other ways, for example by raising prices or by placing a lower priority on new orders. Such actions could do **damage** to both the **efficiency and profitability** of the company.

(4)   Suppliers may place the company **'on stop'** until the account is paid. This can jeopardise supplies of essential raw materials which in turn could cause production to stop: this will obviously provide the company with a high level of unwanted costs.

(b) **Working capital cycle**

This can be defined as the debtor days plus the stock days less the creditor days:

Debtor days:	£0.4m × 365/£10m	14.6 days
Stock days:	£0.7m × 365/(£10m – £2m)	31.9 days
Creditor days:	£1.5m × 365/(£10m – £2m)	68.4 days
Working capital cycle		(21.9 days)

This is a remarkably short working capital cycle which suggests that Keswick is unusually efficient in its management of working capital. The effect of the proposal by the supplier would be to reduce the creditor period for 50% of the purchases from 68.4 days to 15 days. The new creditor days figure would therefore fall to:

$(68.4 \times 50\%) + (15 \times 50\%) = 41.7$ days

The working capital cycle will therefore rise to:

$14.6 + 31.9 - 41.7 = 4.8$ days

Interest cover

Interest cover can be defined as EBIT (earnings before interest and tax) divided by annual interest payments. The current figure for Keswick is four times (£2.0m/£0.5m) which for the majority of companies would be quite reasonable. The effect of the proposal made by the supplier will be to reduce the cost of sales, and therefore increase EBIT, but at the same time increase the level of interest since the company will have to finance the reduction in the working capital cycle. These elements can be calculated as follows.

Improvement in EBIT = $((£10m - £2m) \times 50\%) \times 5\% = £0.2m$

The net advanced payment to the supplier will be:

$((£10m - £2m) \times 50\%) -$ discount $(£0.2m) = £3.8m.$

This must be financed for an additional 53.4 days (68.4 – 15). If this is financed using the overdraft, the interest rate to be paid will be 12%, generating additional interest of £3.8m × 12% × 53.4/365 = £66,700.

The interest cover now becomes:

$(£2.0m + £0.2m)/(£0.5m + £0.0667m) = 3.88$ times

This represents only a very small reduction in the interest cover.

Profits after tax

These will change as follows.

	Before £'000	After £'000
Earnings before interest and tax	2,000	2,200
Interest	(500)	(566)
Taxable profit	1,500	1,634
Tax at 31%	465	507
Profit after tax	1,035	1,127

The proposal should give a small improvement in post-tax profit.

Earnings per share

Earnings attributable to equity have been calculated above (the profit after tax figure). The number of shares in issue is 4m (£1m/25p).

Existing EPS:	£1.035m/4,000,000m	=	25.9 pence
Projected EPS:	£1.127m/4,000,000m	=	28.1 pence

Thus, the EPS is also likely to improve if the proposals are adopted.

Return on equity

Return on shareholders' funds is calculated as profit attributable to equity divided by shareholders' funds (£2m):

Existing:	£1.035/£2m	=	50.25%
Projected:	£1.127/£2m	=	54.75%

The return on equity will also rise if the proposals are adopted.

Capital gearing

Capital gearing is defined as prior charge capital (in this case the bank overdraft of £3m) divided by shareholders' funds (£2m). The existing level of gearing is therefore 150% (£3m/£2m).

If the proposals are adopted, the average level of the overdraft will rise by £3.8m × 53.4/365 = £556,000. The gearing level will therefore increase to 178% (£3.556m/£2m).

Summary

In summary, the effect of the proposal would be to give a slight increase in the profitability of Keswick, as measured by profit after tax, earnings per share and return on equity, but this would be at the expense of a small reduction in the interest cover, a lengthening of the working capital cycle, and a significant increase in the level of capital gearing. It is this final item that gives the greatest cause for concern - to have such a high gearing level based totally on overdraft finance which is repayable on demand is a very dangerous position to be in. It is suggested that Keswick should either attempt to renegotiate its terms with the supplier to give a longer credit period than that being proposed, or alternatively seek to restructure its debt and to convert at least a part of the overdraft into more secure long-term borrowings.

55   FENTON SECURITY PLC

> **Pass marks.** In (a) (i) you will find it helpful to tabulate the calculation of the average collection period, as the 75 day collection period must be split. In (a) (i) you needed to state clearly your assumptions regarding the treatment of bad debts since no specific instructions are given.

(a)   The current position is as follows:

Average collection period

	% value (a)	Av days (b)	(a) x (b)
	5	30	150
	28	45	1,260
	10	60	600
	30	75	2,250
	16	90	1,440
	11	120	1,320
Total	100		7,020

Working capital requirement

Working capital requirement	=	Sales × collection period/365
	=	£67.5m × 70.2/365
	=	£12,982,192

Total funding cost

Funding cost	=	£12.982m × 12%
	=	£1.558m
Add cost of bad debts		£2m
Total funding cost	=	£3.558m

(i) The early settlement discount would **reduce the amount of sales income** by £67.5m × 50% × 1% = £0.3375m

The revised sales income will therefore be £67.163m

The new average collection period can be found as follows.

% value (a)	Av days (b)	(a) x (b)
5	30	150
28	30	840
10	30	300
7	30	210
23	75	1,725
16	90	1,440
11	120	1,320
100		5,985

Average collection period	=	59.85 days
Working capital requirement	=	Sales × collection period/365
Funding cost	=	£11.012m × 12%
Add: cost of bad debts		£2m

	£m
Total funding cost	3.321
Add: cost of discount	0.338
Total cost of proposals	3.659

Adoption of the discount scheme would increase Fenton's annual costs by £0.101m per year.

The scheme should not be introduced.

(ii) Reducing the debtor days by 20 would **reduce the working capital requirement** as follows:

Reduction in overall debt	=	£67.5m × 20/365
Reduction in funding cost	=	£3.699 × 12%
Reduction in bad debts	=	£2.0m × 50%
	=	£1.0m
Cost of service	=	£67.5m × 1%

Total savings = £0.444m + £1.0m – £0.675m = £0.769m

Use of the debt collection service would reduce Fenton's annual costs by £0.769m. This is mainly due to the large reduction in bad debts promised by the service. Fenton should therefore take up this proposal.

(b) Methods that Fenton could use to help reduce the current level of bad debts include the following.

Obtain bank and trade references

One **bank** and two **trade references** should be investigated and followed up with phone calls if necessary. However both sources may be unwilling to give their own customers a bad reference.

Use credit reference agency

Credit reference agencies can be used to check creditworthiness. They may provide a more objective reference or credit rating than that provided by trade or bank sources, but may be using information (statutory accounts) that is some months old.

Visit potential customer

For large potential customers, a **visit** should be made to assess the security of the business.

Compare with other customers

The company may be able to compare key characteristics of the potential customer with other customers, perhaps by using some sort of credit scoring system.

Clarify credit policy

All staff involved should clearly **understand** the credit rules that apply. **Regular checks** should be made to ensure that the policy is being implemented correctly. Particular attention should be given to the **setting** of credit limits, with **management approval** being required for higher than normal levels of credit.

(c) **Invoice discounting** is a method of **raising finance** from the **debtors' ledger**. The invoice discounter does not take over the administration of the client's sales ledger, and the arrangement is purely to secure an **advance of cash**. The discounter will offer to **purchase selected invoices** and **advance** up to 75% of their value. The balance of the purchase price, less charges, will be paid over once the customer has settled the invoices.

Advantages

(i) It is a source of **off balance sheet finance** that can be used to meet one-off requirements.

(ii) **Working capital requirements** are **reduced** and cash flow is improved.

Disadvantages

(i) The service is relatively **expensive**, a typical monthly rate being 1% of the value of the invoices being discounted.

(ii) The discounter will normally only offer the service **with recourse**, the client remaining liable for bad debts. Therefore the risk of bad debts remains.

(iii) The discounter will normally only accept invoices to **customers** with a **good credit rating**. This means that the amount of finance available will depend on the quality of the client's debtors.

Paper 4

Finance

IFIN

INSTRUCTIONS TO CANDIDATES

> *You are allowed three hours to answer this question paper.*
>
> *Answer the ONE question in section A (consisting of twenty sub-questions).*
> *Answer THREE questions ONLY in section B.*

DO NOT OPEN THIS PAPER UNTIL YOU ARE READY
TO START UNDER EXAMINATION CONDITIONS

SECTION A - 40 MARKS

ANSWER ALL TWENTY SUB-QUESTIONS IN THIS SECTION: TWO MARKS EACH

Each of the sub-questions numbered from 1.1 to 1.20 inclusive, given below, has only one right answer.

REQUIREMENT:

*On the SPECIAL ANSWER SHEET provided at the end of this question, place a circle 'O' around the letter (either **A, B, C** or **D**) that gives the right answer to each sub-question.*

If you wish to change your mind about an answer, block out your first attempt and then encircle another letter. If you do not indicate clearly your final choice, or if you encircle more than one letter, no marks will be awarded for the sub-question concerned.

1.1 Which of the following criteria does not form part of the 'value for money' concept used to measure performance in not-for-profit organisation?

- **A** Economy
- **B** Equity
- **C** Efficiency
- **D** Effectiveness

1.2 An arrangement whereby a company's share obtain a quotation and listing on The Stock Exchange, and most of the shares that are made available are bought by a small number of institutional investors (such as pension funds and insurance companies), is known as

- **A** A placing
- **B** An offer for sale
- **C** A prospectus issue
- **D** A Stock Exchange introduction

1.3 Mr Stowe has just received a legacy of £50,000. He intends to invest this to provide himself with an income in retirement. Which of the following factors will be the most important in his choice of appropriate investments?

- **A** Security
- **B** Liquidity
- **C** Return
- **D** Growth prospects

1.4 Mr Flynn holds shares in two different companies. There is a correlation coefficient of −0.9 in their returns. Which of the following combinations of product types is it most likely that are involved?

- **A** Ski-wear and beach balls
- **B** Umbrellas and waterproof clothing
- **C** Bakery and vacuum cleaners
- **D** Cars and bicycles

1.5 Which of the following could be described as a risk-free investment?

- **A** Local Authority deposits
- **B** Clearing bank deposits
- **C** Government stocks
- **D** Shares in 'blue chip' companies

1.6   In portfolio theory, which of the following elements measures the extent to which return exceeds the risk free rate of return?

   A   The standard deviation of expected returns.
   B   A weighted average of expected returns on portfolio investments.
   C   The beta factor.
   D   The correlation coefficient of expected returns.

1.7   For AMZ plc, earnings and interest payments are constant in perpetuity. All prices are ex-divided or ex-interest with payments made annually. The firm has 100 million shares issued and fully paid at a nominal value of 25p and a market price of 120p. The dividends per share are 24p. The issued debt consists of £160m (nominal value) in non-redeemable loans with a coupon rate of 6%. The debt is currently traded at £50 per £100 nominal. The rate of corporation tax is 35%.

   What is the firm's weighted average cost of capital?

   A   5.1%
   B   10.8%
   C   13.0%
   D   15.1%

1.8   A company's 5% irredeemable preference shares (or £1 each) have a market price of 65p. The company is paying corporation tax at a rate of 40%. What is the cost of preference share capital.

   A   3.0%
   B   4.6%
   C   5.0%
   D   7.7%

1.9   Shown below are recent statistics relating to the ordinary shares of Calc plc, a quoted company.

   Last year's net dividend   5p
   Average annual growth rate of dividends   10%
   Dividend cover   2.4
   Price earnings ratio   8

   The company calculates its cost of equity capital using the net dividend growth valuation model.

   The cost of Calc's equity capital is

   A   13.8%
   B   15.2%
   C   15.7%
   D   23.8%

1.10   Quinton plc maintains a ratio of retained earnings to dividends of 1:3. Its summarised profit and loss account for the year ended 31 December 20X5 was as follows.

	£'000
Profit before tax	500
Taxation	(100)
	400
Dividends on ordinary shares	(300)
Retained earnings	100

   The shareholders' equity is £4,500,000.

   What is the dividend growth rate per annum, computed via the Dividend Valuation model?

A	3.70%
B	2.96%
C	2.78%
D	2.22%

1.11 Which of the following theories can be used to account for the yield curve?

A	Market segmentation theory
B	Liquidity preference theory
C	Expectations theory
D	All of theories A, B and C

1.12 Which of the following is not relevant to the decision about whether to borrow over the short term or long term?

A	The purpose of the borrowing
B	The dates at which current debt matures
C	The security available as collateral
D	Possible future government restrictions on lending

1.13 Camilla is thinking about taking out an endowment fund. Her mortgage is £150,000 and is repayable in 20 years time. She does, however, wish to remove £10,000 from the fund in 5 years time in order to pay for a conservatory in her back garden. This will be removed immediately after making the 60th payment. This will leave £5,000 in the fund which, together with the further instalments, will grow to the £150,000 required.

What would be the monthly payment into the fund after the withdrawal of the £10,000 if the nominal interest rate was 18% per annum (work to the nearest £)?

A	£85
B	£103
C	£156
D	£201

1.14 Company F and Company G have current ratios of 0.9 and 2.5 respectively. If each company then makes a purchase of stock on credit what will be the effect on the current ratio of each company;

	Company F	*Company G*
A	Increase	Increase
B	Increase	Decrease
C	Decrease	Increase
D	Decrease	Decrease

1.15 A retailing company earns a gross profit margin at 37.5% on its monthly sales of £20,000.

In order to generate additional working capital, the following changes are proposed.

	Present	*Proposed*
Stock turnover period	1.5 months	1.0 month
Trade creditor payment period	1.0 month	1.3 months

What increase or decrease in working capital will arise at the end of the month in which these changes take place?

A	£13,750
B	£10,000
C	£6,250
D	£2,500

1.16 Which one of the following may be thought of as a stock holding cost?

A   Disruption of production schedules
B   Loss of customer goodwill
C   Shipping and handling costs
D   Stock obsolescence

1.17 The working capital of a company consists of stocks, debtors, cash or bank overdraft and creditors. The following turnover ratios apply.

Debtors	90 days
Stocks	72 days

Assume a 360 day year. Stocks are valued at 50% of sales value.

The ratio of creditors to debtors is 0.8, and during a year when sales turnover was £2,000,000 (achieved at an even monthly rate) the current ratio declined to 1.4 at 31 December. The liquid ratio (or acid test ratio) at 31 December was

A   1.00
B   1.05
C   1.25
D   1.50

1.18 When a company expands too rapidly, it might start overtrading. A symptom of overtrading is

A   High ratio of current assets: current liabilities
B   High ratio of current assets: proprietors' capital
C   Low ratio of current assets: annual sales
D   Shorter credit given by trade creditors

1.19

CY Low Phones Ltd
Extracts from annual accounts

	£
Stock: Raw material	250,000
Work in progress	115,000
Finished goods	186,000
Purchases	1,070,000
Cost of goods sold	1,458,000
Sales	1,636,000
Debtors	345,000
Trade creditors	162,000

On the basis of these figures, the length of the working capital cycle (operating cycle) is

A   182 days
B   193 days
C   210 days
D   293 days

1.20 Pointer Law Ltd is a manufacturing company. It purchases materials each month, and holds them in store for two months before they enter production. The production cycle is one month. Finished goods are held for about three months before sale. Three months credit is taken from suppliers.

Sales are expected to be £100,000 in January, rising by £10,000 per month through the year. Material costs amount to 50% of sales.

The budgeted cash payments for materials in June is

A	£60,000
B	£65,000
C	£90,000
D	£95,000

Total Marks = 40

BPP PUBLISHING

SPECIAL ANSWER SHEET FOR SECTION A

1.1   A   B   C   D

1.2   A   B   C   D

1.3   A   B   C   D

1.4   A   B   C   D

1.5   A   B   C   D

1.6   A   B   C   D

1.7   A   B   C   D

1.8   A   B   C   D

1.9   A   B   C   D

1.10   A   B   C   D

1.11   A   B   C   D

1.12   A   B   C   D

1.13   A   B   C   D

1.14   A   B   C   D

1.15   A   B   C   D

1.16   A   B   C   D

1.17   A   B   C   D

1.18   A   B   C   D

1.19   A   B   C   D

1.20   A   B   C   D

SECTION B – 60 MARKS

ANSWER THREE QUESTIONS ONLY FROM SECTION B

---

2   A number of investigations have been undertaken into the use made by shareholders of the annual reports of companies in which they have invested. Several of these show that the annual report is regarded as an important source of information for making decisions on equity investment.

Other types of study indicate that the market price of the shares in a company does not react in the short term to the publication of the company's annual report.

How would you reconcile these findings with each other, and with the efficient market hypothesis?

Total Marks = 20

---

3   The following financial information is available for Konjic.

	20X6	20X7	20X8	20X9
Earnings attributed to ordinary shareholders	£200m	£225m	£205m	£230m
Number of ordinary shares	2,000m	2,100m	2,100m	1,900m
Price per share	220p	305p	290p	260p
Dividend per share	5p	7p	8p	8p

Assume that share prices are as at the last day of each year.

REQUIREMENTS:

(a) Calculate Konjic's earnings per share, dividend yield, dividend cover and price/ earnings ratio. Explain the meaning of each of these terms and why investors use them. What limitations may they have? **8 Marks**

(b) Give possible explanations for the changes that have occurred in the figures calculated in (a) above over the past four years. **8 Marks**

(c) State briefly why you think that in most capital markets dividend yields are less than bond yields, despite their relative risks. **4 Marks**

Total Marks = 20

---

4   **(a)** Explain the advantages and disadvantages to a company of paying suppliers by using an electronic funds transfer system instead of cheques by post. **5 Marks**

(b) The treasurer of a local government department is reviewing her cash management procedures. She plans to introduce the use of cash management models and has asked you to investigate their applicability to the department. The following information is available.

(i)   The department has agreed with its bank that it will maintain a minimum daily cash balance of £15,000. Severe financial penalties will apply if this balance is not maintained.

(ii)   A forecast of daily cash movements for the next twelve months shows a standard deviation of daily cash flows of £3,000.

(iii)   The daily interest rate is at present 0.0236% and this is not expected to change for the foreseeable future.

(iv)   The transaction cost for each sale or purchase is £25.

Assume you are a newly recruited accountant in the department.

REQUIREMENTS:

Write a report to the treasurer which discusses:

(i)   The advantages and disadvantages of cash management models over more traditional methods of cash forecasting, making specific reference to their applicability to a public sector organisation such as a local authority **6 Marks**

(ii)   How one such model, the Miller-Orr, would operate in practice, using the information given above. Your report should include calculations of the upper and lower limits for cash balances and the return point. Assume a spread of £26,820. **9 Marks**

Total Marks = 20

---

5   PCB plc manufacture printed circuit boards for use in pocket calculators. It is now December 20X8. Since the year 20X5 business has been expanding very rapidly and the company has now encountered a liquidity problem, as illustrated by the most recent balance sheets reproduced below.

PCB company balance sheets

	As at 30 November 20X8 £	As at 30 November 20X7 £
Fixed assets	308,000	264,000
Current assets		
Stock	220,000	95,000
Debtors	210,000	108,000
Cash	Nil	1,750
	430,000	204,750
Current liabilities		
Bank	158,000	41,250
Trade creditors	205,000	82,500
Net current assets	67,000	81,000
Capital and reserves		
Issued share capital	18,000	18,000
Reserves	357,000	327,000
Equity		
Shareholders' funds	375,000	345,000

Other information

1.   Sales for the year to 30 November 20X7 were £1.7 million, yielding a gross profit of £330,000, and a net profit before tax of £82,000.

2.   The corporation tax rate is 30%.

3.   For the year ending 30 November 20X7 dividends of £35,000 were paid out.

4.   At the beginning of the year to 30 November 20X8 the company bought some new manufacturing equipment and recruited six more sales staff.

5.   Sales for the year to 30 November 20X8 were £3 million, with a gross profit of £450,000, and net profit before tax of £60,000.

6.   Dividends payable for the year to 30 November 20X8 amounted to £12,000.

REQUIREMENTS:

(a)   Illustrating your answer with figures taken from the question, explain why it is not unusual for manufacturing companies to face a cash shortage when sales are expanding very rapidly.**4 Marks**

(b)   Explain why PCB plc has not increased its net profit, despite the large increase in sales between 20X7 and 20X8.   **4 Marks**

(c)   How has the mix of funding used by PCB changed between the two years, and what are the implications of such changes in terms of investor and creditor risks?   **6 Marks**

(d)   Suggest ways in which PCB might seek to resolve its current funding problems, and avoid the risks associated with overtrading.   **6 Marks**

Total Marks = 20

6   Burnsall plc is a listed company which manufactures and distributes leisurewear under the brand name Paraffin. It made sales of 10 million units world-wide at an average wholesale price of £10 per unit during its last financial year ending 30 June 20X5. In 20X5-X6, it is planning to introduce a new brand, Meths, which will be sold at a lower unit price to more price-sensitive market segments. Allowing for negative effects on existing sales of Paraffin, the introduction of the new brand is expected to raise total sales value by 20%.

To support greater sales activity, it is expected that additional financing, both capital and working, will be required. Burnsall expects to make capital expenditures of £20m in 20X5-X6, partly to replace worn-out equipment but largely to support sales expansion. You may assume that, except for taxation, all current assets and current liabilities will vary directly in line with sales.

Burnsall's summarised balance sheet for the financial year ending 30 June 20X5 shows the following.

Assets employed	£m	£m	£m
Fixed (net)			120
Current:			
Stocks	16		
Debtors	23		
Cash	6		
		45	
Current liabilities:			
Corporation tax payable	(5)		
Trade creditors	(18)		
		(23)	
Net current assets			22
Long-term debt at 12%			(20)
Net assets			122
Financed by			
Ordinary shares (50p par value)			60
Reserves			62
Shareholders' funds			122

Burnsall's profit before interest and tax in 20X4-X5 was 16% of sales, after deducting depreciation of £5m. The depreciation charge for 20X5-X6 is expected to rise to £9m. Corporation tax is levied at 33%, paid with a one-year delay. Burnsall has an established distribution policy of raising dividends by 10% pa. In 20X4-X5, it paid dividends of £5m net.

You have been approached to advise on the extra financing required to support the sales expansion. Company policy is to avoid cash balances falling below 6% of sales.

REQUIREMENTS:

(a) By projecting its financial statements, calculate how much additional *external* finance Burnsall must raise.

    Notes

    1   It is not necessary to present your projection in FRS 1 format.

    2   You may assume that all depreciation provisions qualify for tax relief.   **9 Marks**

(b) Evaluate the respective merits of *four* possible external long-term financing options open to Burnsall.   **11 Marks**

                                        Total Marks = 20

ANSWERS

DO NOT TURN THIS PAGE UNTIL YOU
HAVE COMPLETED THE MOCK EXAM

A PLAN OF ATTACK

Mock Exam 1 is made up of a mix of questions similar to those you should expect to meet in the exam itself. The mark allocations are the same as in the actual exam. There is a mix of numerical and non-numerical questions or part-questions in both Sections, and you should expect to find such a mix in the exam itself.

First things first

It will probably be best to **start with the objective test questions**. These make up a substantial 40 per cent of the marks for the *Finance* paper. Allow yourself **72 minutes** to do the objective test questions, to reflect the proportion of marks given to these questions in the exam itself. No more. You can always come back to them at the end of the exam if you have some spare time.

The next step

Now spend a good 5 minutes looking through Section B in detail working out which **three** optional questions to do and the order in which to attack the questions. Three out of five is not a very wide choice. If you're a bit worried about the paper, do the questions in the order of how well you think you can answer them.

Question 2 is a non-numerical question. It invites you to consider the efficient market hypothesis in the context of the information included in companies' annual reports. The **Pass marks** section at the beginning of our answer gives suggestions about how to structure the answer.

Question 3, on investor ratios, is partly numerical and partly non-numerical. In any question split into parts with separate mark allocations, you should take note of the split of marks and allocate your time and effort accordingly, allowing yourself 1.8 minutes per mark. The importance of providing explanations to the calculations in part (a) is clear from the 8-mark allocation for part (b). Although only four marks are available for part (c), it is essential that you leave yourself time to get as many of those four marks as possible, in a **brief** answer.

Question 4 covers aspects of cash payment methods and cash management models. Formulae for the Miller-Orr model are provided for you. Make sure that you are familiar with the range of formulae given to you, before entering the exam room. Then, you will know whether to consult the exam formulae in answering any particular question. Since part (b) of this question asks for a report, a report format is what you should provide. You could lose a couple of marks of you don't, and that could be the difference between passing and failing the exam.

Question 5 deals with working capital and overtrading. In part (c), remember that 'investors' in this context includes the providers of both debt and equity. In part (d), take account of of both internal and external sources of finance.

In **Question 6**, you need to calculate the shortfall of funds available for an expansion proposal. Before starting your answer, you should have noticed the mark split between parts (a) and (b). More marks are available for part (b) than part (a), so it is important not to over-run on time doing calculations, as you could be sacrificing more marks on the explanatory part (b) than you would be gaining by putting more time into the calculations. As a general rule, a **law of diminishing marginal returns** applies to effort spent on any particular task in an exam, as on other things: more marks are likely to be gained in the first minutes spent on the task than in later minutes spent on the same task.

Time allocation

Allocate your time strictly according to the marks for the question in total and then according to the parts of the question. And **take care to follow the requirements** exactly.

If you have allocated your time properly then you **won't have time on your hands** at the end of the exam. But if you find yourself with five or ten minutes to spare, you have the opportunity to **go back to the objective test questions** that you couldn't do or to **any parts of questions that you didn't finish** because you ran out of time.

Forget about the exam!

And don't worry if you found the paper difficult. More than likely other candidates will too. If this were the real thing you would need to **forget** the exam the minute you leave the exam hall and **think about the next one**. Or, if it's the last one, **celebrate**!

SECTION A

1.1 B   The 'Three Es' are economy, efficiency and effectiveness.

1.2 A   The most common methods of flotation are placings and offers for sale. Offers for sale are 'bigger' and all the shares are offered to the general investing public. Placings are 'smaller' and although some shares must be made available for the general investing public, most are 'placed' with a small number of institutional investors.

1.3 A   Since the investment is needed to provide a basic income in the future, security is important. Mr Stowe should be confident that the investments should at least maintain their capital value.

1.4 A   This is the combination most likely to have a high negative correlation, since demand for ski-wear is likely to peak when demand for beach balls is at a minimum, and vice versa. B is an example of positive correlation, in that returns are likely to respond in a similar way to given weather conditions. It is unlikely that there will be any correlation in the case of C and D.

1.5 C   It is extremely unlikely that the Government would default on any payment of interest and capital on its stocks, and these stocks can therefore be taken to be effectively risk free. Although the others are relatively low in risk, they are still not as secure as Government stocks.

1.6 C   A measures the risk of the portfolio.
B measures the expected return of a portfolio.
D measures the relationship between returns from different investments.

1.7 D $k_e = \dfrac{0.24}{1.20} = 20\%$ $V_E = \pounds120m$

$k_d = \dfrac{6 \times 0.65}{50} = 7.8\%$ $V_D = \pounds80m$

$\text{WACC} = \dfrac{0.2 \times 120 + 0.78 \times 80}{200}$

$= 15.12\%$

1.8 D $k_e = \dfrac{d}{P_o} = \dfrac{5}{65} = 7.7\%$.

(NB: Dividends are paid out of post-tax income.)

1.9 C $k_e = \dfrac{D_o(1+g)}{MV_e} + g$

Earnings $= 2.4 \times 5p = 12p$
$= 8 \times 12 = 96p$
$= \dfrac{5(1.1)}{96} + 0.1 = 15.7\%$

1.10 D $g = rb$

$r = \dfrac{\text{PAT}}{\text{Equity}} = \dfrac{400}{4,500} = 0.088$

$b = \,^1/_4$

$\therefore g = \dfrac{0.088}{4} = 2.22\%$

1.11 D   All three theories are relevant.

1.12 C   Collateral is relevant to the lender, while the other factors are relevant to the borrower.

1.13   A   Nominal rate = 18%
= 1.5% per month
EAR = $(1.015)^{12} - 1 = 19.562\%$
£5,000 left in fund and further amounts added:

$$150,000 - 5,000 \times 1.1956^{15} = X \left(\frac{1.015^{180} - 1}{0.015} \right)$$

∴ X = £85

1.14   B   F say $\frac{90}{100}$ G say $\frac{250}{100}$

Buy stock of 50 on credit

F now $\frac{140}{150}$ G now $\frac{300}{150}$

= 0.933   = 2.0

1.15   B   Cost of sales £12,500

Stock now   = 1.5 × 12,500 = £18,750
Creditors now = 1 × 12,500 = £12,500

Proposed

Stock   1 × 12,500 = £12,500
Creditors   1.3 × 12,500 = £16,250

	£
Stock decrease	6,250
Creditors increase	3,750
	10,000

1.16   D

1.17   A

	£
Debtors (90/360 × £2,000,000)	500,000
Stocks (72/360 × 50% × £2,000,000)	200,000
	700,000
Creditors (80% of £500,000)	400,000

The ratio of debtors plus stocks to creditors is 1.75, and since the current ratio is less 6than this, there must be a bank overdraft, B.

$$\frac{700,000}{400,000 + B} = 1.4, \text{ and so } B = 100,000$$

$$\text{Liquid ratio} = \frac{\text{Debtors} + \text{Cash}}{\text{Current liabilities}} = \frac{500,000}{400,000 + 100,000} = 1.0$$

1.18   B   Overtrading means trying to carry out an excessive volume of business for the size of the company's capital base (Answer B is a symptom of this). The current ratio (Answer A) is likely to be *low* with *long* periods of credit (Answer D) being taken from creditors.

1.19   A

	Days
Raw material stock turnover (250 ÷ 1,070 × 365 days)	85.3
Less creditors: average payment period (162 ÷ 1,070 × 365)	(55.3)
	30.0
Production cycle (WIP turnover) (115 ÷ 1,458 × 365)	28.8
Finished goods stock turnover (186 ÷ 1,458 × 365)	46.6
Debt collection period (345 ÷ 12,636 × 365)	77.0
Full operating cycle	182.4

1.20   C   In June, the payment will be for material purchases in March. These will relate to sales in September, which are expected to be £180,000.

Budgeted cash payment = 50% of £180,000 = £90,000.

SECTION B

2

> **Pass marks.** You should start by outlining the efficient market hypothesis in general, and you should then distinguish the three forms of the hypothesis.
>
> You should then identify the form of the hypotheses relevant to published information such as companies' annual reports.
>
> Finally, if you feel the form does not explain the observed facts set out in the question, consider whether another form, or some other facts, might do so.

The **efficient market hypothesis** describes an efficient market as one where security prices fully and speedily reflect available information: in other words, the market is efficient in terms of information processing. The result is the product of the actions of market participants actively competing with each other.

The content of any new information becoming available will be quickly digested by market participants and, if the information causes them to change their opinion of the security's intrinsic value, their subsequent actions will rapidly cause an equivalent change in the security's market price.

The hypothesis takes three forms depending upon the extent of the information deemed available to market participants.

(a)   **Weak form**. Information available is restricted to details of past share prices, returns and trading volumes. Hence future prices cannot be predicted from historical price data alone and trading rules based only on such price and volume data, ie the chartist approach, cannot consistently produce excess returns if the hypothesis is correct.

(b)   **Semi-strong form**. Share prices reflect all publicly available information. Reaction to public announcements will not produce excess returns as the information content of such announcements is reflected in share prices.

(c)   **Strong form**. Share prices reflect all information whether publicly available or not.

Since the question refers to published annual reports, it is the **semi-strong form** of the hypothesis that is in question.

This form of the hypothesis is in accord with the results of the first set of investigations, which indicated that the annual report is an important source of information for investment decisions, but appears to conflict with the studies which indicate that market prices of equity do not react in the short term to the publication of the annual report.

There are a **number of factors** which may explain the apparent discrepancy.

(a)   Much information contained in the annual report will already have been published in the financial press before the report appears.

(b)   If the strong form of the hypothesis is valid, share prices may be influenced by information which has not been published. Investors in possession of such information will take action accordingly and if they are large, for example institutional investors, their actions may influence the market price.

175

(c) It is possible that reactions to the annual report take time to affect share prices. This might be because time is needed to weigh up the contents of the report or because investors need time to gather together the funds necessary to give effect to their reactions. Studies based on the short term would then be inadequate as a guide to the effect of the annual report on market prices.

3

> **Pass marks.** In part (a) it is easy to compute the figures, but providing explanations, uses and limitations is a rush for the number of marks awarded. In part (b), avoid the tendency to simply repeat a description of your calculations. Use your imagination to think of *why* the various changes happened. The answer to part (c) is clear once you realise that dividend yield is usually only a fraction of the total yield on shares.

(a)

	Data:	*20X6*	*20X7*	*20X8*	*20X9*
1	Equity earnings (£m)	200	225	205	230
2	Number of shares (m)	2,000	2,100	2,100	1,900
3	Price per share (pence)	220	305	290	260
4	Dividend per share (pence)	5	7	8	8
	Solution:				
5	Earnings per share ($=1 \div 2$)	10.0p	10.7p	9.8p	12.1p
	Dividend yield ($= 4 \div 3$)	2.3%	2.3%	2.8%	3.1%
	Dividend cover ($= 5 \div 4$)	2.0	1.5	1.2	1.5 times
	Price/earnings ratio ($=3 \div 5$)	22.0	28.5	29.6	21.5 times

Earnings per share (eps) shows the amount of profit after corporation tax attributable to each ordinary share. Although a high eps generally indicates success, care must be taken in interpreting the trend in eps when there have been share issues, especially rights issues at heavily discounted prices or bonus issues, both of which result in a fall in eps. Similar problems are encountered when warrants or convertible loan stock are issued.

The **dividend yield** shows the ordinary dividend as a rate of return on the share value. The figures shown in this example are *after* basic rate income tax, whereas they are normally shown gross. The figure is of limited use because it shows only part of the return to the equity investor (see part (c)).

The **dividend cover** shows how many times bigger the eps is than the dividend per share. A high dividend cover shows that a large proportion of equity earnings is being reinvested for growth.

The **price/earnings ratio** (P/E ratio) shows how many times bigger the share price is than the eps. In general, the bigger the eps, the more the share is in demand, though care must be taken when making comparisons because whereas eps is a historical result, the share price is based on future expectations and is affected by both risk and growth factors. Consequently, abnormal results can often arise from a crude use of P/E ratios.

(b) In 20X7, **share capital was increased by 5%**, probably through a **rights issue**. Equity earnings increased more than proportionately, resulting in a 7% increase in eps, indicating a successful year. Demand for the company's shares rose swiftly, either because of a general stock market rise or because of high expectations of Konjic's future growth, and the share price rose by approximately 40%. This caused a big rise in P/E and allowed a 40% increase in dividend per share with no fall in dividend yield. The dividend cover fell, however, because the dividend increased much more than earnings.

The company's **earnings and EPS fell in 20X8**, either because of normal cyclical business risks or possibly because the high 20X7 dividend left insufficient cash for reinvestment. However, the company gave a 'bullish' signal to the market by increasing its dividend per share, indicating future prospects of a swift recovery and increased growth. As a result, the dividend yield increased and there although the share price fell in line with earnings, there was no disproportionate drop in demand for the company's shares, as shown by the stability of the P/E.

There was 12% **earnings growth** in 20X9. The company used some of its cash to buy back ordinary shares. This is possibly because it offered shareholders the choice between a cash and a scrip dividend. Share capital reduced by about 10%, resulting in a big increase in earnings per share. Although 20X9 was a successful year for earnings, demand for the company's shares fell, as shown by the drop in share price and P/E. It is possible that the market has become uncertain of the company's future plans, as a result of the share issue and share buy-back in quick succession.

(c) When making financial decisions, investors trade off **risk** and **return**. An investor will accept a lower rate of return on a fixed interest bond than on an equity share simply because the bond is less risky.

A **bond yield** represents the true rate of return which the investor receives on the bond, taking into account both interest and the eventual redemption value. Its correct name is the 'redemption yield' of the bond.

However, the **dividend yield** on a share is only a partial measure of the investor's return. The shareholder may also receive **gains** in the capital value of the share. Although not reflected in an immediate cash return, this growth in value reflects expectations of increased future dividends and can be realised if the share is sold. The more the company reinvests for future growth, the less cash is available for dividends and the lower the dividend yield. The dividend valuation model summarises the total return on a share as dividend yield + growth percentage.

Although shares provide higher long run rates of return than bonds, much of their returns are via capital growth, leaving limited cash for dividends, and it is not surprising that dividend yields are lower than bond yields.

4

> **Pass marks**. This question covers two important areas of cash management: electronic funds transfer systems and cash models for optimising cash balances. No detailed knowledge was expected of any of these areas but you were expected to provide a reasoned discussion of the advantages and disadvantages of the systems.

(a) **Electronic funds transfer systems** (EFTS) enable funds to be transferred between bank accounts on the same day. Examples in the UK include BACS (Bankers Automated Clearing System) and CHAPS (Clearing House Automated Payment System). International transfers can be made via SWIFT (Society for Worldwide Interbank Financial Telecommunications).

The usual alternative is payment by cheque or bankers draft, which results in delays as the documentation passes through the postal, banking and clearing systems.

From the payer's point of view, the advantages of EFTS are savings in processing time and paperwork and hence in administration costs.

The disadvantages to payers are as follows.

(i)   The prompt processing means here is no excuse for delayed payment (eg the postal system cannot be blamed) and hence there will possibly be an effective reduction in the free credit period and an increase in interest costs.

(ii)   If processing is carried out in batches, an urgent request for payment by one customer may cause a whole batch of payments to be made early, again resulting in an increased interest cost.

(b) To: The Treasurer
     From: A N Recruit, Accounts   Date: 15 May 20X2
     Subject: Cash management models

(i)   **Cash management models** take into account the trade-off between the rate of return which can be earned on surplus funds and the need to maintain liquidity. For example, a company will need to keep a certain amount of cash in a non-interest or low-interest current account in order to meet known and expected liabilities. If, however, the balance in this account becomes unnecessarily high, the company is losing the interest which could be earned by transferring the funds to a higher interest deposit account or other form of investment.

For our department, this is particularly important as the more we can earn in additional interest the more we have to spend on the local community. Local authorities are increasingly being asked to demonstrate efficiency and effective use of resources and one of our largest resources is cash.

Cash management models effectively regard surplus cash as a form of stock. Stock management models attempt to minimise the sum of stock-holding costs, stock ordering costs and stock-out costs. Equivalent costs can be identified for cash balances. The cash model which is closest to the 'Economic Order Quantity' stock model is the Baumol model, but this is unrealistic in that it assumes that cash is used up at an even rate.

(ii)   The **Miller-Orr model**, illustrated below, is more useful because it deals with receipts and payments of cash and provides trigger points for transferring cash to and from investment accounts when the current account balance becomes too high or low respectively. It does, however, make an unrealistic assumption that cash flows are entirely unpredictable.

We have already agreed with our bank that the minimum balance on our current account will be £15,000. This is referred to as the 'lower limit'. Thus when the balance falls to that level we will need to transfer money out of the investment account into the current account. To compute the 'upper limit' the Miller-Orr model uses three data items:

- The transaction cost for each cash transfer in or out of the account: £25
- The variance of daily cash flows: $(£3,000)^2 = £9,000,000$
- The daily interest rate on invested cash: 0.0236%

Using these items of data it can be shown that the 'spread' between the upper and lower limits is £26,820. This means that the upper limit is £15,000 + £26,820 = £41,820. When the current account reaches this high level, money will be transferred out into the investment account.

The final question is how much needs to be transferred in and out when the lower and upper limits are reached. The Miller-Orr model sets the 'return point' at a figure one third of the way between the upper and lower limits.

The return point is £15,000 + $\frac{1}{3}$ × £26,820 = £15,000 + £8,940 = £23,940.

In summary, then, when the balance falls to £15,000, £8,940 is transferred into the account to bring it up to £23,940. When the balance rises to £41,820, £17,880 is transferred out of the account to return the balance to £23,940.

Signed: AN Recruit

Pass marks. You do not need to compute the spread in this question because it is given to you. However, future questions might not be so generous! Using the formula for the Miller-Orr model, the spread is $3\left(\dfrac{\frac{3}{4}\ TV}{R}\right)^{1/3}$ where T is the transaction cost, V is the variance of daily cash flows and R is daily interest rate. Hence the spread is

$$3\left(\dfrac{\frac{3}{4}\times25\times9,000,000}{0.000236\%}\right)^{1/3} = £26,827.$$

This is approximately the same as the spread given in the question.

5

Pass marks. This question requires an understanding of working capital and the causes and consequences of overtrading. There is plenty of information available in the example that you will find helpful to analyse and incorporate in your answer in order to provide a good illustration of the theoretical points that you make.

In part (c), don't forget that 'investors' in this context include the providers of both debt and equity.

In part (d), you should take into account both internal and external sources of finance.

(a)   Manufacturing companies generally have a relatively long operating cycle and a correspondingly large working capital requirement. When the level of sales increases, there is an increased investment in:

(i)   **Stock,** as additional raw materials are purchased to produce the additional goods.

(ii)   **Staff costs,** both direct in production, and indirect in sales and credit control overhead.

(iii)   **Debtors** since most manufacturing companies sell on credit, and additional sales will therefore translate into a higher level of debtors.

The company may also need to purchase equipment to increase its capacity. All of these areas require an immediate investment of cash, in advance of the cash flow benefits of the additional sales and operating profits being felt. Although the company may also benefit from an increased level of creditors, this will not be enough to offset the other factors, and therefore additional cash will be required to finance this process.

This problem can be illustrated using PCB as an example.

(i)   During the last year, sales have increased by £1.3m from £1.7m to £3m, an increase of 76%.

(ii)   There has been additional investment of £44,000 in fixed assets during the same period.

(iii)   The level of stock has more than doubled from £95,000 to £220,000.

(iv)   Debtors have increased by £102,000 from £108,000 to £210,000, an increase of 94%.

(v)   Six additional sales staff have been recruited.

(vi)   This has resulted in a massive increase in the bank overdraft of £116,750 from £41,250 to £158,000, and in the level of trade creditors, which has increased by nearly 150% from £82,500 to £205,000.

The cash resources at the start of the year were only £1,750, and the increased level of trading has been financed entirely from short-term bank borrowings and trade creditors.

(b)   The change in the trading position has been as follows.

	Y/e 30.11.X8		Y/e 30.11.X7		Change
Sales	3,000,000		1,700,000		+76%
Gross profit	450,000	15%	330,000	19%	+36%
Net profit before tax	60,000	2%	82,000	5%	−26%

Both gross and net margins have fallen.

Contributory factors

(i)   **Selling prices may have been reduced** to achieve the increase in sales. This will result in depressed gross margins.

(ii)   The additional investment in fixed assets will have led to an **increase in the depreciation charge**.

(iii)   **Interest costs will have increased** due to the higher level of bank borrowings.

(iv)   **Staff costs will have increased** because of the larger number of sales staff now employed.

(c)   It has been seen that there has been a large increase in the level of short-term borrowings in the form of bank loans and trade creditors. The ratio of equity: bank debt has fallen from 8.4 times (£345,000 ÷ £41,250) to 2.4 times (£375,000 ÷ £158,000), and the real level of reliance on debt is even higher if the increase in the level of trade creditors is taken into account.

In effect, PCB has financed its expansion wholly by using short-term debt. This is a dangerous position for the following **reasons.**

The company should **match long-term assets with long-term funds**. At present, both the increase in working capital and the increase in fixed assets are being financed out of short-term debt.

Although the use of trade creditors as a source of finance is attractive because there is rarely any interest charge, it is likely that PCB **is exceeding its terms of trade,** since the increase in the level of creditors is so much greater than the increase in the level of sales. It is therefore running the risk of losing the goodwill of its suppliers.

The current state of the funding means that, on the basis of the balance sheet figures, PCB may find it **hard to obtain additional credit** from existing or new suppliers. This is because of the high level of financial risk now being carried by the trade creditors who have no security for their credit.

There is **no information on the nature of any agreements** that PCB has with the bank over funding, or any indication as to the size of the overdraft limit. However, as the level of short-term funding increases, the bank will want to review the current and forecast trading situation with the company before increasing its stake in the company any further. It would be in the interest of both parties if the existing overdraft were replaced with some form of secured medium-term bank debt.

The current situation represents an **increase in the level of risk** carried by the equity shareholders. As the gearing increases, so the level of the interest charge will increase, and thus there will be greater volatility in the level of returns to equity, particularly if the business is cyclical in nature.

The current cash shortage also means that even if the company continues to be profitable, it will be difficult to sustain the level of dividend payments. This situation is already arising, since dividends have been cut drastically from £35,000 in 20X7 to £12,000 in 20X8.

(d) The main needs of PCB are to reduce its reliance on short-term debt and to ease its current cash shortage. This could be achieved in the **following ways.**

The short-term bank loan could be **converted to a longer-term loan** or debenture as discussed in (c) above.

The company could seek to **increase the level of equity investment**, which would reduce the level of gearing to a safer level. The exact means by which this should be achieved is difficult to specify, since it is not clear from the question whether PCB is a quoted or unquoted company.

It is possible that **additional funding in the form of venture capital** could be appropriate, given the fact that the company is growing. However, PCB would need to satisfy potential investors that it will be able to improve its earnings performance as well as its sales performance.

As has already been shown, certain elements of working capital have increased at a faster rate than the sales growth would appear to warrant. In particular, there appears to be scope for improving the control of stock and debtors. If both these elements were restricted to a 76% increase in line with the growth in sales, this would release over £72,000 of working capital. This would **reduce the need for additional external funding.**

6

> **Pass marks**. In part (a) the approach is to calculate the amount of additional working and fixed capital required, and then to compare this with the level of internally generated funds in order to establish the external financing requirement. You will need to make an assumption about the operating margin for 20X5/X6. In part (b) take into account the size and status of the company (ie listed) as well as the funds required when deciding on the appropriate financing alternatives.

(a) The first step is to calculate Burnsall's total additional financing requirement.

	£m
Existing working capital:	
Current assets	45
Creditors	(18)
	27
Additional working capital (+20%)	5.4
Additional fixed capital	20.0
Total	25.4

This can be met in part from internal sources as follows. It is assumed that the margin before depreciation will remain unchanged. The profit in 20X4/X5 before depreciation was £100m × 16% + £5m = £21m.

	£m
20X5/X6 profit before depreciation (£21m × 120%)	25.2
Less outflows:	
Interest (£20m × 12%)	(2.4)
Corporation tax (20X4/X5)	(5.0)
Dividends (£5m × 110%)	(5.5)
Net additional internal funds generated	12.3

Internally generated funds are therefore inadequate to finance the costs of expansion, there being a shortfall of £13.1m (£25.4m – £12.3m) which will have to be raised externally.

(b) Financing options include the following.

    (i)   **Leasing capital equipment.** Some of the new capital equipment could be acquired using some form of leasing agreement. This would have the added benefits that rental payments qualify for tax relief, and that the cost of the assets is spread more evenly over their useful life.

           Alternatively Burnsall could consider a sale and leaseback agreement on some of the assets that it already owns.

    (ii)   **Raising additional debt.** Since the gearing level at present is low at 16.4% (£20m/£122m) and the interest cover is good at 6.67 times (£16m/£2.4m), Burnsall could take on significant amounts of additional debt without too much risk.

           This could be in the form of a debenture or medium-term bank loan. It is likely that the rate of interest would have to be higher than that on the existing debt.

    (iii)   **Venture capital.** Burnsall is of a sufficient size and with growth prospects that should make it appropriate for some form of development capital from an organisation such as 3i.

           The venture capital company is likely to require an equity stake and a seat on the board in return for its investment and the directors must therefore accept that there is likely to be some loss of control.

    (iv)   **Raising additional equity.** Since Burnsall is already listed it has access to a wide range of investors. Given the size of the sum required this should be possible to attain by means of a rights issue at a discount to the current market price of the shares.

           Although the effect of this would be to reduce EPS and hence the market price, the wealth of the ordinary shareholders would be unaffected providing that the issue was well subscribed.

Other points. Other methods include:

(i)   Regional assistance, if available

(ii)   A mortgage on property

Paper 4

Pilot paper

Finance

IFIN

INSTRUCTIONS TO CANDIDATES

You are allowed three hours to answer this question paper.
Answer the ONE question in section A (consisting of twenty sub-questions). *Answer THREE questions ONLY from section B.*

DO NOT OPEN THIS PAPER UNTIL YOU ARE READY
TO START UNDER EXAMINATION CONDITIONS

SECTION A – 40 MARKS

ANSWER ALL TWENTY SUB-QUESTIONS IN THIS SECTION: TWO MARKS EACH

Each of the sub-questions numbered from 1.1 to 1.20 inclusive, given below, has only one right answer.

REQUIREMENT:

*On the SPECIAL ANSWER SHEET provided at the end of this question, place a circle 'O' around the letter (either **A, B, C, or D**) that gives the right answer to each sub-question.*

If you wish to change your mind about an answer, block out your first attempt and then encircle another letter. If you do not indicate clearly your final choice, or if you encircle more than one letter, no marks will be awarded for the sub-question concerned.

1.1   A yield curve shows the relationship between the yield and term to maturity for a number of financial assets, eg government stock. In theory, the yield curve will normally be upward sloping so that long-term financial assets offer a higher yield than short-term financial assets.

Which of the following best explains the reason for this?

A   Interest rates are expected to fall in the future.

B   Interest rates have been increased on a number of occasions in the past year in an attempt to combat high inflation.

C   The investor must be compensated for the additional risk to tying up money in the asset for a longer period to time.

D   The market prices of long-term financial assets will tend to be lower than for short-term financial assets.

1.2   The ordinary share price of NS plc is currently 150p. Dividends are paid once a year, and the dividend for the previous year has very recently been paid. The net dividend for the year was 3p and 15% annual growth rate is expected for dividend payments for the foreseeable future.

Using the dividend growth model, what is the cost of equity for NS plc?

A   2.4%
B   15.0%
C   17.0%
D   17.3%

1.3   The following data relates to shares of RB plc at the end of the day on 20 July 20X2.

Share price		Closing prices, 20 July		
High for year	Low for year	Selling price	Mid-market price	Buying price
330p	205p	280p	290p	300p

The earnings per share for the year to 31 January 20X2 were 20p

What is the P/E for the company that would be reported in the financial press on 21 July 20X2?

A   14.0
B   14.5
C   15.0
D   16.5

1.4   In certain circumstances the Stock Exchange may grant a quotation for a company, even though the company is not making any new shares or existing shares available to the market.

This method of obtaining a quotation is known as a:

A	Placing
B	Prospectus issue
C	Tender issue
D	Introduction

1.5   Which of the following is *not* true for a financial lease?

A	The lessee receives capital allowances for the asset.
B	The lease has a primary period which covers all or most of the useful economic life of the asset.
C	The lessee is responsible for servicing and maintenance of the asset.
D	The lessee records the leased asset as a fixed asset in its balance sheet.

1.6   SB plc has a published equity beta of 1.4. The expected return on three-month Treasury bills is 6%. The expected return on the market is 11%.

The cost of equity for SB plc may be estimated as:

A	11%
B	12.4%
C	13%
D	15.4%

1.7   Which of the following statements about certificates of deposits is *not* true?

A	Certificates of deposits are negotiable deposits issued by banks.
B	Certificates of deposits will typically have maturity periods of between one months and five years.
C	Certificates of deposits are non-negotiable.
D	Certificates of deposits are issued in bearer form.

1.8   AC Ltd is a new company, whose directors have approached its bank for financial assistance. The bank has asked for draft profit and loss balance sheet information to support the request for finance. The only information the directors have available is an estimate of sales for the first year, together with some industry averages for the current year.

Industry averages	
Cost of sales to sales	50%
Sales to capital employed	2.5 times
Fixed assets to capital employed	70%
Current ratio	1.5:1
Estimated sales for the year	£760,000

In the draft balance sheet for AC Ltd, what would be the total of current assets?

A	£91,200
B	£182,400
C	£273,600
D	£570,000

1.9   PB Ltd uses 2,500 units of component X per year. The company has calculated that the cost of placing and processing a purchase order for component X is £185, and the cost of holding one unit of component X for a year is £25.

What is the economic order quantity (EOQ) for component X, and assuming a 52-week year, what is the average frequency at which purchase orders should be placed?

	EOQ	*Frequency of orders*
A	136 units	3 weeks
B	136 units	6 weeks
C	192 units	4 weeks
D	192 units	5 weeks

1.10 BACS (Bankers Automated Clearing Services) is an example of an electronic funds transfer system.

Which of the following best describes the system?

A   Provides same-day settlement for large sums of money

B   Is mostly concerned with processing payrolls and transactions involving standing orders and direct debits

C   Is a network for rapid transmission of international remittances between participating banks

D   Requires cheques to be completed to ensure settlement of a transaction

---

1.11 Which one of the following statements about the efficiency markets hypothesis is *false*?

A   The strong form of the hypothesis implies that it is possible to predict changes in share price.

B   The strong form of the hypothesis implies that share prices will reflect all available information that could possible affect the share price.

C   The semi-strong form of the hypothesis implies that share prices will reflect information such as earning forecasts and announcements of acquisitions.

D   The semi-strong form of the hypothesis implies that it is not worthwhile for an investor to study company reports and try to achieve superior terms.

1.12 ABC plc and DEF plc are listed companies in the same country. Their P/E ratios and share prices are shown below.

	P/E ratio	*Current share price ex div*
ABC plc	8	£5.00
DEF plc	12	£3.90

Which of the following statements will best explain the higher P/E ratio of DEF plc?

A   DEF plc is a much larger company that ABC plc.
B   DEF plc is regarded as a higher risk investment than ABC plc.
C   DEF plc has higher earnings per share growth prospects than ABC plc.
D   DEF plc retains a higher proportion of its annual post-tax profits than ABC plc.

1.13 A company maintains a minimum cash holding of £1,000. The variance its daily cash flows has been measured as £250,000. The transaction cost for each sale or purchase of treasury bills is £20. The daily interest rate is 0.025% per day and is not expected to change in the foreseeable future. Using the Miller-Orr cash management model, the maximum cash holding level would be:

A   £1,594
B   £2,594
C   £7,400
D   £8,400

1.14 The following information relates to the ordinary shares of BC plc.

Earnings per share	50p
Dividend cover	2.5
Published dividend yield	3.2%

The price of BC plc's ordinary shares implied by the data above is:

A   78p
B   153p
C   625p
D   3,906p

1.15   The projected profit and loss account of SD plc for the year to 30 June 20X1 shows the following figures.

	£ '000
Operating profit	100
Interest payable	40
Profit before tax	60
Corporation tax (30%)	18
Profit after tax	42

The directors of SD plc estimate that the additional purchase of new equipment on 1 July 20X0 for £140,000 would increase the projected profit for the year by £18,000. The machine would be financed by a loan raised on 1 July 20X with a coupon rate of 5%.

What would the projected interest cover for the company become if the directors purchased the new machine?

A   0.66
B   0.94
C   2.13
D   2.51

1.16   If £1,700 is invested at an interest rate of 9% per annum, compounded monthly, the sum it will give in three years' time is:

A   £1,738
B   £2,159
C   £2,202
D   £2,225

1.17   Which of the following is *not* a method used for raising finance to fund export sales?

A   Bills of exchange
B   Credit insurance
C   Documentary credits
D   Countertrade

1.18   Which of the following statements about warrants is incorrect?

A   Warrants are a device sometimes offered by a company to its ordinary shareholders, or attached to a loan issue as part of a package.

B   Warrants are sometimes issues by investment trusts in a bid to compensate investors for the discount to net asset backing at which the shares often trade.

C   Warrants have a fixed life, and once this has expired, the warrant may be sold back to the issuing company at the nominal value of the ordinary shares.

D   Warrants offer no income, but give the holder the right to apply for the ordinary shares of the company at a fixed price.

1.19   A company has cash outgoings of £1,260,000 per annum, spread evenly throughout the year. The interest rate on Treasury Bills is 8% per annum, and every sale of Treasury Bills costs £20. According to the Baumol cash management model, the optimum amount of Treasury Bills to be sold each time cash is replenished is:

A   £7,937
B   £17,748
C   £25,100
D   £88,741

1.20 Which of the following statements about venture capital is correct?

A   Venture capital would not be appropriate to finance a management buyout.

B   Venture capital organisations may provide loan finance as well as equity finance to a company.

C   Secured medium-term bank loans are a form of venture capital.

D   Companies with a stock market quotation would have no difficulty raising finance from a venture capital organisation.

Total Marks = 40

SPECIAL ANSWER SHEET FOR SECTION A

1.1	A	B	C	D
1.2	A	B	C	D
1.3	A	B	C	D
1.4	A	B	C	D
1.5	A	B	C	D
1.6	A	B	C	D
1.7	A	B	C	D
1.8	A	B	C	D
1.9	A	B	C	D
1.10	A	B	C	D
1.11	A	B	C	D
1.12	A	B	C	D
1.13	A	B	C	D
1.14	A	B	C	D
1.15	A	B	C	D
1.16	A	B	C	D
1.17	A	B	C	D
1.18	A	B	C	D
1.19	A	B	C	D
1.20	A	B	C	D

190

SECTION B – 60 MARKS

ANSWER THREE QUESTIONS ONLY FROM SECTION B

2   The finance director of KM plc has recently reorganised the finance department following a number of years of growth within the business, which now includes a number of overseas operations. The company now has separate treasury and financial control departments.

REQUIREMENTS:

(a)   Describe the main responsibilities of a treasury department, and comment on the advantages to KM plc of having separate treasury and financial control departments.   **14 Marks**

(b)   Identify the advantages and disadvantages of operating the treasury department as a profit centre rather than a cost centre.   **6 Marks**

Total Marks = 20

3   SF Ltd is a family-owned private company with five main shareholders.

SF Ltd has just prepared its cash budget for the year ahead, details of which are shown below. The current overdraft facility is £50,000 and the bank has stated that it would not be willing to increase the facility at present, without a substantial increase in the interest rate charged, due to the lack of assets to offer as security.

The shareholders are concerned by the cash projections, and have sought advice from external consultants.

All figures, £'000	J	F	M	A	M	J	J	A	S	O	N	D
						Month						
Collections from customers	55	60	30	10	15	20	20	25	30	40	55	80
Dividend on investment	—	—	—	—	—	10	—	—	—	—	—	—
Total inflows	55	60	30	10	15	30	20	25	30	40	55	80
Payments to suppliers		20		20		25		28		27		25
Wages and salaries	15	15	15	15	15	20	20	15	15	15	15	15
Payments for fixed assets			2		5	10		15				
Dividend payable				25								
Corporation tax									30			
Other operating expenses	5	5	5	5	7	7	7	7	7	7	8	8
Total outflows	20	40	22	65	27	62	27	65	52	49	23	48
Net in or (out)	35	20	8	(55)	(12)	(32)	(7)	(40)	(22)	(9)	32	32
Bank balance (overdraft)												
Opening	20	55	75	83	28	16	(16)	(23)	(63)	(85)	(94)	(62)
Closing	55	75	83	28	16	(16)	(23)	(63)	(85)	(94)	(62)	(30)

The following additional information relating to the cash budget has been provided by SF Ltd.

   (i)   All sales are on credit. Two months' credit on average is granted to customers.

   (ii)   Production is scheduled evenly throughout the year. Year-end stocks of finished goods are forecast to be £30,000 higher than at the beginning of the year.

   (iii)   Purchases of raw materials are made at two-monthly intervals. SF Ltd typically takes up to 90 days to pay for goods supplied. Other expenses are paid in the month in which they arise.

   (iv)   The capital expenditure budget comprises:

Office furniture	March	£2,000
Progress payments on building extensions	May	£5,000
Car	June	£10,000
New equipment	August	£15,000

REQUIREMENT:

Assume you are an external consultant employed by SF Ltd. Prepare a report for the board advising on the possible actions it might take to improve its budgeted cash flow for the year, and consider the possible impact of these actions on the company's business. Your report should also identify possible short-term investment opportunities for the cash surpluses identified in the first part of the budget year.

20 Marks

4   The summarised balance sheet of D plc at 30 June 20X9 was as follows.

	£'000	£'000
Fixed assets		15,350
Current assets	5,900	
Creditors falling due within one year	(2,600)	
Net current assets		3,300
9% debentures		(8,000)
		10,650
Ordinary share capital (25p shares)		2,000
7% preference shares (£1 shares)		1,000
Share premium account		1,100
Profit and loss account		6,550
		10,650

The current price of the ordinary shares is 135p ex dividend. The dividend of 10p is payable during the next few days. The expected rate of growth of the dividend is 9% per annum. The current price of the preference shares is 77p and the dividend has recently been paid. The debenture interest has also been paid recently and the debentures are currently trading at £80 per £100 nominal. Corporation tax is at the rate of 30%.

REQUIREMENTS:

(a)   Calculate the gearing ratio for D plc using:

(i)   Book values
(ii)   Market values   **4 Marks**

(b)   Calculate the company's weighted average cost of capital (WACC), using the respective market values as weighting factors.   **6 Marks**

Assume that D plc issued the debentures one year ago to finance a new investment.

(c)   Discuss the reasons why D plc may have issued debentures rather than preference shares to raise the required finance.   **4 Marks**

(d)   Explain what services a merchant bank may have provided to D plc in connection with the raising of this finance.   **6 Marks**

Total Marks = 20

---

5   ABC Ltd is a small manufacturing company which is suffering cash flow difficulties. The company already utilises its maximum overdraft facility. ABC Ltd sells an average of £400,000 of goods per month at invoice value, and customers are allowed 40 days to pay from the date of invoice. Two possible solutions to the company's cash flow problems have been suggested.

- **Option 1** The company could factor its trade debts. A factor has been found who would advance ABC Ltd 75% of the value of its invoices immediately on receipt of the invoices, at an interest rate of 10% per annum. The factor would also charge a service fee amounting to 2% of the total invoices. As a result of using the factor, ABC Ltd would save administration costs estimated at £5,000 per month.

- **Option 2** The company could offer a cash discount to customers for prompt payment. It has been suggested that customer could be offered a 2% discount for payments made within ten days of invoicing.

REQUIREMENTS:

(a)   Identify the services that may be provided by factoring organisations.   **4 Marks**

(b)   Calculate the annual net cost (in £) of the proposed factoring agreement.   **6 Marks**

(c)   Calculate the annualised cost (in percentage terms) of offering a cash discount to customers.
                                                                                                                  3 Marks

(d)   Discuss the relative merits of the two proposals.   **7 Marks**

Total Marks = 20

6   **(a)**   KB plc has a paid-up ordinary share capital of £1,500,000 represented by 6 million shares of 25p each. It has no loan capital. Earnings after tax in the most recent year were £1,200,000. The P/E ratio of the company is 12.

The company is planning to make a large new investment which will cost £5,040,000, and is considering raising the necessary finance through a rights issue at 192p.

REQUIREMENTS:

(i)   Calculate the current market price KB plc's ordinary shares.   **2 Marks**

(ii)   Calculate the theoretical ex-rights price, and state what factors in practice might invalidate your calculation.   **6 Marks**

(iii)   Briefly explain what is meant by a deep-discounted rights issue, identifying the main reasons why a company might raise finance by this method.   **3 Marks**

(b)   As an alternative to a rights issue, KB plc might raise the £5,040,000 required by means of an issue of convertible loan stock at par, with a coupon rate of 6%. The loan stock would be redeemable in seven years' time. Prior to redemption, the loan stock may be converted at a rate of 35 ordinary shares per £100 nominal loan stock.

REQUIREMENTS:

(i)   Explain the term *conversion premium* and calculate the conversion premium at the date of issue implicit in the data given.   **4 Marks**

(ii)   Identify the advantages to KB plc of issuing convertible loan stock instead of the rights issue to raise the necessary finance.   **5 Marks**

Total Marks = 20

ANSWERS

DO NOT TURN THIS PAGE UNTIL YOU
HAVE COMPLETED THE MOCK EXAM

A PLAN OF ATTACK

What's the worst thing you could be doing right now if this was the actual exam paper? Sharpening your pencil? Wondering how to celebrate the end of the exam in 2 hours 59 minutes time? Panicking, flapping and generally getting in a right old state?

Well, they're all pretty bad! But what you should be doing is spending a good **5 minutes looking through the paper in detail**, working out which questions to do and the order in which to attempt them. So turn back to the paper and let's sort out a **plan of attack**.

First things first

It's usually best to **start with the objective test questions**. You'll always be able to do some of them, even if you really haven't done as much preparation as you should have done. There is a mix of numerical and non-numerical questions. And answering even a couple of them will give you the confidence to attack the rest of the paper. **Don't even look at the other questions before doing Section A.** If you see something you don't recognise or which you don't think you can do, you'll only panic! Allow yourself **72 minutes** to do the objective test questions. No more. You can always come back to them at the end of the exam if you have some spare time.

The next step

Now move on to make your choice of **three questions** from **Section B**.

Question 2 deals with the role and management of the treasury function which forms one of the key elements of section (i) of the syllabus: **The finance function.** You are asked to comment on the advantages of establishing a separate treasury function, and the advantages and disadvantages of operating this function as a profit centre.

Question 3 deals with analysis of cash-flow forecasts. The question tests for your ability to evaluate working capital control and cash management techniques, and asks you to consider the possible impact of their suggested actions on the business. The question is drawn mainly from section (iv) of the syllabus: **Working capital management,** but also draws from topic areas in section (iii) of the syllabus: **Sources of short-term finance,** as the question also asks you to consider opportunities for investing short-term cash surpluses.

Question 4 is aimed at testing gearing ratios, the cost of capital and the role of merchant banks in connection with an issue of new finance. It asks you to discuss why a particular form of financing might be preferred. The topics covered here are from section (ii) of the syllabus: **Sources of long-term finance** and section (i): **The finance function.**

Question 5 requires you to summarise the services provided by factoring organisations and to calculate the net cost of a particular factoring agreement. The question also tests knowledge of alternative methods of managing debtors, requiring the calculation of cash discounts and an evaluation of cash discounts as against factoring. This question is drawn from topics within section (iv) of the syllabus: **Working capital management.**

Question 6 tests knowledge of two potential long-term sources of finance. The question asks candidates to carry out relevant calculations for both sources, to discuss the advantages of issuing convertible loan stock rather than making a rights issue, and to briefly explain what is meant by a deep-discounted rights issue. The question is drawn from topic areas in section (ii) of the syllabus: **Sources of long-term finance.**

No matter how many times we remind you....

Always **allocate your time** according to the marks for the question in total and then according to the parts of the question. And **always follow the requirements** exactly.

You've got spare time at the end of the exam.....?

If you have allocated your time properly then you **shouldn't have time on your hands** at the end of the exam. But if you find yourself with five or ten minutes to spare, **go back to the objective test questions** that you couldn't do or to **any parts of Section B questions that you didn't finish** because you ran out of time.

Forget about it!

And don't worry if you found the paper difficult. More than likely other candidates will too. If this were the real thing you would need to **forget** the exam the minute you leave the exam hall and **think about the next one**. Or, if it's the last one, **celebrate**!

SECTION A

1.1   C

1.2   D $K_e = \dfrac{d_1}{P_0} + g = \dfrac{3(1.15)}{150} + 0.15 = 0.173$, or 17.3%.

1.3   B $\dfrac{\text{Mid-market price}}{\text{EPS}} = \dfrac{290p}{20p} = 14.5$

1.4   D

1.5   A

1.6   C $K_e = R_f + (R_m - R_f)\beta$
        $K_e = 0.06 + (0.11 - 0.06)\,1.14 = 0.13$ or 13%

1.7   C

1.8   C   Capital employed: $^{760,000}/_{2.5}$ £304,000
        Fixed assets: £304,000 × 70%   £212,800
        Working capital   £91,200

    Current assets (CA) – Current liabilities (falling due within one year) (CL) = £91,200

    CA   = 1.5CL
    ∴ CL   = £182,400
    and CA = £273,600

1.9   C $EOQ = \sqrt{\dfrac{2C_0 D}{C_h}}$

    Economic order quantity = $\sqrt{\dfrac{2 \times 185 \times 2,500}{25}} = 192$ units

    Frequency of ordering = $\dfrac{192}{2,500} \times 52$ weeks = 4 weeks

1.10   B

1.11   A

1.12   C

1.13   D   Spread = $3 \times \left(\dfrac{\frac{3}{4} \times 20 \times 250,000}{0.00025}\right)^{1/3} = £7,400$

    Upper limit = £7,400 + £1,000 = £8,400

1.14   C   Dividend cover = $\dfrac{\text{EPS}}{\text{DPS}}$ ∴ DPS = $\dfrac{50}{2.5} = 20p$

    Dividend yield = $\dfrac{\text{DPS}}{\text{MPS}}$ ∴ MPS = $\dfrac{20}{0.032} = 625p$

1.15   D   Operating profit will increase by £18,000

    Interest payable will increase by £140,000 × 5% = £7,000

    Interest cover = $\dfrac{\text{Profit before interest payable}}{\text{Interest payable}} = \dfrac{£118,000}{£47,000} = 2.51$

1.16   D $V = X(1 + r)^n = 1,700\,(1 + 0.0075)^{36} = £2,225$

1.17   B

1.18 C

1.19 C   Optimal sale $= \sqrt{\dfrac{2 \times 1,260,000 \times 20}{0.08}} = £25,100$

1.20 B

SECTION B

2

> **Pass marks**. This question requires a factual knowledge of the role of the treasury department and the ways in which this function may be managed within the company. To answer it well, you should also take account of the specific circumstances of KM plc.

(a) Treasurership has been defined as 'the function concerned with the provision and use of finance. It includes provision of capital, short-term borrowing, foreign currency management, banking, collections and money market investment'.

The main responsibilities of the treasury function include:

(i) **Liquidity management**

- Working capital and money transmission management
- Banking relationships and arrangements
- Money management

This involves making sure that the organisation has the liquid funds it needs and invests any surplus funds, even for very short terms. The treasurer should maintain a good relationship with one or more banks to ensure that negotiations are as swift as possible, and that rates are reasonable.

(ii) **Funding management**

- Funding policies and procedures
- Sources of funds
- Types of funds

Funding management is concerned with all forms of borrowing, and alternative sources of funds, such as leasing and factoring.

(iii) **Currency management**

- Exposure policies and procedures
- Exchange dealing, including futures and options
- International monetary economics and exchange regulations

(iv) **Corporate finance**

- Equity capital management
- Business acquisitions and disposals
- Project finance and joint ventures

(v) **Corporate taxation**

(vi) **Risk management and insurance**

(vii) **Pension fund investment management**

The financial control function is concerned with determining whether the various activities of the organisation are meeting their financial objectives. This function will therefore be interested in a wide variety of stakeholder relationships, for example, with customers, suppliers and employees. By contrast, the treasury function is mainly concerned with the relationship of the company to the providers of finance. In a geographically dispersed company such as KM plc, it is likely that financial control functions will exist at a variety of local levels, while the treasury department will be centralised at the head office. The advantages of having a specialist treasury department include the following.

(i) Centralised liquidity management avoids having a **mix of cash surpluses and overdrafts in different localised bank accounts,** particularly in a company such as KM plc, which now includes a number of overseas operations.

(ii) **Bulk cash flows** are possible, allowing lower bank charges to be negotiated.

(iii) **Larger volumes of cash** are available to invest, giving better **short-term** investment opportunities.

(iv) Any borrowing can be arranged in **bulk,** at **lower interest rates** than for smaller borrowings.

(v) **Foreign currency risk management** should be improved, with matching of cash flows in different subsidiaries being possible. This means that there should be less need to use expensive hedging instruments such as option contracts. This is particularly valuable in a company such as KM plc where there are a number of overseas operations.

(vi) A specialist department can employ **staff with a greater level of expertise** than would be possible in a local, more broadly based, finance department.

(vii) Centralisation will allow the company to benefit from the use of **specialised cash management software.**

(viii) Access to treasury expertise should improve the quality of **strategic planning and decision making.**

(b) The **advantages** of operating the treasury department as a **profit centre** rather than a **cost centre** include the following.

(i) This approach recognises the fact that some companies are able to make **significant profits** from their treasury activities. Treating the department as a profit centre may make treasury staff more motivated to achieve the best possible return for the company.

(ii) If it is treated as a profit centre, the department will have to **charge for its services** to other parts of the organisation. This may make the subsidiaries more aware of the true cost of the services they use, and encourage them to use the department more efficiently.

The main **disadvantages** are as follows.

(i) Treasury staff may be tempted to **speculate,** and to ignore the risk criteria that they should be using.

(ii) **Internal charging** may mean that **some subsidiaries go outside the organisation** for treasury services and thus reduce the overall benefit to the organisation of having a centralised treasury function.

(iii) **Performance evaluation** may be difficult, since the success of the function may sometimes involve the avoidance of costs rather than the maximisation of profits.

(iv) **Administrative costs** may be increased.

3

> **Pass marks**. Read the question carefully – this is a small family owned private company, not a large plc listed on the Stock Exchange. Your suggestions should be reflect this and be ones which such a company might reasonably be expected to adopt.
>
> Make an assessment of the underlying profitability of the business and try to understand in your own mind the key reasons for the cash-flow problems before starting to propose possible solutions.

To: Board of Directors, SF Ltd

From: External consultant

Date: 12 November 20X1

Subject: Cash flow budget

Introduction

The budget shows that the company will experience a positive cash position for the first quarter of the year, there being a net inflow of cash during this time as well as no use of the overdraft facility. However, thereafter the position deteriorates, with the company being forecast to exceed its overdraft limit from August to November. By the end of the year, the company's cash reserves will be £50,000 lower than at the start of the period.

Possible remedial actions

1   **Production scheduling.** Sales show a cyclical movement, with receipts from customers being highest during the winter months. However, production is scheduled evenly throughout the year. If production could be scheduled to match the pattern of demand, the cash balance would remain more even throughout the year. Any resulting increase in the overall level of production costs could be quantified and compared with the savings in interest costs to assess the viability of such a proposal.

2   **Reducing the debt collection period.** SF Ltd currently allows its customers two months' credit. It is not known how this compares with the industry norms, but it is unlikely to be excessive. However, there may be some scope for reducing the credit period for at least some of the customers, and thereby reducing the average for the business as a whole.

3   **Tightening the credit control procedures.** It is not known what level of bad debts is incurred by SF Ltd, but even if it is low, tightening up the credit control and debt collection procedures could improve the speed with which money is collected.

4   **Factoring the sales ledger.** The use of a factor to administer the sales ledger might reduce the collection period and save administration costs. An evaluation of the relevant costs and benefits could be undertaken to see whether it is worth pursuing this option.

5   **Reduce the stockholding period.** At present it is forecast that stocks will be £30,000 higher by the end of the year. This represents three months' worth of purchases from suppliers. It is not clear to what extent this increase is predicated upon increasing sales, although since the building is being extended it is assumed that there will be some increase in the level of production and sales in the near future. However, the size of the increase seems excessive.

6   **Increase the credit period taken.** Since SF Ltd already takes 90 days credit, it is unlikely that it will be able to increase this further without jeopardising the relationship with its suppliers.

7   **Defer payment for fixed assets**

Presumably the purchase of the office furniture could be deferred, although the sums involved are relatively insignificant.

The progress payment on the building extension is likely to be a contractual commitment that cannot be deferred.

The purchase of the car could reasonably be deferred until the cash position improves. If it is essential to the needs of the business, the company could consider spreading the cost through some form of leasing or hire purchase agreement.

It is not clear why the new equipment is being purchased. Presumably some form of investment appraisal has been undertaken to establish the financial benefits of the acquisition. However, if it is being purchased in advance of an increase in production then it may be possible to defer it slightly. The company could also look at alternative methods of financing it, as have been suggested in the case of the car.

8   **Dividend.** SF Ltd is a private company, and therefore the shareholders could agree to forego or defer the dividend. The practicality of this will depend on the personal situation of the five shareholders.

9   **Defer the corporation tax payment.** This might be possible by agreement with the Inland Revenue. The company should consider the relative costs of the interest that would be charged if this were done, and the cost of financing the payment through some form of debt.

10   **Realise the investment.** The dividend from this is £10,000, and therefore assuming an interest rate of, say, 5%, it could be worth in the region of £200,000. It is not clear what form this takes or for what purpose it is being held, but it may be possible to dispose of a part of it without jeopardising the long-term strategic future of the business.

11   **Inject additional long-term capital.** The budget assumes that both fixed and working capital will increase by £30,000 during the year, and the directors should therefore consider seeking additional long term capital to finance at least the fixed asset acquisitions. Possible sources of capital include:

- Injection of funds from the existing shareholders
- The use of venture capital
- Long-term bank loan, debenture or mortgage

Conclusions

It can be seen that there are a number of avenues that SF could explore. It appears that the company is fundamentally profitable, given the size of the corporation tax bill, and the fact that were it not for the fixed asset additions and the investment in stock the cash balance would increase by £10,000 during the year. However, the liquidity issues must be addressed now to avoid exceeding the overdraft limit.

The company should also consider investing its cash surpluses during the first quarter of the year to earn at least some interest, although this will be restricted by the short periods for which funds are likely to be available . Possible investments include:

- Bank deposits
- Short-term gilts
- Bills of exchange

SECTION C

4

> **Pass marks**. This question requires the calculation of gearing ratios and weighted **average** cost of capital for a company that includes both preference shares and debentures in **its** capital structure. You should be careful in your treatment of these items and **explain your** reasoning. As always with gearing calculations, you must state the formula you **are using** since more than one approach is possible.
>
> In section (c) you should consider the needs of investors as well as the position **of the** company, since these will be relevant in ensuring the success of the issue.

(a) The gearing ratio can be calculated using the following expression:

$$\text{Gearing} = \frac{\text{Prior charge capital}}{\text{Prior charge capital} + \text{equity}}$$

(i) Using book values, prior charge capital includes:

	Book value
	£'000
9% debentures	8,000
7% preference shares	1,000
	9,000
Equity:	
Ordinary share capital	2,000
Share premium account	1,100
Profit and loss account	6,550
	9,650

$$\text{Gearing} = \frac{9,000}{9,000 + 9,650} = 48.3\%$$

(ii) Using market values, prior charge capital includes:

	Market value
	£'000
9% debentures @ 80p per £1	6,400
7% preference shares @ 77p per £1	770
	7,170

Equity:

Ordinary shares @ £1.35 per 25p nominal value	10,800

$$\text{Gearing} = \frac{7,710}{7,170 + 10,800} = 39.9\%$$

(b) The weighted average cost of capital (WACC) can be found using the **following** expression:

$$\text{WACC} = k_e \frac{V_E}{V_E + V_D} + k_d \frac{V_D}{V_E + V_D}$$

where:

k_e	= cost of equity
k_d	= cost of debt (after tax)
V_E	= market value of equity in the firm
V_D	= market value of debt in the firm

In this case, there are three sources of capital to be included. k_d and V_D will **therefore** be replaced by k_p (cost of preference shares) and P (market value of **preference shares),** and k_g (cost of debentures) and G (market value of debentures).

The next step is to calculate the cost of the different sources of capital in D plc:

Cost of equity (k_e)

This can be found using the dividend growth model:

$$k_e = \frac{d(1+g)}{P} + g$$

where:

d = current level of dividends
g = dividend growth rate in perpetuity
P = current market price of equity

$$k_e = \frac{10(1+0.09)}{135} + 0.09$$

$$k_e = 17.1\%$$

Cost of preference shares (k_p)

This can be found by dividing the preference dividend rate by the market price of the shares:

$$k_p = \frac{7}{77}$$

$$k_p = 9.1\%$$

Although preference shares are included with prior charge capital, the dividend is not allowable for tax, and therefore no adjustment needs to be made for this.

Cost of debentures (k_g)

The after tax cost of the debentures can be found using the following expression:

$$k_g = \frac{I(1-t)}{P}$$

where:

I = rate of debenture interest
P = market price of debentures
t = rate of corporation tax

$$k_g = \frac{9(1-0.3)}{80}$$

$$k_g = 7.9\%$$

The WACC can now be calculated:

$$\text{WACC} = \frac{(17.1 \times 10,800)}{17,970} + \frac{(9.1 \times 770)}{17,970} + \frac{(7.9 \times 6,400)}{17,970}$$

$$\text{WACC} = 13.5\%$$

(c) Possible reasons why D plc may have chosen to raise additional finance using debentures rather than preference shares include the following.

(i) Debentures are a cheaper form of finance than preference shares because debenture interest is tax deductible, unlike preference dividends.

(ii) Debentures are more attractive to investors because they are secured against the company's assets.

(iii) Debenture holders rank before preference shareholders in the event of a liquidation.

(iv) Issue costs should be lower for debentures than for preference shares.

(d)   **Services of a merchant bank in this situation**

(i)   Advice on the most appropriate form of capital to be raised, ie equity or debt

(ii)   Advice on the precise form that the issue of debt should take, for instance, whether it should be secured, and if so, against which assets; whether the issue should be made more attractive to investors by the use of devices such as warrants

(iii)   Advice on the price at which the issue should be made

(iv)   Advice on the coupon rate and term of the debenture

(v)   Identifying appropriate investors and marketing the issue

(vi)   Administration of the issue, including making sure that the terms of the issue comply with statutory and regulatory requirements

5

> **Pass marks**. This question requires you to calculate the cost of the two proposals in different ways, one being an actual annual cost, and the other an annualised percentage. This means that you cannot make a clear comparison of the two on cost terms on the basis of these calculations.
>
> It is unusual to have to calculate the annualised percentage cost of offering a cash discount. However, this is not difficult if you apply your knowledge of compounding. If your calculator is not capable of raising numbers to larger powers you can approximate the rate, as explained in the suggested solution.

(a)   A factor normally manages the debts owed to a client on the client's behalf.

Services provided by factoring organisations

(i)   **Administration** of the client's invoicing, sales accounting and debt collection service.

(ii)   **Credit protection** for the client's debts, whereby the factor takes over the risk of loss from bad debts and so 'insures' the client against such losses. The factor usually purchases these debts 'without recourse' to the client, which means that if the client's debtors do not pay what they owe, the factor will not ask for the money back from the client.

(iii)   **'Factor finance'** may be provided, the factor advancing cash to the client against outstanding debts. The factor may advance up to 85% of approved debts from the date of invoice.

(iv)   A **confidentiality agreement** may be offered to conceal the existence of the arrangement from customers.

(b)   It will be assumed that the factor finance will not be replacing any existing credit lines, and therefore the full interest cost of the agreement will be relevant when determining the cost of factoring.

Annual sales are £400,000 × 12 = £4.8m

Daily sales are £4.8m/365 = £13,151

The annual cost of factoring can now be found:

	£
Interest (£13,151 × 40 days × 75% × 10%)	39,452
Service fee (£4.8m × 2%)	96,000
Total annual charge	135,452
Less internal cost savings (£5,000 × 12)	60,000
Net annual cost	75,452

(c) The first stage is to calculate the monthly cost in percentage terms. Assuming that all customers take up the discount, each month the company would receive a cash inflow after ten days of £392,000 (£400,000 x 98%), and would forego a cash inflow after forty days of £400,000. If 'r' is the percentage cost of this, the situation can be expressed as follows:

$$392,000 = \frac{4000,000}{1+r}$$

$$r = 2.04\%$$

This is the cost of offering the discount over a 30 day period (40 days minus ten days). There are 12.17 (365/30) of these periods in a year.

The period rate can be converted into an annual rate (Ra) using the following expression:

$$(1 + Ra) = (1 + \text{periodic rate})^{\text{number of periods in year}}$$
$$(1 + Ra) = (1 + 0.0204)^{12.17}$$
$$(1 + Ra) = 1.2786$$
$$Ra = 27.9\%$$

The true cost of the cash discount is therefore **27.9% per annum**.

Pass marks. If you cannot calculate to the power of 12.17, you could estimate the solution as $(1.0204)^{12} = 27.4\%$. Alternatively, once the monthly rate has been found, the annual rate could be approximated as follows:

$$Ra \approx 2.04 \times 365 \div 30$$
$$Ra \approx 24.8\%$$

(d) **Key issues in the discounting option**

The proposal is expensive. The company should be able to get cheaper overdraft finance than this, and longer-term debt should cost even less.

The company may need to offer a discount in order to make its terms competitive with other firms in the industry.

The level of take-up among customers is uncertain, and will affect the cash flow position.

Problems may arise when customers take both the discount and the full forty day credit period. This will increase administrative costs in seeking repayment.

Key issues in the factoring option

The factor may be able to exercise better credit control than is possible in a small company.

The amount of finance that will be received is much more certain than for the discounting option *less* 75% of the value of the invoices will be provided immediately.

The relationship with the customers may deteriorate due partly to the reduction in the level of contact with the company, and partly to the historical view of the factor as the lender of last resort.

Conclusion

The final decision must take into account all the above issues. However, the **most important points** to consider are the ability of each proposal to meet the financing requirements, and the relative costs of the different sources of finance.

6

> **Pass marks**. This is a relatively simple question that tests your knowledge of the theory surrounding rights issues and convertibles. When considering in (a)(ii) the likely price following the rights issue, you should take into account external market factors as well as the performance of the company.

(a) (i) The current market price can be found by multiplying the earnings per share (EPS) by the price/earnings (P/E) ratio.

EPS is £1.2m/6m = 20 pence per share
P/E ratio is 12
Market price of shares is 12 × 20p = **£2.40 per share**

(ii) In order to raise £5,040,000 at a price of 192 pence, the company will need to issue an additional 2,625,000 (£5,040,000/£1.92) shares.

Following the investment, the total number of shares in issue will be 8,625,000 (6,000,000 + 2,625,000).

At this point, the total value of the company will be:

(6m × £2.40) + £5,040,000 = £19,440,000

The theoretical ex-rights price will therefore be £19.44m/8.625m = **£2.25.**

The **following factors** might invalidate this in practice.

(1) The costs of arranging the issue have not been included in the calculations.

(2) The market view of the quality of the new investment will affect the actual price of the company's shares.

(3) If the issue is not fully subscribed and a significant number of shares remain with the underwriters, this will depress the share price.

(4) The effect of the new investment on the risk profile of the company and the expected future dividend stream could also cause the share price to differ from that predicted.

(5) The price of the shares depends not only on the financial performance of the company, but also on the overall level of demand in the stock market. If the market moves significantly following the announcement of the issue, this will affect the actual price at which the shares are traded.

(iii) In a **deep-discounted** rights issue, the new shares are priced at a large discount to the current market price of the shares. The purpose of this is to ensure that the issue is well subscribed and that shares are not left with the underwriters, and thus this form of issue pricing is attractive when the stock market is particularly volatile. However, the shares cannot be issued at a price which is below their nominal value.

The main drawback to this approach is that a larger number of shares will need to be issued in order to raise the required amount of finance, and this will lead to a larger dilution of earnings per share and dividends per share.

(b) (i) The **conversion premium** is the difference between the issue value of the stock and the conversion value as at the date of issue. In other words it is the measure of the additional expense involved in buying shares via the convertible stock as compared with buying the shares on the open market immediately.

In this case, £100 loan stock can be converted into 35 ordinary shares. The effective price of these shares is therefore £2.86 (£100/35) per share.

The current market price of the shares is £2.40. The conversion premium is therefore £2.86 – £2.40 = **46 pence**. This can also be expressed in percentage terms as **19%** (0.46/2.40).

(ii)   The **advantages** to KB plc of **issuing convertible loan stock** as compared with a rights issue include the following.

(1)   Convertibles should be cheaper than equity because they offer greater security to the investor. This may make them particularly attractive in fast growing but high-risk companies.

(2)   Issue costs are lower for loan stock than for equity.

(3)   Interest on the loan stock is tax deductible, unlike dividends on ordinary shares.

(4)   There is no immediate change in the existing structure of control, although this will change over time as conversion rights are exercised.

(5)   There is no immediate dilution in earnings and dividends per share.

BPP PUBLISHING

Mathematical tables and exam formulae

PRESENT VALUE TABLE

Present value of £1 ie $(1+r)^{-n}$ where r = interest rate, n = number of periods until payment or receipt.

Periods					Interest rates (r)					
(n)	1%	2%	3%	4%	5%	6%	7%	8%	9%	10%
1	0.990	0.980	0.971	0.962	0.952	0.943	0.935	0.926	0.917	0.909
2	0.980	0.961	0.943	0.925	0.907	0.890	0.873	0.857	0.842	0.826
3	0.971	0.942	0.915	0.889	0.864	0.840	0.816	0.794	0.772	0.751
4	0.961	0.924	0.888	0.855	0.823	0.792	0.763	0.735	0.708	0.683
5	0.951	0.906	0.863	0.822	0.784	0.747	0.713	0.681	0.650	0.621
6	0.942	0.888	0.837	0.790	0.746	0.705	0.666	0.630	0.596	0.564
7	0.933	0.871	0.813	0.760	0.711	0.665	0.623	0.583	0.547	0.513
8	0.923	0.853	0.789	0.731	0.677	0.627	0.582	0.540	0.502	0.467
9	0.914	0.837	0.766	0.703	0.645	0.592	0.544	0.500	0.460	0.424
10	0.905	0.820	0.744	0.676	0.614	0.558	0.508	0.463	0.422	0.386
11	0.896	0.804	0.722	0.650	0.585	0.527	0.475	0.429	0.388	0.350
12	0.887	0.788	0.701	0.625	0.557	0.497	0.444	0.397	0.356	0.319
13	0.879	0.773	0.681	0.601	0.530	0.469	0.415	0.368	0.326	0.290
14	0.870	0.758	0.661	0.577	0.505	0.442	0.388	0.340	0.299	0.263
15	0.861	0.743	0.642	0.555	0.481	0.417	0.362	0.315	0.275	0.239
16	0.853	0.728	0.623	0.534	0.458	0.394	0.339	0.292	0.252	0.218
17	0.844	0.714	0.605	0.513	0.436	0.371	0.317	0.270	0.231	0.198
18	0.836	0.700	0.587	0.494	0.416	0.350	0.296	0.250	0.212	0.180
19	0.828	0.686	0.570	0.475	0.396	0.331	0.277	0.232	0.194	0.164
20	0.820	0.673	0.554	0.456	0.377	0.312	0.258	0.215	0.178	0.149

Periods					Interest rates (r)					
(n)	11%	12%	13%	14%	15%	16%	17%	18%	19%	20%
1	0.901	0.893	0.885	0.877	0.870	0.862	0.855	0.847	0.840	0.833
2	0.812	0.797	0.783	0.769	0.756	0.743	0.731	0.718	0.706	0.694
3	0.731	0.712	0.693	0.675	0.658	0.641	0.624	0.609	0.593	0.579
4	0.659	0.636	0.613	0.592	0.572	0.552	0.534	0.516	0.499	0.482
5	0.593	0.567	0.543	0.519	0.497	0.476	0.456	0.437	0.419	0.402
6	0.535	0.507	0.480	0.456	0.432	0.410	0.390	0.370	0.352	0.335
7	0.482	0.452	0.425	0.400	0.376	0.354	0.333	0.314	0.296	0.279
8	0.434	0.404	0.376	0.351	0.327	0.305	0.285	0.266	0.249	0.233
9	0.391	0.361	0.333	0.308	0.284	0.263	0.243	0.225	0.209	0.194
10	0.352	0.322	0.295	0.270	0.247	0.227	0.208	0.191	0.176	0.162
11	0.317	0.287	0.261	0.237	0.215	0.195	0.178	0.162	0.148	0.135
12	0.286	0.257	0.231	0.208	0.187	0.168	0.152	0.137	0.124	0.112
13	0.258	0.229	0.204	0.182	0.163	0.145	0.130	0.116	0.104	0.093
14	0.232	0.205	0.181	0.160	0.141	0.125	0.111	0.099	0.088	0.078
15	0.209	0.183	0.160	0.140	0.123	0.108	0.095	0.084	0.074	0.065
16	0.188	0.163	0.141	0.123	0.107	0.093	0.081	0.071	0.062	0.054
17	0.170	0.146	0.125	0.108	0.093	0.080	0.069	0.060	0.052	0.045
18	0.153	0.130	0.111	0.095	0.081	0.069	0.059	0.051	0.044	0.038
19	0.138	0.116	0.098	0.083	0.070	0.060	0.051	0.043	0.037	0.031
20	0.124	0.104	0.087	0.073	0.061	0.051	0.043	0.037	0.031	0.026

CUMULATIVE PRESENT VALUE TABLE

This table shows the present value of £1 per annum, receivable or payable at the end of each year for n years $\dfrac{1-(1+r)^{-n}}{r}$.

Periods					Interest rates (r)					
(n)	1%	2%	3%	4%	5%	6%	7%	8%	9%	10%
1	0.990	0.980	0.971	0.962	0.952	0.943	0.935	0.926	0.917	0.909
2	1.970	1.942	1.913	1.886	1.859	1.833	1.808	1.783	1.759	1.736
3	2.941	2.884	2.829	2.775	2.723	2.673	2.624	2.577	2.531	2.487
4	3.902	3.808	3.717	3.630	3.546	3.465	3.387	3.312	3.240	3.170
5	4.853	4.713	4.580	4.452	4.329	4.212	4.100	3.993	3.890	3.791
6	5.795	5.601	5.417	5.242	5.076	4.917	4.767	4.623	4.486	4.355
7	6.728	6.472	6.230	6.002	5.786	5.582	5.389	5.206	5.033	4.868
8	7.652	7.325	7.020	6.733	6.463	6.210	5.971	5.747	5.535	5.335
9	8.566	8.162	7.786	7.435	7.108	6.802	6.515	6.247	5.995	5.759
10	9.471	8.983	8.530	8.111	7.722	7.360	7.024	6.710	6.418	6.145
11	10.368	9.787	9.253	8.760	8.306	7.887	7.499	7.139	6.805	6.495
12	11.255	10.575	9.954	9.385	8.863	8.384	7.943	7.536	7.161	6.814
13	12.134	11.348	10.635	9.986	9.394	8.853	8.358	7.904	7.487	7.103
14	13.004	12.106	11.296	10.563	9.899	9.295	8.745	8.244	7.786	7.367
15	13.865	12.849	11.938	11.118	10.380	9.712	9.108	8.559	8.061	7.606
16	14.718	13.578	12.561	11.652	10.838	10.106	9.447	8.851	8.313	7.824
17	15.562	14.292	13.166	12.166	11.274	10.477	9.763	9.122	8.544	8.022
18	16.398	14.992	13.754	12.659	11.690	10.828	10.059	9.372	8.756	8.201
19	17.226	15.679	14.324	13.134	12.085	11.158	10.336	9.604	8.950	8.365
20	18.046	16.351	14.878	13.590	12.462	11.470	10.594	9.818	9.129	8.514

Periods					Interest rates (r)					
(n)	11%	12%	13%	14%	15%	16%	17%	18%	19%	20%
1	0.901	0.893	0.885	0.877	0.870	0.862	0.855	0.847	0.840	0.833
2	1.713	1.690	1.668	1.647	1.626	1.605	1.585	1.566	1.547	1.528
3	2.444	2.402	2.361	2.322	2.283	2.246	2.210	2.174	2.140	2.106
4	3.102	3.037	2.974	2.914	2.855	2.798	2.743	2.690	2.639	2.589
5	3.696	3.605	3.517	3.433	3.352	3.274	3.199	3.127	3.058	2.991
6	4.231	4.111	3.998	3.889	3.784	3.685	3.589	3.498	3.410	3.326
7	4.712	4.564	4.423	4.288	4.160	4.039	3.922	3.812	3.706	3.605
8	5.146	4.968	4.799	4.639	4.487	4.344	4.207	4.078	3.954	3.837
9	5.537	5.328	5.132	4.946	4.772	4.607	4.451	4.303	4.163	4.031
10	5.889	5.650	5.426	5.216	5.019	4.833	4.659	4.494	4.339	4.192
11	6.207	5.938	5.687	5.453	5.234	5.029	4.836	4.656	4.486	4.327
12	6.492	6.194	5.918	5.660	5.421	5.197	4.988	4.793	4.611	4.439
13	6.750	6.424	6.122	5.842	5.583	5.342	5.118	4.910	4.715	4.533
14	6.982	6.628	6.302	6.002	5.724	5.468	5.229	5.008	4.802	4.611
15	7.191	6.811	6.462	6.142	5.847	5.575	5.324	5.092	4.876	4.675
16	7.379	6.974	6.604	6.265	5.954	5.668	5.405	5.162	4.938	4.730
17	7.549	7.120	6.729	6.373	6.047	5.749	5.475	5.222	4.990	4.775
18	7.702	7.250	6.840	6.467	6.128	5.818	5.534	5.273	5.033	4.812
19	7.839	7.366	6.938	6.550	6.198	5.877	5.584	5.316	5.070	4.843
20	7.963	7.469	7.025	6.623	6.259	5.929	5.628	5.353	5.101	4.870

EXAM FORMULAE

Valuation models

(i)   Irredeemable preference share, paying a constant annual dividend, d, in perpetuity, where P_0 is the ex-div value:

$$P_0 = \frac{d}{k_{pref}}$$

(ii)   Ordinary (equity) share, paying a constant annual dividend, d, in perpetuity, where P_0 is the ex-div value:

$$P_0 = \frac{d}{k_e}$$

(iii)   Ordinary (equity) share, paying an annual dividend, d, growing in perpetuity at a constant rate, g, where P_0 is the ex-div value:

$$P_0 = \frac{d_1}{k_e - g} \text{ or } P_0 = \frac{d_0[1 + g]}{k_e - g}$$

(iv)   Irredeemable (undated) debt, paying annual after tax interest, i(1 − t), in perpetuity, where P_0 is the ex-interest value:

$$P_0 = \frac{i[1 - t]}{k_{d\,net}}$$

or, without tax:

$$P_0 = \frac{i}{k_d}$$

(v)   Future value of S, of a sum X, invested for n periods, discounted at r% interest per annum:

$$S = X[1 + r]^n$$

(vi)   Present value of £1 payable or receivable in n years, discounted at r% per annum:

$$PV = \frac{1}{[1 + r]^n}$$

(vii)   Present value of an annuity of £1 per annum, receivable or payable for n years, commencing in one year, discounted at r% per annum:

$$PV = \frac{1}{r}\left[1 - \frac{1}{[1 + r]^n}\right]$$

(viii)   Present value of £1 per annum, payable or receivable in perpetuity, commencing in one year, discounted at r% per annum:

$$PV = \frac{1}{r}$$

(ix)   Present value of £1 per annum, receivable or payable, commencing in one year, growing in perpetuity at a constant rate of g% per annum, discounted at r% per annum:

$$PV = \frac{1}{r - g}$$

Cost of capital

(i) Cost of irredeemable preference capital, paying an annual dividend d in perpetuity, and having a current ex-div price P_0:

$$k_{pref} = \frac{d}{P_0}$$

(ii) Cost of irredeemable debt capital, paying annual net interest $i(1-t)$, and having a current ex-interest price P_0:

$$K_{d\,net} = \frac{i[1-t]}{P_0}$$

(iii) Cost of ordinary (equity) share capital, paying an annual dividend d in perpetuity, and having a current ex div price P_0:

$$k_e = \frac{d}{P_0}$$

(iv) Cost of ordinary (equity) share capital, having a current ex div price, P_0, having just paid a dividend, d_0, with the dividend growing in perpetuity by a constant g% per annum:

$$k_e = \frac{d_1}{P_0} + g \ \text{ or } k_e = \frac{d_0[1+g]}{P_0} + g$$

(v) Cost of ordinary (equity) share capital, using the CAPM:

$$k_e = R_f + [R_m - R_f]\beta$$

(vi) Weighted average cost of capital, k_0:

$$k_0 = k_e\left[\frac{V_E}{V_E + V_D}\right] + k_d\left[\frac{V_D}{V_E + V_D}\right]$$

Stock management

(i) Economic Order Quantity

$$EOQ = \sqrt{\frac{2C_0 D}{C_h}}$$

Where C_o = cost of placing an order
        C_h = stockcarrying cost
        D = annual demand

Cash management

(i) Optimal sale of securities, Baumol model:

$$\text{Optimal sale} = \sqrt{\frac{2 \times \text{Annual cash disbursements} \times \text{Cost per sale of securities}}{\text{Interest rate}}}$$

(ii) Spread between upper and lower cash balance limits, Miller-Orr model:

$$\text{Spread} = 3\left[\frac{\frac{3}{4} \times \text{transaction cost} \times \text{variance of cash flows}}{\text{Interest rate}}\right]^{\frac{1}{3}}$$

BPP PUBLISHING

REVIEW FORM & FREE PRIZE DRAW

All original review forms from the entire BPP range, completed with genuine comments, will be entered into one of two draws on 31 July 2001 and 31 January 2002. The names on the first four forms picked out on each occasion will be sent a cheque for £50.

Name: _____   Address: _____

_____

_____

How have you used this Kit?
(Tick one box only)

☐ Self study (book only)

☐ On a course: college (please state)_____

_____

☐ With 'correspondence' package

☐ Other _____

Why did you decide to purchase this Kit?
(Tick one box only)

☐ Have used the complementary Study Text

☐ Have used other BPP products in the past

☐ Recommendation by friend/colleague

☐ Recommendation by a lecturer at college

☐ Saw advertising in journals

☐ Saw website

☐ Other _____

During the past six months do you recall seeing/receiving any of the following?
(Tick as many boxes as are relevant)

☐ Our advertisement in *CIMA Insider*

☐ Our advertisement in *Financial Management*

☐ Our advertisement in *Pass*

☐ Our brochure with a letter through the post

☐ Our website

Which (if any) aspects of our advertising do you find useful?
(Tick as many boxes as are relevant)

☐ Prices and publication dates of new editions

☐ Information on product content

☐ Facility to order books off-the-page

☐ None of the above

When did you sit the exam? _____

Which of the following BPP products have you used for this paper?

☐ Study Text   ☐ MCQ Cards   ☑ Kit   ☐ Passcards   ☐ Success Tape   ☐ Breakthrough Video

Your ratings, comments and suggestions would be appreciated on the following areas of this Kit.

	Very useful	Useful	Not useful
'Question search tools'	☐	☐	☐
'The exam'	☐	☐	☐
'Background	☐	☐	☐
Preparation questions	☐	☐	☐
Exam standard questions	☐	☐	☐
'Pass marks' section in answers	☐	☐	☐
Content and structure of answers	☐	☐	☐
Mock exams	☐	☐	☐
'Plan of attack'	☐	☐	☐
Mock exam answers	☐	☐	☐

	Excellent	Good	Adequate	Poor
Overall opinion of this Kit	☐	☐	☐	☐

Do you intend to continue using BPP products?   ☐ Yes   ☐ No

Please note any further comments and suggestions/errors on the reverse of this page.

Please return this form to: Alison McHugh, CIMA Range Manager, BPP Publishing Ltd, FREEPOST, London, W12 8BR

REVIEW FORM & FREE PRIZE DRAW (continued)

Please note any further comments and suggestions/errors below.

FREE PRIZE DRAW RULES

1   Closing date for 31 July 2001 draw is 30 June 2001. Closing date for 31 January 2002 draw is 31 December 2001.

2   Restricted to entries with UK and Eire addresses only. BPP employees, their families and business associates are excluded.

3   No purchase necessary. Entry forms are available upon request from BPP Publishing. No more than one entry per title, per person. Draw restricted to persons aged 16 and over.

4   Winners will be notified by post and receive their cheques not later than 6 weeks after the relevant draw date.

5   The decision of the promoter in all matters is final and binding. No correspondence will be entered into.

See overleaf for information on other
BPP products and how to order

Mr/Mrs/Ms (Full name)

Daytime delivery address

Postcode

Daytime Tel   E-mail

Date of exam (month/year)

CIMA Order

To BPP Publishing Ltd, Aldine Place, London W12 8AW
Tel: 020 8740 2211. Fax: 020 8740 1184
www.bpp.com.

	7/00 Texts	1/01 Kits	1/01 Passcards	9/00 Tapes	7/00 Videos	MCQ cards**
FOUNDATION *						
1 Financial Accounting Fundamentals	£19.95 ☐	£10.95 ☐	£5.95 ☐	£12.95 ☐	£25.00 ☐	£4.50 ☐
2 Management Accounting Fundamentals	£19.95 ☐	£10.95 ☐	£5.95 ☐	£12.95 ☐	£25.00 ☐	£4.50 ☐
3A Economics for Business	£19.95 ☐	£10.95 ☐	£5.95 ☐	£12.95 ☐	£25.00 ☐	£4.50 ☐
3B Business Law	£19.95 ☐	£10.95 ☐	£5.95 ☐	£12.95 ☐	£25.00 ☐	£4.50 ☐
3C Business Mathematics	£19.95 ☐	£10.95 ☐	£5.95 ☐	£12.95 ☐	£25.00 ☐	£4.50 ☐
INTERMEDIATE *						
4 Finance	£19.95 ☐	£10.95 ☐	£5.95 ☐	£12.95 ☐	£25.00 ☐	£4.50 ☐
5 Business Tax (FA 2000)	£19.95 ☐	(9/00)£10.95 ☐	£5.95 ☐	£12.95 ☐		£3.50 ☐
6 Financial Accounting	£19.95 ☐	£10.95 ☐	£5.95 ☐	£12.95 ☐	£25.00 ☐	
6I Financial Accounting International	£19.95 ☐	£10.95 ☐				
7 Financial Reporting	£19.95 ☐	£10.95 ☐	£5.95 ☐	£12.95 ☐	£25.00 ☐	
7I Financial Reporting International	£19.95 ☐	£10.95 ☐				
8 Management Accounting - Performance Mgmt	£19.95 ☐	£10.95 ☐	£5.95 ☐	£12.95 ☐	£25.00 ☐	£3.50 ☐
9 Management Accounting - Decision Making	£19.95 ☐	£10.95 ☐	£5.95 ☐	£12.95 ☐	£25.00 ☐	£3.50 ☐
10 Systems and Project Management	£19.95 ☐	£10.95 ☐	£5.95 ☐	£12.95 ☐	£25.00 ☐	
11 Organisational Management	£19.95 ☐	£10.95 ☐	£5.95 ☐	£12.95 ☐	£25.00 ☐	
FINAL						
12 Management Accounting - Business Strategy	£20.95 ☐	£10.95 ☐	£5.95 ☐	£12.95 ☐	£25.00 ☐	
13 Management Accounting - Financial Strategy	£20.95 ☐	£10.95 ☐	£5.95 ☐	£12.95 ☐	£25.00 ☐	
14 Management Accounting - Information Strategy	£20.95 ☐	£10.95 ☐	£5.95 ☐	£12.95 ☐	£25.00 ☐	
15 Case Study	£15.95 ☐ (1)	£15.95 ☐ (2)		£15.95 ☐ (12/00)	£15.95 ☐ (12/00)	

(1) Workbook   (2) Case Question Bank

* There will also be a selection of Master CDs available in 2001
** (FREE WITH TEXT)

POSTAGE & PACKING

Study Texts

	First	Each extra	
UK	£3.00	£2.00	£ ☐
Europe***	£5.00	£4.00	£ ☐
Rest of world	£20.00	£10.00	£ ☐

Kits/Passcards/Success Tapes

	First	Each extra	
UK	£2.00	£1.00	£ ☐
Europe***	£2.50	£1.00	£ ☐
Rest of world	£15.00	£8.00	£ ☐

Master CDs(2001)/Breakthrough Videos

	First	Each extra	
UK	£2.00	£2.00	£ ☐
Europe***	£2.00	£2.00	£ ☐
Rest of world	£20.00	£10.00	£ ☐
MCQ cards	£1.00	£1.00	£ ☐

Grand Total (Cheques to *BPP Publishing*) I enclose a cheque for (incl. Postage) £ ☐

Or charge to Access/Visa/Switch

Card Number

Expiry date   Start Date

Issue Number (Switch Only)

Signature

We aim to deliver to all UK addresses inside 5 working days. A signature will be required. Orders to all EU addresses should be delivered within 6 working days. All other orders to overseas addresses should be delivered within 8 working days.